AF580675

AUTHENTIC PR

HOW TRANSPARENCY CAN TRANSFORM YOUR BUSINESS

AUTHENTIC PR

HOW TRANSPARENCY CAN TRANSFORM YOUR BUSINESS

MICHAEL LEVINE

RARE BIRD
LOS ANGELES, CALIF.

THIS IS A GENUINE RARE BIRD BOOK

Rare Bird Books
6044 North Figueroa Street
Los Angeles, California 90042
rarebirdbooks.com

FIRST HARDCOVER EDITION

ISBN-13: 9781644285527 (hardcover edition)
ISBN-13: 9781644286036 (e-book edition)

For more information, address:
Rare Bird Books Subsidiary Rights Department
6044 North Figueroa Street
Los Angeles, California 90042

Set in Minion Pro
Printed in the United States

10 9 8 7 6 5 4 3 2 1

Library of Congress Cataloging-in-Publication Data
available on request

Contents

Preface: *The Authentic Age* 9
Introduction: *The Promise* 13
Chapter One: *Augmenting Authenticity* 15
Chapter Two: *The History of Personal Branding* 19
Chapter Three: *The Personal Connection* 21
Chapter Four: *Your Challenge as a Brand* 23
Case Study One: *The Antique Advantage* 25
The Strategies 26
Case Study Two: *Swing and a Hit* 28
Chapter Five: *How to Get on Radio and Television* 30
Case Study Three: *Eyes and Ears* 38
Chapter Six: *Advantage: "Mom and Pop"* 40
Chapter Seven: *The Six As* 42
Case Study Four: *The Haircuts for the Homeless* 46
Case Study Five: *The X Games* 49
Case Study Six: *Cleaning Up* 50
Case Study Seven: *Games On* 51
Case Study Eight: *The Crypto Contest* 52
Case Study Nine: *Guns for Grub* 53
Chapter Eight: *The Experience Economy* 54
Case Study Ten: *Good Sports* 56
Case Study Eleven: *Going Green* 58
Chapter Nine: *Gaining Visibility in the Age of Transparency* 60
Chapter Ten: *First, Do No Harm* 62
Chapter Eleven: *How to Do No Harm* 64
Case Study Twelve: *X Success* 65
Chapter Twelve: *Tell the Truth* 67
Case Study Thirteen: *Diamonds Are Forever* 70
Case Study Fourteen: *Flying the Coop* 72
Case Study Fifteen: *On the Job* 75
Chapter Thirteen: *Get Real* 76
Case Study Sixteen: *Systems Down* 77
Case Study Seventeen: *Food for Thought* 78
Chapter Fourteen: *Post It and Pitch It* 81
Case Study Eighteen: *First Come, First Served* 92
Case Study Nineteen: *The Brand-Boosting Virtual Job Fair* 95

Chapter Fifteen: *Television and Radio—*
More Thoughts About the "Non-Social" Media 97
Chapter Sixteen: *The Phone—The Forgotten Medium?* 99
Case Study Twenty: *The Human Factor* 100
Chapter Seventeen: *When Is a Phone Not a Phone?*
When It Is a Camera. 103
Case Study Twenty-One: *Twenty-Four Hours of Moments* 104
Chapter Eighteen: *Prankster Public Relations* 106
Case Study Twenty-Two: *Sundaes Will Never Be the Same* 110
Case Study Twenty-Three: *By Comparison* 111
Chapter Nineteen: *The Campaign* 116
Chapter Twenty: *To Your Health* 118
Case Study Twenty-Four: *Healing the Community* 118
Case Study Twenty-Five: *A Shot in the Arm* 120
Chapter Twenty-One: *Influencers, Influencing the Internet* 124
Case Study Twenty-Six: *Building a Better Business* 125
Chapter Twenty-Two: *To Be Real* 127
Case Study Twenty-Seven: *Knowing the Lingo* 128
Case Study Twenty-Eight: *The Play's the Thing* 130
Chapter Twenty-Three: *Seasoned Public Relations* 132
Case Study Twenty-Nine: *Batter Up* 134
Chapter Twenty-Four: *Pop-Up Events* 136
Case Study Thirty: *A Winter Wonderland in July* 137
Case Study Thirty-One: *Spring Cleaning* 138
Chapter Twenty-Five: *Adrenaline Public Relations* 140
Case Study Thirty-Two: *Summer Surprise* 142
Case Study Thirty-Three: *Peak Performance* 144
Chapter Twenty-Six: *Restoring Reputations* 146
Case Study Thirty-Four: *Under the Influence* 147
Chapter Twenty-Seven: *AI PR* 152
Case Study Thirty-Five: *Faking It* 154
Case Study Thirty-Six: *The Newsletter* 155
Case Study Thirty-Seven: *The Cyber Comic* 157
Chapter Twenty-Eight: *The Quest for Influence* 160
Case Study Thirty-Eight: *See You on the Radio* 162
Case Study Thirty-Nine: *Influencer 101* 164
Case Study Thirty-Nine A: *Influencer 102* 165
Case Study Forty: *Passion to Profession* 170

Chapter Twenty-Nine: *Marketing Your Product or Service—What Could Possibly Go Right?* 174
Case Study Forty-One: *Cars on Parade* 177
Case Study Forty-Two: *Budget Battles* 178
Chapter Thirty: *About Your Image* 181
Chapter Thirty-One: *A Child's Garden of Public Relations* 183
Case Study Forty-Three: *World's Most Important Art Auction* 184
Case Study Forty-Four: *Going, Going, Gone* 185
Chapter Thirty-Two: *Building a Campaign* 187
Case Study Forty-Five: *Yes, And...* 190
Case Study Forty-Six: *The Ugliest Vehicle Contest* 191
Chapter Thirty-Three: *Fire, Police, and PR* 195
Case Study Forty-Seven: *Halls of Justice 1* 197
Case Study Forty-Eight: *Halls of Justice 2* 198
Case Study Forty-Nine: *Happy Days* 200
Chapter Thirty-Four: *If You Are the Media* 201
Case Study Fifty: *The Front Page* 204
Case Study Fifty-One: *Putting Together a Podcast* 206
Chapter Thirty-Five: *PR and Marketing—What's the Difference?* 208
Case Study Fifty-Two: *Step by Step* 209
Chapter Thirty-Six: *How to Recover When Something Goes Wrong* 211
Case Study Fifty-Three: *Searching for the Key* 212
Case Study Fifty-Four: *There's a Fly in My Soup* 213
Case Study Fifty-Five: *Be True to Your Word* 214
Chapter Thirty-Seven: *How to Start a Trend* 216
Case Study Fifty-Six: *A Holiday for No Reason* 218
Case Study Fifty-Seven: *The Sustainability Rally* 219
Chapter Thirty-Eight: *The Customer Service Factor* 221
Chapter Thirty-Nine: *How to Write a News Release* 224
Chapter Forty: *Internal Communications* 228
Case Study Fifty-Eight: *Honing the Core* 230
Chapter Forty-One: *Doing Well by Doing Good* 233
Chapter Forty-Two: *Takeaways* 235
Epilogue 236
Index 239
Glossary 245
Authentic PR *Toolkit* 247

Preface

The Authentic Age

It's 1993. The height of the Clinton presidency, lodged somewhere between the end of the Cold War and the heyday of the Information Age. Mikhail Gorbachev had torn down the wall, but the walls between people remained standing. Silicon Valley was about to go into overdrive, and little did anyone know that someday, after the Millennium, people would become addicted to personal devices that would fit in the palm of your hand yet have more computing power than an Apollo mission. Not yet would people crouch as they walked down the sidewalk, thumbs seemingly doing a jaunty two-step on a keyboard, carrying on a text conversation with someone thousands of miles away while ignoring every passing soul and, perhaps, the "Do Not Walk" icon. "Read my lips" had come and gone, but read my text was not yet *en vogue*.

This was also the year my most successful business book ever was published. *Guerrilla PR: Waging an Effective Publicity Campaign Without Growing Broke* was, as the title suggested, a handbook on how to wage a successful, big-budget public relations effort without the big budget. To do that in 1993, we followed some cardinal rules:

- **We knew the players.** The anchors, the reporters, the editors, the writers, the critics; we knew about their interests, their awards, their insecurities, their senses of humor and their dreams. They were the gatekeepers, but we knew how to get through the gate. There's a very famous bit of dialogue in the movie *Broadcast News* that epitomizes the volatility of the television industry. I always made it a point to be able to answer the question, to be "in the loop," so that I became a confidante of many in the media. When they came to recognize that I understood their business and their lives, they became more likely to trust me when I came to them with a pitch.

- **We practiced journalism.** Because of that trust we established, journalists came to rely on us for story ideas. Quite frankly, there were times when we were doing most of their work—originating story ideas, and tracking down sources—but we recognized that journalists were stretched very thin because of the nature of the business. Journalism is, in part, the process of becoming an instant expert one day on something you knew nothing about the previous day. (If you don't think that's difficult, try it at home.) Journalists are harried, distracted, and working on deadline. If an interview doesn't come through, it's like the first in a set of dominoes falling. So, we turned our clients' narratives into saleable stories, we vetted the sources, and we made sure everything came through on time.
- **We practiced the "5:30 Rule."** If it was after the end of the business day, and the light on the phone was blinking, we answered it. To ignore it would be to, potentially, miss a column on the front page or a slot on *Good Morning America* the following day. In public relations, as in the news business, tomorrow never comes. News is perishable; it's only appealing when it's fresh.

Guerrilla PR, though, was more than just a handbook of professional public relations. As the title suggests, the thesis of the book was that you didn't have to spend a fortune to get the same results as Fortune 500 companies. The title was meant to describe a dominant public relations idea in 1993 about the capacity of people to do for themselves what literally had been done by companies with large budgets. *Guerrilla PR* was a title meant to describe how you could do the very same thing those companies could do for the cost of a postage stamp. (At the time, email wasn't commonly used by the general public.) So I wrote the book, and it went on to become the best-selling PR book of all time all over the world, taught in twenty-five of the top business schools in America. It was the right message for that time. The advice in it was keyed to professionals but meant for anyone who wants to be a strong voice amid murmurs. As I explained in an interview with *PR Week*, our philosophy was based on my "Tiffany Theory": *If you give someone a present in a Tiffany box, it has a higher perceived value than if you give it to them in no box.*

In the years that followed, it became clear to me that the world was changing rapidly, with technology—and social media in particular—reshaping the way public relations and communications function. I came to conclude that the message I had written twenty-five years ago, while valuable, was outdated. I've now come to conclude that, after consideration, the most appropriate message for *this* time, as opposed to 1993, is a phrase called *Authentic PR*.

Introduction

The Promise

For a book to work, it must make a promise to the reader; preferably, a big promise. The promise is that if I give you twenty-five dollars and ten to twelve hours of my time, I will get something productive for it. So, with *Guerrilla PR*, the promise was that, if I gave my twenty-five dollars and twelve hours of my time, I would get a roadmap of how to do *Guerrilla PR*.

So, the first thing a book has got to do is make this big promise to the reader and articulate that promise well. The second thing it has to do is *deliver* on the promise. The book about *Guerrilla PR* was executed well, judging by its sales and popularity with readers. *Authentic PR* is the right message for this time. Jack Benny and Bob Hope were the right comedians for the age in which they lived, but their material would likely be out of sync in the era of YouTube moments.

That doesn't mean that *Authentic PR* is a complete break from the past. *Guerrilla PR* was a usable, practical book that didn't pretend to pretense. It was *USA Today*, not *The New York Times*. It was Denny's, not Spago. *Authentic PR: How Transparency Can Transform Your Business* is a step forward, from Denny's to Uber Eats, from the McIntosh to the Metaverse.

Chapter One

Augmenting Authenticity

"The public is the only critic whose opinion is worth anything at all."

—Mark Twain

The Mission: You are a brand. You live, you breathe, you articulate, and you present yourself whenever you're in public. You are unique. With some of those you meet, you mesh; with others, you clash; and with others, you're like the proverbial ships passing in the night. You may be well defined, or you may be vaguely outlined, or you may be a total enigma, but the image you project has an impact on people. It may attract, it may repel, or it may make no discernible difference whatsoever. Either way, your "brand" will help determine where you live, how well you live and what you do for a living.

Why It's Important: Your brand is crucial in any event; but if you own a business, it's critical. As Tom Goodwin, former Head of Futures & Insight—Publicis Groupe, writes, "Brands are essentially patterns of familiarity, meaning, fondness and assurance that exist in the minds of people." And in the minds of people today, the perception of a business is inseparable from the perception of whoever runs it. At a time when social media can amplify a customer's compliment, concern or complaint around the world, your branding and that of your business can foster or hinder your success.

But how can you burnish your image? How can you not only increase your name recognition and make people aware of your brand, but also propagate a perception that will get people drawn to your brand? Multi-billion-dollar corporations turn to well-established public relations firms that you may not be able to afford. But there are techniques that may not be out of reach and that do not require you to hire public relations professionals. It's the mission of this book to give you some of those techniques.

With *Guerrilla PR*, as the title suggested, it offered strategies designed to shock, awe, and work. LinkedIn, Facebook, and Twitter hadn't become part of life then. Yelp hadn't yet become a tool for the satisfied or dissatisfied customer. That book was published at a time when social media had yet to change the conversation; and different times call for different strategies.

For example: In *Guerrilla PR*, I note how a restaurant named Mel's Diner, which I described as "a kitschy, fifties-style eatery," elevated its profile after a water main burst in Southern California. In 1991, a persistent drought in the state was followed by a deluge, and a water main burst under Ventura Boulevard in the San Fernando Valley. The break decimated the lunch crowd at the restaurant, but rather than sit around apprehensively, David "Mel" Weiss transformed what had happened into an opportunity. As I put it then, "He gave away free hamburgers to the street maintenance crew; and he invited local TV news outlets to witness this noble act of charity. For the cost of a couple of dozen beef patties and a few phone calls, Mel's Diner was all over the airwaves that night, and ever since, business has been better than ever." Mel's Diner became a nightly news hero because Weiss waged *Guerrilla PR*.

Suppose that had happened in the 2020s. In some ways, the strategy might have been similar: make the hamburgers and alert the local television news outlets. But the recipe for success in this "guerrilla" campaign might have also included instructions to "add social media and stir." Such a gesture could have gone global and viral. Social media are force multipliers because they create a virtuous cycle: Users become aware of a good deed by a business or a good experience at that business and they spread the word to their friends, connections and followers, who, in turn, send the message to their networks. It can become what might be called a geometric progression of goodwill.

In today's more volatile weather environment, this sort of campaign could become more commonplace. According to the National Interagency Fire Center, as cited by the Insurance Information Institute, there were 58,985 wildfires in 2021, and 58,950 in 2020. Restaurants could publicize spontaneous efforts to furnish food to firefighters who are battling the blazes that are now appearing year-round in parts of the US. The same rule applies in the aftermath of any life-changing weather event, such as a hurricane or a tornado.

That's not to say that you need to wait for an apocalyptic event to garner some goodwill. Opportunities are everywhere if you know where to find them. Think of this book as a sort of Public Relations 101, or, if you wish, public relations for dummies. Public relations is a fascinating field, but its practitioners may not be available or affordable for some businesses. *Authentic PR* will fill the gap, offering a readable guide to raising your visibility and burnishing your reputation.

Chapter Two

The History of Personal Branding

Mass Production, Mass Communication: Personal branding started coming into its own in the Industrial Revolution. Mass production and advances in infrastructure and transportation allowed people to engage in specialized work. For the first time in history, people asked routinely what others did for a living, since, for the first time in history, the answer didn't routinely involve a reference to the family farm. This diversification led to the rise of multi-million-dollar businesses specializing in the industrial technologies that were being developed.

Some of the founders of those businesses are easily identifiable: Think of John D. Rockefeller and Henry Ford. These industrial pioneers were wealthy and remote. Their companies surrounded them like fortresses, and a budding public relations industry arose to ensure that potential customers perceived those companies as rock solid and here to stay. It was all very impersonal and institutional.

The movie industry was also very remote. Actors' images were well manufactured. The heroes of the latest Westerns had no flaws. If you believed their publicity staff, they could lasso three bulls while signing an autograph—and the leading lady was glamor personified in the spotlight. Nothing was known about her flawed personal life because studios were as adept as the Central Intelligence Agency in keeping secrets.

Even small businesses could afford to be somewhat impersonal. If you were deciding whether to patronize a restaurant in the mid-twentieth century, you would have been likely to have based that decision solely on how tasty the food was and how courteous the waiters and waitresses (servers in today's parlance) were. You wouldn't have investigated whether the owner of the restaurant dined only on organically grown food or whether the chicken on your plate had been caged for most of its life.

That was then.

Chapter Three

The Personal Connection

People are connected today like never before. Social media have transformed the remote into the reachable. A corporate CEO who in past decades might have been a virtual unknown to most people may be your LinkedIn connection. In the words of Sasha Strauss, founder of Innovation Protocol, "One of my favorite coworkers often says Elon Musk has more followers than SpaceX and Tesla combined. And that says a lot about this time, where the leader of the organization often has more attention than the brand itself. And so, this is a whole new expectation, where, honestly, if you traded stocks in the '80s you rarely heard from the CEO of an organization." He continued, "Now, now we're hearing from the CEO at four in the morning, and it may affect the stock price for the day. And so, it's this really interesting situation where we used to expect a leader to lead economically, financially, and now we're expecting them to lead with voice. And that's why this is so trying is that they weren't prepared. Their voices weren't ready."

No wonder *Bloomberg Businessweek* titles a weekly podcast "Elon, Inc." The face of the corporation is the fate of the corporation.

Voice and Volatility: Social media has created a more volatile environment in which to do business. If you had bought a Model T Ford back when they were coming off the production line and the engine kept breaking down, you might have railed to some friends or written a letter to the company; but it would have been difficult to get the manufacturer to take notice. If the same thing happened today with the newest model of automobile, your outrage could reach not only your friends, your acquaintances, and members of your family, but also everyone who is on social media, and you could singlehandedly send the company and the dealership into damage control mode. Furious customers on websites such as Yelp can deliver a billion unkind cuts to a business. And cell phone cameras can literally catch businesses and their proprietors in the act, whatever act that is.

A Time of Transparency: Privacy is at a premium in the digital age. At a time when Google can aggregate all of our triumphs and transgressions in one search and Siri and Alexa can blab about us if we ask, it is impossible for owners of businesses of any size to hide. Some owners and CEOs have embraced high visibility or had it thrust upon them by millions of inquisitive and appreciative social media users. Bill Gates keeps in touch with the public online through emails of "Gates Notes." Elon Musk posts. And posts. And posts. And Richard Branson at least once used artificial intelligence to offer a personalized phone call to anyone who requested it.

For Branson, visibility is a key to customer service. Carmine Gallo, Senior Contributor to *Forbes*, spent time with Branson on the occasion of the first Virgin America flight from Los Angeles to Las Vegas. She quotes Branson as saying, "A good leader doesn't get stuck behind a desk," and writes, "Branson is always on the move, meeting employees, talking to cabin crews, and soliciting feedback from passengers. He's constantly asking for their opinions and he keeps a notebook of the ideas and the feedback he receives. Branson believes that a leader's creativity is nourished by the time he or she spends out of the office and in the field."

Decision makers are no longer out of the public's reach. They may be secure at home in gated communities, but there are no gates online. The time of faceless companies and institutional public relations is over. Corporate public relations must be personalized and nimble. CEOs must be ready at a moment's notice to handle memes as competently as they handle mergers.

That same accessibility is not only available to smaller businesses; it's essential to their survival. If you're a business owner, it behooves you to get in front of your business, the way Branson does. Not only should you be the face of your business to your customers; you should also aggressively find out what's on their minds and cater to that. But above all, you have to make members of the public aware that your business exists and then find ways to attract them. The only difference between smaller and larger businesses is the size of their public relations budgets. Think of *Authentic PR* as a force multiplier for the smaller business.

Chapter Four

Your Challenge as a Brand

If you have a business, you are just as visible and vulnerable as Elon Musk, Bill Gates or Jeff Bezos. And in the minds of the public, you and your business are inseparable. For example, in my book *Broken Windows, Broken Business: The Revolutionary Broken Windows Theory: How the Smallest Remedies Reap the Biggest Rewards*, I mention the story of a vegan restaurant owner who resigned after she posted in an online forum that she had "spiked a vegan meal."

As recounted in *The Guardian*, "A group of diners had booked a table on Friday evening, and in the early hours of Saturday [Laura] Goodman posted: Pious, judgmental vegan (who I spent all day cooking for) has gone to bed, still believing she was a vegan. And on a separate post she writes, Spiked a vegan meal a few hours ago." The response on social media was vehement.

According to Goodman's co-owner and fiancé, they received death threats and threats of lawsuits.

Goodman resigned.

It's not enough to say that you have the best vegan restaurant, *please come here*. You have to communicate that you *have a wonderful vegan restaurant run by an authentic vegan who raises his children to be vegans and who donates to vegan causes*. And you need to offer evidence. That's the authentic part.

Building Your Business with Background: Customers want to know the people with whom they're doing business, and they want to be assured that the business is acting ethically. Generations of people who were raised to be health-conscious and socially conscious want to make sure that their food is ethically sourced. In the case of restaurants, it's no longer enough to know that the food is good. Potential diners are likely to scrutinize the lives of the owners of restaurants, and learn something about the histories of those restaurants.

Starbucks is a prime example of a company that celebrates the background of its product rather than just the product. As the company notes on Starbucks.com, "Helping people thrive helps ensure the long-term sustainability of the premium products we provide. Whether it's arabica coffee, tea, cocoa or manufactured goods, we're committed to offering ethically purchased and responsibly produced sustainable products of the highest quality." Without such an assurance, Starbucks would arguably be unsuccessful. Customers want to identify with the businesses they patronize. But they won't identify with the business if the owner doesn't share their values.

Being Authentic—The Value of Vulnerability: You might say that Starbucks adds value through vulnerability. In an interview with *The Associated Press* posted by Business Writer Dee-Ann Durbin, former Starbucks CEO Kevin Johnson is quoted as saying, "[I]f I think back to my life journey the advice, I would give to the younger version of myself is be authentic. I went through life maybe not having the courage to show vulnerability or the confidence to really be who I was and as I got later in my life, I figured out that authenticity is the fastest way to create human connection and to lead people. That means having the courage to show vulnerability, show empathy and compassion, and in doing that, you're demonstrating something that every single one of us on this planet has in common. That's the human experience, and that's what makes us great leaders."

Vulnerability spawns credibility. Everyone has flaws. Would you be more likely to buy from a business that's opaque with its flaws and spin-doctors its image? Or a business that's transparent with its flaws and pursues its vision? A business's vision should be in line with its values. When the two are in sync, consumers get a message that keeps them coming back for more. For example, Ben & Jerry's Homemade Ice Cream Holdings, Inc. attracted customers because of its founders' commitment to the values associated with the 1960s. When it was sold to Unilever in 2000, part of the deal was that its social mission would be protected. Today, it has a separate board of directors charged with assuring that its social mission gets the same attention as its profit picture. In an age of authenticity, the two are related.

Case Study One: The Antique Advantage

The Challenge: You have opened a new restaurant based on home cooking that was handed down in your family over the generations. You want to showcase your place as an authentic part of the community, with shared roots and shared values.

The Strategy: Most communities have some kind of heritage festival designed to focus on their history and cultural heritage. Set up a space at that festival offering not only free food, but a look at family artifacts, photographs and perhaps a vintage vehicle. Then, offer an appraiser's services to evaluate some of your customers' antiques and collectibles. Allow the appraiser to preview the items, then hold the appraisals at the event. Invite television coverage, and shoot a video of some of the appraisals for your website. If you're living in a smaller city, such a festival probably commemorates the entire community. In larger cities, the focus may be on neighborhoods.

The Rationale: People love history, and they have a keen interest in the artifacts that make it live today. Look at the success of the PBS program *Antiques Roadshow*. Daphne Northrop writes on wgbh.org, "With about five million viewers each week. *Antiques Roadshow* is not only PBS's most-watched ongoing series. It is a local phenomenon—wherever it goes." Just as history is an anchor for one of the most popular programs on PBS, so can it be a touchstone for a restaurant with deep roots in the community.

Nelson's, a restaurant in Rancho Palos Verdes, California, is another case in point. The restaurant commemorates Mike Nelson, a former Navy diver portrayed by actor Lloyd Bridges in the syndicated television series *Sea Hunt*, which ran in original episodes from 1958 through 1961. Food may lure the curious to the restaurant, but the artifacts on display from the television show help to establish an emotional bond, both culinary and cultural, that keeps them coming back. And just as *Antiques Roadshow* uses history to attract a following around the country, you can use it to create a clientele in your community.

One strategy: Call a local television station and invite them to do a story about your collectibles and your cuisine. You might be surprised at how receptive a television producer may be to a "kicker" story about history on a slow day.

The Costs: Booth space rental, and, possibly, food permits. But you need more than roots. You need wings. For a smaller business, the question becomes how to get the message out. A company like Starbucks may have employees whose sole job is to reassure customers that its products will salve their consciences while satisfying their yearnings for a morning beverage, but smaller businesses can promote an image of sustainability without increasing their budgets.

For example, the chef at a locally owned restaurant could create a YouTube video showing how one of the eatery's dishes is prepared and talking about how it is sourced. (Customers in the restaurant could access those videos quickly by scanning a QR Code strategically placed at the table.) That same chef could do the same demonstration at a farmers market. And, who knows? That chef could approach the producer of a local morning television news program and offer to do a regular cooking segment. (Producers of these morning shows, which typically run before *Today, Good Morning America* or *CBS Mornings*, may be hungry for time fillers. (Non-network affiliates may have their own morning shows with even more time available for segments such as these.)

Conscience drives commerce.

The Strategies

In Sync with the 2020s: Society today is much more cynical than it was decades ago. In those days, 78 percent of American adults felt that authorities—attorneys, doctors, priests, military, teachers—would do the right thing or try to do the right thing. Today, that number is 18 percent. When you measure people under thirty years old, the number goes to two percent. *Authentic PR* is a way of people communicating messages of credibility. Do you trust someone you've known and met in person more than someone you haven't? Of course. Because in person, they become *authentic*. All their strengths and frailties are on display. Do they speak knowledgeably? Do they present themselves well? Are they committed to certain ideals? Are they just in it for the money, whatever "it" is? People you meet become *authentic*. They're not avatars (unless they live exclusively in the metaverse). *Authentic PR* is a way of communicating messages for today's cynical audiences. And you don't need a Fortune 500 budget to practice it.

A Multi-Dimensional Approach: In today's world, you have to communicate your message to the audience in many multi-dimensional ways. You can't rely on any one mode. Instagram isn't enough. Social media is wonderful, but it's only one piece of a puzzle. When you're communicating a message to an audience, you have to communicate in many, many venues, including radio, television, newspapers, magazines, the internet, and social media. American audiences today are so distracted that to communicate with them, you must have a multi-dimensional approach.

The Authenticity Advantage: Audiences and customers want (in fact, demand) to know that the people who are trying to sell them something are who they appear to be, that they're *credible*, that they're *trustable*, that they're *believable*. If you have a restaurant today, it's very important that you have good Yelp reviews. It's also important that the physical experience is consistent with the promise of the restaurant. You want to be *consistent*, *authentic*, *transparent*, and *vulnerable*. You want to teach your audience, or potential audience, about the restaurant, about the food you serve, about where that food is sourced, and about who prepares it. Who's the chef? What were the founding ideas of the restaurant? What are some customer testimonials? What you say about yourself is not nearly as important as what others say about you. Website testimonials are great, but social media testimonials are even greater because you can't edit them. If you have a Jewish deli, it would be important to have the testimonials come from prominent people in the Jewish community. If you had a Mexican restaurant, it would be important to have testimonials from people in the in the Hispanic community. You're creating proof to confirm the believability of your message.

No Targeting Required: The key in *Authentic PR* is not to figure out how to target messages to certain audiences, but to reveal who you truly are, then let the right audiences find you. If you have a sports bar and the owner of the bar has an extensive baseball card collection that they began to amass when they were a kid, it would be important maybe to get pictures of them when they ere that age to tell the story. How did their childhood lead to them owning a sports bar? Their journey to sports began at a young age with a card collection that was started by their uncle, and they still have many of those cards today. This is the kind of thing that creates an *authenticity* to the audience. It's very appealing at a time when so much human interaction has been lost to work-at-home days and shop-at-home evenings.

"Cell" the Business: Technology has been an accelerator of low-cost communication. It's been said that every cell phone in use right now has more computing power than the entire Apollo program. The cell phone is an effective, efficient, and low-cost way of communicating a potentially powerful message. If you own a restaurant or another type of business where people congregate, you can record thirty-second videos on your cell phone of a happy customers and upload them for free. The only investment is a few minutes of your time. (Standard message and data rates may apply.)

Keep in mind, though, that the cell phone you use to record a happy diner enjoying a Salisbury steak can also be used by an unhappy diner to document a hair in their chicken sandwich or a dirty restroom, but the advantage of technology is that the images it records are real. They have the feel of cinema verite on the fly. That gives those images enhanced credibility. They can also be used to tell the story of how a business is striving to be an integral part of the community and a powerful force in enhancing the quality of life.

Case Study Two: Swing and a Hit

The Challenge: Owners of a dry-cleaning establishment want to enhance their visibility and reputation in a community. To that end, they've decided to sponsor a local Little League team.

The Strategy: Create a section in your website devoted to the team, showing highlights of each game, especially improbable highlights, like the 450-foot home run hit by one of the players. Then, call a local television station and tell the producer about the surprise you're going to stage at a specific game. That surprise is a parachutist who is going to land on the field between innings.

The key is the element of surprise. People may or may not attend a Little League game to see someone jump out of a perfectly good airplane, but if they're already at the game, they'll have their cell phone cameras out to record the aerial maneuvers.

The Rationale: Some of the greatest moments in baseball don't involve players. *Case in Point*: the sixth game of the 1986 World Series between the Boston Red Sox and the New York Mets, when a man parachuted onto the field at Shea Stadium in the first inning of play. Later in that same game, Bill Buckner of Boston would allow a ball hit by Mookie Wilson of the Mets to roll through his legs. The error gave New York the win. And then there was the time a goose landed on the field during a game between the Los Angeles Dodgers and the San Diego Padres.

Baseball is a game of both triumph and tedium. And it's the surprises and the electric moments that make it such a crowd pleaser. You can't affect the outcome of the game, but you can affect its impact in person and on social media. Hiring a skydiver to glide into the stadium or onto the field is one way of galvanizing media coverage and social media visibility. All the better if your team is in the championship series. Perhaps the parachute jump could be augmented by a grand slam that clears the bases and wins the night for your team.

The Cost: Hiring the parachutist and renting the plane, plus the ongoing cost of team sponsorship.

Chapter Five

How to Get on Radio and Television

The Talk of the Airwaves: Think a radio talk show of your own is out of the question? Then you must not have heard of Tom and Ray Magliozzi. In 1977, radio station WBUR-FM in Boston tried to assemble a panel of car mechanics to talk about car repairs on the air. Tom Magliozzi was the only one who showed up, and his performance was so good, he was invited back as a guest, and he brought along his brother Ray. The two were eventually offered their own show on WBUR-FM, then NPR decided to distribute it nationally beginning in 1986. *Car Talk* won a Peabody Award in 1992. The brothers retired in 2012.

Tom and Ray Magliozzi didn't set out to be professional broadcasters. *It just happened*. And who's to say it couldn't happen to you? All it takes is a little chutzpah to get you on the air, and a little charisma to keep you on the air.

Automobile repair, do-it-yourself home maintenance, hunting, fishing, boating, and antiques are just some of the business sectors that are perfectly suited for podcasting. In fact, any business sector in which some expertise is required is the starting point for a podcast and a call-in radio show. The best of these shows follow what might be called the Three Hs: They have a personable *host*, a sense of *humor*, and no *hard* sell. They give the business a mention perhaps twice an hour. The best of the best of these shows are accessible to, and even sought out by, a listener who would otherwise have no interest in the subject. That listener may patronize your store just to check it out and invite friends who will, in turn, invite friends who will spend money and leave you with enough disposable income for this year's cruise to Antigua.

Engaging the Media: There's no question that television has changed over the decades. Where once there were three over-the-air networks, today there's a bevy of streaming services and cable channels in the mix as well, not to mention online entertainment and gaming. And the news media, which have become the bedrock of cost-effective television programming, have taken a hit. According to Elisa Shearer, Katerina Eva Matsa, Michael Lipka, Kirsten Eddy, and Naomi Forsten-Katz, writing for the Pew Research Center, "The local news landscape in America is going through profound changes as both news consumers and producers adapt to a more digital news environment."

Nevertheless, local television remains a visible part of the media ecosystem in most communities, and savvy business owners would do well to cultivate relationships with the local media. They will learn that most of the anchors and reporters they see on television are not the decision makers. They will learn to check the credits of popular news programs and reach out to the producers, the real powers behind the rundown. These for-the-most-part unsung visionaries make the decisions that determine what will be covered on any given day. Because they have to respond to breaking news, they normally have "go-to" sources with expertise on different types of breaking news, whether it be brush fires, earthquakes, crime or international terrorism. A former firefighter who owns a store that sells fire suppression equipment would be an excellent go-to resource for a harried producer at a time when news is breaking and a fire department spokesperson may be unavailable.

A garden shop owner who happens to be a master gardener is in an excellent position to become a personality on local media. Morning news programs perennially search for experts in a wide variety of fields to populate segments that may be of interest to the waking audience. Physicians can offer to do regular health segments. My friend Jerry Edling worked at a television station in Florida where a local dermatologist did a five-days-a-week segment titled, "To Your Health." He became possibly as recognizable as a billboard lawyer, and it didn't cost him a penny.

And then, there's food. Everyone has to eat, so food shows on television are a natural way to soft-sell restaurants. There are a number of different career paths that can lead to a show of your own. You could follow the career path of Chef Emeril Lagasse, opening restaurants, writing cookbooks and amassing awards and Michelin stars. Or you could take a lesson from Rachael Ray and travel a simpler route, from conducting cooking lessons in a store to being on national television.

Ray told *Forbes* (as quoted by Sophie McEvoy on The List), "My mom worked in restaurants for sixty years, and what I learned from her is a lot." According to IMDb, while working at a shop in Albany, New York, "she held cooking lessons in the store and caught the attention of a local television station. The station began cooking segments, which later became 30 Minute Meals…" She has since hosted shows on the Food Network, along with a nationally syndicated show, written cookbooks, and had a word added to The Oxford American College Dictionary. (The word is EVOO, her shortened depiction of "extra-virgin olive oil.")

She is not the only one who took culinary skills from local television to a national audience. The late Art Ginsburg had a catering business when he started a cooking segment on a station in Schenectady, New York. He parlayed that into a nationally syndicated segment in which he was known as "Mr. Food."

There's no reason these sorts of show business sagas couldn't happen to other businesses. All it takes is skills, savvy, and the "it" factor. But even if you don't become the next continent-wide cook, a segment on a local TV station could add the visibility and name recognition you're seeking in your market.

All or Nothing: So many businesses miss out on opportunities to be on the air because they want it all. No television or radio news producer is going to give you an opportunity to broadcast an infomercial about your business, unless, of course, you buy the airtime. But that same producer may want to tap into your expertise about a specific subject and offer your business a mention on the air. The owner of a business offering whale-watching tours, for example, may be asked about certain endangered species of whales. A coin shop owner might be asked whether an economic downturn has led to a spike in the purchase of gold. An anchor or reporter isn't going to ask about weekly specials, but they will likely name the business and create the opportunity for thousands, perhaps millions, of impressions on viewers or listeners.

***Case in Point*:** One of the principals of a river cruise company was offered a segment on a network affiliate about trends in his business. He later complained that he didn't get an opportunity to discuss specifics about upcoming cruises. The producer of that segment heard about the complaint and muttered about referring the cruise guy to the sales department the next time he wants publicity.

Proximity, Proximity, Proximity: Does the name Rupert Jee sound familiar? It should if you were a regular viewer of *The Late Show with David Letterman*. Jee owns Hello Deli, which is literally around the corner from the front entrance to The Ed Sullivan Theater, where the show was recorded. After it debuted in the 1990s, the show had a "meet the neighbors" segment, taking cameras past businesses within a one-block radius of the theater. Letterman talked with various people the camera encounters. (Two people were asked to Xerox their faces.) Letterman asked Jee if he had ever had a standing ovation. He asked him to leave the cash register in the custody of a customer and to come to the theater, where the audience cheered him.

That was the first in a number of comedic segments in which Jee participated. He became familiar to regular viewers. You can imagine the effect his television appearances had on sales and name recognition. Even after the show went off the air, Hello Deli remained an iconic part of the neighborhood. On January 31, 2022, the City of New York proclaimed "Hello Deli Day" in honor of its 30th anniversary.

There's a saying that the three most important considerations in real estate are "location, location, location." A mansion in an unpopular area of the city may be worth less than a small townhouse in a desirable area. For a business, proximity to a media outlet can unlock hours of good publicity. Hello Deli may be a fine eatery, but it was its proximity to The Ed Sullivan Theater, not its cuisine, that made it nationally known.

This is an unvarnished example of *Authentic PR*. There were no sophisticated marketing messages vetted by layers and layers of publicists and message customizers here; just the owner of a business who was willing to act as a comic foil on national television.

Of course, not every business can be around the corner from a national late-night talk show, but taking advantage of proximity to a media outlet works at any market level. A friend of mine worked at a television station where he was asked once how he would fashion a segment with a gourmet chef. He replied that he would take a camera across the street to Denny's, and have the chef teach one of the short-order cooks how to make one of his dishes. You don't have to be an advertising executive to figure out the value of that kind of publicity in brand recognition and sales.

With radio and television, there are a number of people you need to get to know, and you need to know how each media outlet really works. If you've ever been in a television station within one hour of news time, you've probably seen what appears to be chaos. People are running around and yelling. It looks like the New York Stock Exchange the day of the crash in 1929. Again, if you're familiar with the movie *Broadcast News*, you may recall the scene in which the producer was in an editing booth, working with the editor, trying to finish putting together the story with seconds to spare. The reporter runs down the hall as the editor smirks and says, "She's not gonna make it." The producer then jumps over a baby to get the story to the control room on time.

That type of scenario is not the exception to the rule in broadcast news. It's *the* rule. And now, you're going to try to cut through the maelstrom of frantic producers and flapping identification tags to get a story on the air? It's easier than you think if you get to know broadcast journalists, respect their schedules and deadlines, and go out of your way to help them with breaking news.

The Players: Story selection begins with the assignment editors. Their job is to bring stories to the attention of producers and then assign videographers, and, in some cases, reporters to the stories that are due to be covered that day. In smaller markets, there may be one person on the assignment desk at any one time, while in larger markets the area around it may resemble a beehive, especially if there's breaking news, the reporter van had a flat tire, or the helicopter is running low on gasoline.

Knowing people who work the assignment desk (or "the desk," as it's called in newsrooms) will put you ahead in getting coverage because they're the ones who will determine whether your story gets "staffed"—that is, if they have the resources to send a videographer, a reporter, or both to your story. The desk is your first hurdle.

Suppose they staff the story. Your next challenge is to get it included in the show. That's the producer's job. He or she has the final say as to whether your story will get on the rundown—the list of stories, in order, that comprise the show. Once you're in the rundown, you're home free, sort of. Breaking news supersedes everything and could kill your story at any time. Sure, it would be a shame if your promotional event, which you have spent months planning, is deleted from the rundown because of a car chase—but that's the way it is.

How to Get Face Time: First, you need to do some investigative work. Watch local television news programs and find the shows in which you think a segment about your business would fit. Remember to think like a producer. If *you* were the producer of the show, what sorts of features would you include to appeal to the available audience? Remember that daytime audiences tend to be primarily people who are not working at that time, while prime time and 11:00 p.m. audiences tend to be in the workforce. What would appeal to them? Also, check the lead-in. What show precedes the one you're targeting. Is it a soap opera? A court show? The audience for the show that precedes a television news programs will sometimes (but not always) carry over to the show.

After you decide which show(s) to target, find out the name of the producer(s). This is easier to do than you might think. One way to find out is to check the credits for the show. (They will probably run on Fridays, if at all.) A better way is to call the newsroom and ask who produces the show in which you're interested. Don't ask for the anchor, who may have little to do with the actual production and brainstorming that go into the show. Producers are the unsung creative forces and decision makers behind television news shows. They, not the anchors or reporters, are the ones who make the decisions. So, keep calling until you reach them and then make your pitch.

One note of caution: Don't try to call them close to the time at which the show airs. Producers will probably be distracted then, and your call will be dismissed quickly. If you're pitching the producer of a news program that airs at, say, 2:00 p.m. or 4:00 p.m., call in the morning. You *could* call right after the show airs, though keep in mind that producers generally leave very soon after their programs end, and that they may not be in the mood to hear your pitch. But if you're pitching to the producer of a show that airs at 6:00 a.m. or 7:00 a.m., it's actually wise to call after the show airs because the producer will often be working then on the next day's show. Most of those shows begin production at about 11:30 p.m. or midnight. If you can stay awake and get through to the newsroom at around 12:00 a.m., those producers may be receptive to a pitch well before the rush begins.

Keep in mind that producers are human beings, and that they're in an industry in which compliments are few and most accolades go to the anchors. They'll be receptive to any compliments you might want to pass along, especially if it involves their shows' quality of writing. (Producers are chosen, in part, for their ability to write.) Then, make your pitch and offer to send more information about your business. If you get the sense that they'd like to break off the call, thank them, get their phone numbers (including, for example, their direct lines and, possibly, their company cell phone numbers.) And ask them for the best time(s) to contact them.

Always follow up immediately with an email or a text (if the contact number is a cell phone) thanking them for their time and reiterating your interest. You can follow up the pitch with another phone call in about a week.

How to Get Voice Time: Radio is the original electronic mass medium, and it all began with AM. In the 20th century, according to the Federal Communications Commission, the first radio broadcast went on the air in 1920, "when Westinghouse Electric and Manufacturing Company in Pittsburgh, under the call sign KDKA, broadcast the live returns of the Harding-Cox presidential election." The FCC states, "Within four years of the initial KDKA broadcast, 600 stations existed in the US and radio's rapid popularity contributed to our shared national identity by providing syndicated news, sports and music."

AM radio and FM radio are propagated in different ways. Both generate a ground wave that travels from transmitter to receiver via line of sight. But AM radio also generates a sky wave that can travel hundreds of miles at night because it bounces off the ionosphere. The sky wave is the reason AM radio signals can travel so far at night. They bounce up and down and travel hundreds, sometimes thousands of miles.

Listening to AM radio at night used to have the air of a mystery. Big rig drivers would ply slush-covered highways, and their only companionship was a mellifluous voice crackling through the static or a big band love song shimmering off the dashboard. Fifty-thousand watt stations with three-letter, and then four-letter, call signs blanketed the country with news, sports and prime-time entertainment until FM, which was less vulnerable to static and produced a mellower sound, became the medium of choice for music. AM radio turned to news and talk, then faded.

Today, radio is seen as a legacy medium, but it still attracts audiences, and should be on most lists of broadcast outlets to contact.

If you're pitching yourself as a guest on a radio talk show, there are some people you need to know. The producers of the shows you are targeting are your direct links to the station(s). Do whatever it takes to be nice to them: Laugh at their jokes. Root for their sports teams. Offer to change their tires. They are the gatekeepers. They are the ones who stand between being anonymous and being asked by strangers if you're that guy on the radio.

You also need to know the program director, who may have another title, like brand manager. That's a producer's boss. The program director is responsible for the overall sound of the radio station, so he or she wields power over your future as a regular guest. And, by all means, defer to the receptionist(s), as they're the ones who truly run the stations.

When it comes to radio, the procedure for pitching is about the same as in television, but the qualities they are seeking in a guest may be quite different. Unless you're a celebrity and you're being invited to talk with the morning team of the hippest music station in your market, you're most likely going to want to be interviewed on a news/talk station. On radio, they're not looking for clever visuals such as was the case in the gourmet-chef-at-Denny's scenario; they're looking for expertise. If you own a tour company, for example, a radio news producer might be very interested in tapping your expertise on travel. Where is it safe to go? Will airfares go up? Where are the deals? Are Americans leaving the country or exploring the US? Owners of independent moving companies could talk about where people are going and why. Are housing costs driving people away? If so, where are they going? Retirement planners could offer advice to Baby Boomers who are about to retire, and Millennials and Generation Zers who are planning for retirement or early retirement.

The procedure for getting on the radio is very similar to the approach you would take in getting on television: find out the names of producers of the shows on which you want to be a guest, then pitch them. The same rules apply: don't call just before airtime, be yourself and follow up. Remember that radio, like television, is a business, that producers are human, and that they like to have their work acknowledged. One difference from television is that, when you're pitching radio stations, you may be pitching a longer segment, so adjust accordingly—and keep in mind that radio producers are always looking for expertise and credentials to back up that expertise.

Perhaps in your reading you have come across Michael Levine's Ten Commandments for Dealing with Media:

- *Never be boring. Never!*
- *Know your subject thoroughly.*
- *Review the media you contact. Read the paper, watch the newscast.*
- *Cover your bases.*
- *Don't just take "yes" for an answer. Follow through.*
- *Never feel satisfied.*

- *Always maintain your composure.*
- *Think several moves ahead.*
- *Be persistent, but move on when you're getting nowhere.*
- *Remember, this isn't brain surgery.*
- *Don't take yourself seriously (like too many publicists I know).*
- *Have fun.*

Case Study Three: Eyes and Ears

The Challenge: You've just opened a gym or fitness center and hope to raise its profile in the community by getting television exposure.

The Strategy: Approach the producer of the local morning news program, which will usually begin between 4:00 a.m. and 6:00 a.m., and last up to seven hours. Offer to do a daily segment on fitness live from your business. Open your business to all comers for that segment. That way, you get a double benefit: access to the television audience, *and* new business from those who hope to be seen on camera. If your business is located in a mall, especially in a colder region of the US, chances are the mall opens its doors in the morning to walkers who don't want to brave the chill outside. Chances are, mall owners will be as eager as you are to get television exposure, especially in a business environment in which shopping at home has become the new normal.

The Rationale: Television news is ubiquitous. It's not unusual to find local television stations carrying eleven or more hours of news programming each day. *Why*? For one thing, it's cheaper to produce than other types of programming. In general, afternoon and evening news programs have a more attentive audience than their counterparts in the morning because people are well into their days and have a sense of what is going on in their lives. In the morning, television news is a bit more like wallpaper. It's on in the background as people run around, get the kids ready for school, and prepare for their own appointments. In such an environment, participatory programming, which involves interacting with, rather than talking to, the audience is an ideal way to engage people.

It may surprise you to learn that morning network shows are bigger money-makers than evening shows. Peoples' lifestyles have changed. In the days of Walter Cronkite, people had received comparatively little news by the time dinner was served. An audience of tens of millions of people were as hungry for news as they were for meatloaf and sweet potatoes by the time "Uncle Walter" was on the air. Today, news consumers are bombarded with information on their devices twenty-four hours a day. By the time the evening news programs are on, audiences may be as well informed as the anchor. The typical audience for an evening news program now is in the millions, not the tens-of-millions, but the morning shows are longer and offer more diversified content. Such as fitness.

The Cost: Hourly wage for the fitness instructor (unless you *are* the fitness instructor). When you pitch to the morning news programs, don't ignore the non-network affiliates, Some of them originate their own morning news programs between 7:00 a.m. and 9:00 a.m., or 10:00 a.m., whereas the network affiliates may just have news and weather cut-ins during those times. If you're pitching a network affiliate, you'll be angling to get a segment before the network morning shows go on the air. (Note: Even though FOX stations are network affiliates, the network doesno't have a morning show. If you pitch to a FOX affiliate, you'll generally be trying for a time slot somewhere between 6:00 a.m. and 10:00 a.m.)

Chapter Six

Advantage: "Mom and Pop"

When it comes to *Authentic PR*, the "small guys" have the advantage. Big businesses can't be nearly as quick and as nimble as small businesses. They can make a decision at any moment. If there's a dental office in Southern California and they decide that, starting next week, they're going to be open on Saturdays, they can do it quickly. It would take two years for those who run a big business to make a decision like that, if they were able to do it at all. And probably, the idea would never get ratified because it would be blocked in some kind of committee. So, small businesses have a tremendous opportunity.

And in the current environment, it's vital for businesses of all sizes to take advantage of whatever opportunities they can get. A startup today may become a trillion-dollar corporation tomorrow, only to be disrupted by a college sophomore tinkering in a garage. A big business can outspend you, but if you're a smaller and hungrier entrepreneur, you have the advantage of flexibility. And there's a great attraction among audiences today to *authentic* things. That's the repeated parable message of the book, that *real* is good, vulnerable is good, *transparency* is good. *Authentic* is good because it responds to the malady of our time: cynicism.

Small businesses are fast and local; and because they're local, they're potentially more credible. If you're part of a community, you understand that community's rhythm, and you understand its nuances. Those subtleties may be opaque to the manager of a big-box store. That manager might be here this week, maybe they won't. Chances are, that manager transferred from another location and will have to play catch-up to feel even a remote sense of community. Local business owners are generally networked more tightly into the community. They're members of civic groups, possibly, the Chamber of Commerce. In some communities, they may even be part of the private groups that have founded events, such as

Mardi Gras or the West Hollywood Book Fair. In a sense, local businesses that network in their own communities may be fundamentally more powerful than large corporations seeking simply to build an outpost of commerce there. And they may have more ties to local media.

Chapter Seven

The Six As

Customers want a number of things from businesses, but above all they want the Six As: *Attendance, Authenticity, Access, Acknowledgement, Attitude,* and *Aspiration.*

Attendance is pretty simple: You have to show up. You can tell when the owner and the managers aren't at a restaurant. It's a soulless experience. It shows that whoever runs this business cares only about measuring out the correct portions on each plate, in line with corporate policy, possibly dictated from a distant city. When the owners and the managers are present, they often talk with the customers, answer questions about the cuisine, discuss sports or a past community events.

To achieve *authenticity* in your personal branding and your business branding, don't pretend to be something you aren't. Always conduct your business with liberal amounts of candor, admit your mistakes, and be consistent. That candor should be accompanied by a commitment to openness. Let customers have the *access* they want to information about you and your business, and *acknowledge* how much you appreciate their patronage.

While *attendance, authenticity, access,* and *acknowledgement* are four qualities that can give your business a solid foundation, *attitude* and *aspiration* can take it to entirely new levels. If your *attitude* toward certain values and goals is aligned with your customer's values and goals, that customer may develop a fierce loyalty to your brand. The need for affiliation with a cause or with like-minded people is basic to humanity. We are social beings. We want to join with others, especially if our group is exclusive. Country clubs use exclusivity as a business model. That same principle applies to choices in commerce. If you live near a university, go to the faculty parking lot and count the number of Toyota Priuses and other hybrid vehicles there. Professors may very well believe that they could never be caught driving a gas guzzler, or even a fuel-efficient but fossil-fuel-powered vehicle. Electric vehicles and hybrids are *de rigueur* on campus. (If you want to have more fun, count the number of drivers who are listening to NPR as they drive out of the parking lot. If you happen to be following them, see if they stop at Starbucks for an ethically sourced beverage, then Whole Foods Market for some low-impact shopping.) You're not likely to witness a stop at Burger King.

This sort of groupthink is a powerful force in commerce. Your job in business is to know your customers' expectations, and to create a desire by your customers to affiliate with you. *Authentic PR* can show you how to share not only your business's narrative and values, but also your personal narrative and values to achieve your personal mission and financial goals, keeping in mind that community drives commerce. *Authentic PR* is a tool for creating that community, which should be your core mission as a business owner. Remember that, to succeed, you must reach your customers individually and the community as a whole. *Authentic PR* is the most potent tool to help you accomplish this.

As I mentioned in my book *Guerrilla PR,* we all think of ourselves as unique, unlike any person past or present. Indeed, what gives humanity its divine spark is the distinct quality of every individual. Yet, in so many ways, we're all the same. The task of market analysts, pollsters, and demographers is to identify those characteristics we share, and group us accordingly. If you were in your early forties when the earlier book came out and you were male, Caucasian, a father of two, earned $50,000 or more, and listen to a Top 40 radio station, there were total strangers out there who knew a lot about you.

"That's because they understood your upbringing. They know you watched *The Mickey Mouse Club* in the fifties, *The Man From U.N.C.L.E.* in the sixties, *Saturday Night Live* in the seventies, became environmentally conscious in the eighties, and were probably sorry ABC canceled *Thirtysomething* in the nineties." Of course, the shows have changed since that book was published in 1994. According to Christopher Edling, "if you are in your early forties today, Caucasian, male, you might have watched *He-Man* in the 1980s, *TGIF* on Fridy nights in the 1990s, *The Wire* in the 2000s, *Game of Thrones* in the 2010 s, and *Ted Lasso* in the 2020s." Life has also changed in other ways since that earlier book came out. The generations that succeeded the Baby Boomers have developed entirely new ways of communicating. Millenials and Generation Zers may share preferences for streaming series and music, but they also share their thoughts on social media. Life is a constant conversation today. That's something the Baby Boomers could only imagine. Little did they know that their children and grandchildren would be texting at the dinner table with a device that appeared to be straight out of *Star Trek*. The digital age is the age of sharing, a time of transparency. In such an environment, *Authentic PR* answers the zeitgeist with reality.

Reputational Advantage: This is a concept I introduced in my book *Broken Windows, Broken Business*. Reputational advantage is the use of your brand's reputation, your reputation, and the reputations of your employees to gain a business advantage over your competitors—and it's best accomplished through *authenticity*. If you deliver a product or service that has value, and if you have a reputation for being ethical and for acknowledging your mistakes and dealing with them immediately, your business is likely to succeed. If you develop a reputation for whitewashing and spin-doctoring your mistakes, you're likely to fail, even if what you produce has value. Keep in mind that your reputation is intertwined with your business's reputation.

Customers can sense when a company's "commitment" is nothing of the sort. Virtue signaling may sound like a bold move by a company to associate itself with one side of a controversial issue, but if it isn't sincere, it can tarnish your credibility. You don't have to signal your virtue if you live it. In a similar way, aspiration is a potent quality that can grow the stature of a business as well as its revenue. What could be better than having a customer who believes your company could help with personal growth? When a customer sees your company as a way forward, you have done your job.

JetBlue, for example, is a business that strives to be affordable but aspirational. Their fares are competitive, yet their flights have a high technology aura. They have screens on every plane, a blue cabin motif that buttresses the brand even as it adds a futuristic air to the experience, and a tiered fare system that doesn't leave its more cost-conscious customers feeling like outcasts. It's also created a website, Paisly, which offers à la carte add-ons to JetBlue reservations. In the words of Edward Russell Skift, "the launch [of Paisly] is the latest step in what JetBlue chief digital and technology officer Eash Sundaram has called the airline's evolution into a 'travel tech company.'" That evolution further creates the aura of a future-conscious company, an aura that attracts customers who want to affiliate with that image—and the image must resonate with customers' values, visions, or both.

The lesson here to smaller businesses is that image matters, because when customers affiliate with that image, they become loyal repeat customers. A technology-oriented company, for example, might host a high school robotics competition. A gourmet restaurant might print out a new menu every month highlighting the cuisine of one specific region of the world, then offer its chef to do once-a-month segments on a local television station and in-person classes on international cuisine. That restaurant could also offer amateur chef competitions, adding the winner's creation to the restaurant's menu. Imagine the diner loyalty that can foster. A dentist's office could do something similar to what my friend Doctor Jay Grossman does: he founded Homeless Not Toothless, described on its website as "a 501c3 nonprofit that has provided free dental care to disadvantaged populations including Veterans, the homeless, poor, mentally ill, physically disabled, foster youth, domestic violence survivors and the elderly, in the greater Los Angeles and surrounding areas since 1991." (The program either pays laboratory costs or works with laboratories that offer voluntary services.)

"Just over a decade after opening the HNT doors, Dr. Jay had the opportunity to join forces with actress and philanthropist Sharon Stone in her nonprofit, Planet Hope. Since then and together, the two rebuilt a dental facility to extend free dental care to the 28,000 foster youth living in Los Angeles.

"Some of HNT's pro bono patients have included an elderly ex-convict who had no teeth and had had to survive on a liquid diet for forty years; a five-year-old whose teeth were so blackened by decay that they'd been ridiculed at school; and a fifty-year-old, John, who had spiraled into homelessness as a result of a methamphetamine addiction, losing his construction business and his family in the process.

"As of today, HNT has treated more than 124,000 patients, including veterans, homeless, and foster youth, providing more than $9.7 million in services."

Case Study Four: Haircuts for the Homeless

The Challenge: Owners of a barber shop or styling salon want to increase their revenue during the holidays while cultivating the image that it's an active and generous citizen of the community.

The Strategy: Hold a "Haircuts for the Homeless" event at a local shelter or a public park on Saturday morning, offering haircuts, shaves, and shampoos for free. If possible, partner with a local restaurant to offer free meals at the shelter as well. Use AI to produce "before" pictures of the homeless, suggest styles, then produce "after" photos, all of which could be displayed on the shop's website. (This technology could be incorporated into the barber shop's website so that customers could take photos of themselves and pre-order a look or a style.)

The website could also use AI to book appointments, specify what works needs to be doe, and, through the camera, make recommendations for the style of haircut, hair color, or beard shaping. This information could be available to the barber when the customer arrives.

The day before the business opens, barbers from the shop could show up at the nearest homeless shelter and offer free haircuts and shampoos to the residents there. The owners of the barber shop could cooperate with the administrators of the homeless shelter and pitch the story to the media.

You don't have to be a dentist like Dr. Grossman to offer free services to the homeless. Like anyone else, homeless or housed, people like to look good. This is especially true for people for whom even getting a shower is a challenge and an ordeal—and it's vital for anyone who hopes to get a job and move into his or her own home.

This could be accomplished as a stand-alone event with the cooperation of local shelters and soup kitchens, or, during the holidays, it could be coupled with an annual holiday meal (such as those served *en masse* on Easter, Christmas and Thanksgiving).

The Rationale: This is an example of a values-driven approach. In fact, any outreach to the homeless or to underprivileged communities is likely to generate television coverage, especially around religious holidays. In part, that's because the story "fits" the zeitgeist of the season; but there's another, simpler reason: hard news tends to take a holiday on holidays and on weekends. If you watch local news on weekends, you might notice that the newscasts are populated with twenty-second voiceovers about weekend events, such as 5K runs and the like. *Why shouldn't your business's event be one of them?* You don't have to prepare in advance to pitch. (Just call the assignment desk and tell them what's going on.)

It's not unusual for the lead story on the local evening news on Christmas to be Christmas in the city. Producers are hungry for stories on holidays. A day when they are hungry for news is a day on which business owners should be feeding them heartwarming content that will elevate the image of their brands.

Case in Point: Jamie Masada, owner of the Laugh Factory in Los Angeles. He opens his business to all comers every Christmas and offers free food and a lineup of comedians, some of whom are known to television and movie audiences. Gestures like these help the community, and they also communicate the message that patronizing your business would be a fun and worthwhile experience.

Decades ago, the barber shop was something of a man cave where guys could go for a haircut, a shave, and a conversation about sports. Today, the haircut is still an in-person ritual, matched by the cut-and-color routine of the styling salon. Barber shops tend to be more lived-in, while styling salons tend to resemble the battle bridge of the Starship Enterprise—but the logic is the same: It's a place where you can get your scalp revitalized while someone listens to your gripes.

A post titled, "16 Barbershop Marketing Ideas to Grow Your Business and Attract More Customers" states, "marketing plays a vital role in the success of your barbershop business." With an excellent barbershop marketing plan in place, you can aim high. For example, why not use YouTube as a site for before and after shots? On business cards, a QR code could be a shortcut to your booking page. Most of the suggestions involve using social media and Google Business to the fullest through advertising, articles, and reviews.

One idea could be to set up a selfie station. In the words of the article, "because social media is such a powerful tool, another way to take advantage of it is by setting up an Instagtrammable corner in your barbershop where customers can take a selfie after a hair service and post it to their Facebook or Instagram page. Make sure to promote a hashtag that represents your brand."

Among the other recommendations from InTheChair.com:

- *Request reviews and showcase them online*
- *Tap influencers to help with your barber marketing*
- *Producer branded promotional items*

Reviews are some of the most *authentic* tools of *Authentic PR.* They're unvarnished, uncensored, and unimpeded. Before the advent of social media, messages about a product, or a service were "sanitized for the business's protection." Today, a raw and articulate review can be a business's best offense and defense. If the review *praises* a business, it can draw customers. If it *pans* a business, it can draw attention to a problem that needs to be solved.

The Cost: Hair care supplies, labor costs (unless stylists volunteer), possible insurance premiums. Some of the items, such as business cards and gift certificates, should probably be included among standard start-up costs, although all are forms of marketing. Website development is one cost, but it's a one-and-done expense, and can accommodate future promotions. Designing a selfie station may incur some expenses. The more elaborate it is, the higher the cost. If barbers donate their time for haircutting and shampooing event at the homeless shelter, there would be no labor costs. You may also be able to trim your budget for the grand opening and the trip to the shelter by enlisting the additional support from barbers and partners in other creative ways

In *Guerrilla PR*, I mentioned how "Los Angeles radio station KTWV, known as The Wave, scored points by dotting Southern California beaches with Wave trash cans." This sort of campaign can work for businesses in any beachside or lakeside community. Municipal governments tend to search for campaigns that spruce up public areas, and they can be open to public-private partnerships.

The aim of my earlier book was to outline some affordable techniques that could catapult a business to the next level or beyond. Some of the strategies included a national campaign by two college administrators on Long Island to get *The Honeymooners* back on the air; a marketing campaign by Domino's Pizza during the recession in 1992 called "Eat Your Rejection Letter," in which patrons would get one dollar off the price of their pizza by showing an employment rejection letter; a petition campaign by the founders of the Improvisation Comedy Club to persuade the Academy of Motion Picture Arts and Sciences to add Best Comedy and Best Comic Acting categories to the Academy Awards; an offer of a free seventy-two-ounce steak by the Big Texan Steak Ranch in Amarillo, Texas to anyone who can eat it in an hour; and a joint campaign by an auto detailing firm and a publicist to find America's Long-Distance Commuter Champ. (The winner commuted from Darien, Connecticut to Boston every day: 408 miles round trip.)

A number of those strategies are still relevant today, but it's important to keep up with the times—that means being savvy in social media, which offer new tools for attention-getting public relations and the ability to organize and register people for group evenings online.

Case Study Five: The X Games

The Challenge: A digital strategy firm wants to create a niche as a company that values originality and creativity above all else, a vital skill in a sector where digital marketing startups seem to sprout like mushrooms.

The Strategy: Conduct an online contest on X to find the most creative post.

The Rationale: Facebook is a place where you share your accomplishments; Instagram is a place where you share your photos; LinkedIn is a place where you share your aspirations; and X is a place where you share your opinions. It's like a bullhorn, an amplifier of short bursts of sound—and the message length is limited to 280 characters, which forces you to be concise and to the point.

Lorne Michaels, executive producer of *Saturday Night Live*, is quoted onBrooklyn.com as saying, "To me, there's no creativity without boundaries. If you're gonna write a sonnet, it's fourteen lines, so it's solving the problem within the container...and I think for me commercial television and its boundaries, I like it."

Tylor Mint, writing in *Republican Eagle*, quotes Orson Welles as saying, "The Enemy of Art is the Absence of Limitations." X allows businesses to tout and customers to vent. In a competitive environment, contestants are likely to value victory over venting.

The Cost: The value of the grand prize. No external costs.

Case Study Six: Cleaning Up

The Challenge: A housekeeping services company with a next-to-nothing advertising budget seeks visibility and acceptance in the community.

The Strategy: Organize a "Clean Sweep" campaign that would attract volunteers to help clean up various neighborhoods, in exchange for discount services. Limit the number of attendees to make the discount financially feasible and to convey the aura of exclusivity. Coordinate with the Department of Public Works to publicize the event, including a brief message on the city's 511 or 311 service if available.

The Rationale: States have hosted Adopt-A-Highway programs for many years. Businesses sign up to be responsible for cleaning up and maintaining certain stretches of highway in exchange for a sign, visible to motorists, that announces their involvement. Even people in the entertainment industry got into the act, such as Jennie Garth, who played Kelly Taylor on *Beverly Hills 90210*, and adopted a highway in Southern California. Bette Midler adopted sections of the Long Island Expressway and the Bronx River Parkway in New York.

The Clean Sweep Campaign is similar, only it would apply for neighborhood upkeep rather than highway maintenance. As it grows, perhaps the local municipality could be persuaded to erect signs in the neighborhood akin to the Adopt-A-Highway signs. If it becomes a long-term campaign, businesses could reap extraordinary public relations rewards, especially if owners can take credit for helping to transform the neighborhood from blighted to booming.

Eventually, as publicity for it proliferates, Clean Sweep could go national, with ongoing cleanup campaigns from Connecticut to California and beyond.

The Cost: Discount coupons, permits, and, potentially, insurance (unless the city underwrites the event).

Case Study Seven: Games On

The Challenge: Developers of a just-released video game want to gain visibility around the world and find their niche in the field.

The Strategy: Organize a World Games competition to begin the day the game is released. Announce it in an interactive teaser two weeks to a month before the game goes public and allow potential participants to register. Solicit prizes that would go to the first contestant to reach the highest level of the game and the participant who reaches that highest level the most times during a specified period. Prizes can be bartered in exchange for visibility on the game site in a manner similar to product placement in movies. This may sound out of reach, but it's not. Even the heavy hitters are hungry for visibility, whether they're long-established and deep-pocketed, or less than a year old and ambitious. The prospect of getting their logos in front of millions of people may be all that's needed to get them in the game.

The Rationale: According to Gil Press, "As of 2023, there were 3.220 billion gamers worldwide. The number of gamers worldwide [was] predicted to 3.320 billion by the end of 2024. Asia has the highest number of gamers 1.48 billion followed by Europe with 715 million. Fifty-five percent of the gamers are males in the United States." All of them could potentially rally around your video game if you are savvy about the grand opening. You'd be surprised how easy it is to partner with multi-billion dollar players to enhance revenue streams beyond the usual subscription fees and advertising. Airlines, technology companies, and streaming services may all want to get in line for a global grand opening. Your audience is potentially huge because you don't have to deal with the logistics and limitations of working in real space.

The Costs: Zero for public relations if the prizes are bartered.

Case Study Eight: The Crypto Contest

The Challenge: A cryptocurrency firm wants to raise its visibility and become a "go to" and trusted trader online and in its home community.

The Strategy: Hold an NFT creation contest for artists, display the work online, then allow the public to critique and rate the NFTs. If the firm has a home office that's open to the public, print out and display the NFTs, and encourage customers and passers-by to critique and rate the artists' work. To add a twist to the contest, intersperse the human-created NFTs with some created by AI NFT generators. The contest could be titled "Everyone's a Critic," and the prize could be a year's worth of cryptocurrency counseling.

The Rationale: Cryptocurrency is now everywhere, though it isn't yet fully adopted or trusted. Perhaps, ironically, traders aren't favoring the cryptocurrency environment because it's unregulated. They want boundaries to be set so that more people feel comfortable owning and relying on cryptocurrencies, allowing their values to increase in a less volatile environment.

As James Royal, PhD, states on Bankrate.com, "The volatility of cryptocurrencies such as Bitcoin makes them difficult, if not impossible, to use as currencies. Major currencies need to be more stable in order to act as a medium of exchange. So the ideas that cryptocurrencies can be both trading vehicles for profit and functional currencies to transact are at odds with each other."

According to my friend Jerry Edling, NFTs are essentially throwbacks to the Renaissance, when artwork was a form of commerce as well as creativity. The Renaissance was also a time when the first currency (the Florentine Florin) was introduced. Today, the first cryptourrencies are being accepted widely, and NFTs are being bought and sold for millions of dollars. They can be a fun way for traders to introduce cryptocurrency in a painless way, and a great opportunity to get to know customers and potential customers as creators and critics.

The Cost: The value of the grand prize and fees for website development.

Case Study Nine: Guns for Grub

The Challenge: Bodegas and other markets want to tamp down crime in their neighborhoods and increase their own visibility and popularity as good citizens as well as solid businesses.

The Strategy: Team up with other markets, contact the police department and offer to sponsor a gun buyback program.

The Rationale: Gun buyback programs allow people who own firearms to turn them in with no questions asked in exchange for some kind of compensation, such as a coupon from a supermarket chain. Amanda Charbonneau, writing on Rand.org, states, "The primary goal of gun buyback programs is to prevent firearm violence by reducing the stock of firearms in a community. Gun buybacks can also serve as venues for increasing awareness of the risks associated with firearms, educating participants about safe firearm storage, and connecting violence prevention organizations, all of which could potentially lead to reductions in firearm crimes, injuries, or deaths." While larger supermarkets may furnish the largest share of coupons, smaller markets could team up and donate enough coupons to help sustain the buyback. This would be especially effective on Small Business Saturday, which is held annually on the first Saturday after Thanksgiving. Police could provide space for signage at the gun buyback point so that the smaller business will get their names on local television.

Another possibility would be to hold the gun buyback the weekend before the Major League Baseball All-Star Game, which is held on a Tuesday in July, and call it "All Stars for Peace."

Chapter Eight

The Experience Economy

"The entire history of economic progress
can be recapitulated in the four-stage evolution of the birthday cake."
—B. Joseph Pine II and James H. Gilmore,
"Welcome to the Experience Economy," Harvard Business Review

It's easy to believe that the birthday cake is about as unchanging as an asteroid floating through an uncluttered region of the solar system. It's cake topped by frosting and arrayed with lit candles that are blown out to the cheers of family and friends. But the cake is only part of a ritual that's been around for *decades*. The song "Happy Birthday to You" was written in 1893, and the preparation for that ritual traces the history of an economy that changed in fundamental ways.

According to B. Joseph Pine II and James H. Gilmore, writing in *Harvard Business Review*, the birthday cake in the agrarian economy was made from commodities produced on the family farm and cost "mere dimes." The industrial economy commodified food production and made available packaged goods in the supermarket, and "moms paid a dollar or two to Betty Crocker for premixed ingredients." Pine and Gilmore continue, "Later, when the service economy took hold, busy parents ordered cakes from the bakery or the grocery store, which, at $10 or $15, cost ten times as much as the packaged ingredients." Then came the experience economy, when "they spend $100. Or more to 'outsource' the entire event to Chuck E. Cheese, Discovery Zone, The Mining Company, or some other business that stages a memorable event for the kids." Pine and Gilmore argue that "leading edge companies—whether they sell to consumers or businesses—will find that the next competitive battleground lies in staging experiences."

The Authenticity Factor: As Lionel Valdellon writes in *CleverTap* ("The New Experience Economy: Establishing Authentic Connections With Customers"), "Ecommerce leaders are increasingly leaning into the 'Experience Economy'—the cultivation of authentic, non-transactional brand experiences—to win long-term customer loyalty." In the twenty-first century, it's not enough to produce a good product. There are two ways to transform customers into repeat customers. One of them is to demonstrate that you offer a unique and welcoming experience, while the other is to demonstrate that you share their values.

Experience-Driven: Apple is a master of the customer experience. When Steve Jobs was alive, product launches were cult-like experiences that began with the demonstration of the features of the product by Jobs himself at public gatherings that were mandatory calendar entries for many. Hours, sometimes days, before the producs were launched, people would line up at the local Apple store to purchase them, but transactions aren't the main purpose of the Apple Store: customer experiences are. You might call them technology oases, where even the most confirmed digital duffers can go and have their questions answered by smart and savvy tutors. Apple was, in effect, allowing customers to affiliate with genius.

Values-Driven: One so-called genius of our time is Jeff Bezos, who has at least one obsession: *the customer*. Of course, he stresses convenience, but he also understands that any company hoping to survive in the third decade of the 21st century will want to appear to align with its customers' values, or, at least, not appear to work against them. Amazon, for example, which could conceivably leave a significant carbon footprint with its delivery business, stresses conscience as much as, or more than, customer service.

On AboutAmazon.com, Amazon pledges, "Net-Zero Carbon by 2040": "As part of Amazon's mission to be Earth's most customer-centric company, we are committed to building a sustainable business for our employees, customers and communities. We are driving toward a net-zero carbon future where the people that support our entire value chain are treated with dignity and respect." The company goes on to state that "[i]n 2020, Amazon became the world's largest corporate purchaser of renewable energy."

Virtue signaling? Perhaps. But this isn't an example of a company aligning itself with the popular side of a controversial social issue. As a delivery company, Amazon is savvy enough to recognize that its customers might feel uncomfortable making purchases without an assurance that they're patronizing a company that cares about its impact on climate. In that sense, committing to Net-Zero Carbon by 2040 is at least an attempt at good corporate strategy.

Your Experience: Smaller businesses are not immune to this transformation of the economy. It applies to both Costco and the corner bakery, to Boston Markets and the barber shop.

Many Americans say their favorite restaurant is the one in which they are known by name. So, when you walk into a restaurant and someone says, "Hey, Harry…Hi, Sally…Hi, Matilda…or Hi, Jose," that begins an emotional journey. That's part of the experience economy. If you're a restaurant owner, you can cater to the experience economy and buck up your revenues simply by asking your employees to interact with customers and get to know them on a first-name basis if possible. And even if they don't know them personally, they should treat all customers with respect and attentiveness. Customers should never have to raise their hands to get a server's attention.

The first rule of the experience economy is to cater to your customer. The food at your restaurant may be Wolfgang-Puck quality, but if it's delivered by a surly or indifferent server who disappears for thirty minutes while diners are craving more ice water, those diners are not likely to return. The second rule of the experience economy is to cater to your customer, as is the third rule, the fourth rule, the fifth rule, and so forth.

Then, once you've transformed your restaurant into a worthy successor to *Cheers*, how do you get the word out that yours is a restaurant where conviviality complements the cuisine? And how does any other business get name recognition and brand affinity on a budget?

Case Study Ten: Good Sports

The Challenge: Owners of a sports bar that opened within a month of the World Series or the Super Bowl hopes to attract a crowd of regulars who will patronize their establishment during all sporting events, and eventually, even on slow sports nights.

The Strategy: Invite a local television station to send a crew to a sports bar to observe patrons watching the game.

This challenge is easily met, but there are pitfalls that might get in the way. The first step is to call a local television station, ask for the assignment editor, and invite whoever answers the phone to send a crew to the bar. The second step is to ask for the assignment desk's email address, and the name of the person with whom you are speaking. If the people at the assignment desk say they already have a sports bar in mind, thank them for their time and follow up with an email and offering to help in the future. If they say they might be sending a crew, follow up via email with all the details.

If the bar has a parking lot, make sure to let the station know that there will be a space reserved for their truck. There's nothing more frustrating to a television crew than puttering around, looking for a parking space on the street, only to finally find one a mile away. If you make it difficult for the crew, you may have to settle with a forty-five second story with one sound bite instead of two live shots with five-to-six minutes of crowd excitement. And be persistent. If three television stations turn you down, don't get discouraged and fail to get in touch with the fourth.

The Rationale: This is an example of an experience-driven approach. By inviting coverage of people enjoying a television event, you're not touting how scrumptious your wings are; you're inviting an audience of thousands, perhaps millions, of people to share in the experience of a sporting event.

The Cost: Zero. There are a number of ways to market a sports bar. Otilia Dobos, writing on GloriaFood, suggests choosing a theme. In Dobos' words, "Owning a sports bar already gives you the advantage of having a niche audience composed of people who like sports. When you know who your potential customers are, you can transform your sports bar to better cater to their needs and convince them to spend more time at your place." Among the suggestions, "Focus on a single sport; Honor all the teams in your area; and Choose a popular team with fans in your area."

Case Study Eleven: Going Green

The Challenge: A garden supply store wants to burnish its image as a responsible environmental member of the community by offsetting its carbon footprint.

The Strategy: Conduct a community composting campaign to reduce methane emissions at a local landfill. Purchase a sufficient number of recyclable lawn waste bags with your logo on them and a slogan such as "Going Green." Distribute them to members of the community and ask them to fill it with grass, twigs, and leaves, take them to a composting facility, then hold composting days on weekends and invite the media.

The Rationale: As noted on Cal Recycle, "Compost is the finished product that results from composting. It's a soil amendment containing a wide variety of nutrients, micronutrients, and organic matter, all of which benefit the soil. Whether it's done on site, at the point of waste generation, or in a large-scale, centralized facility, composting helps to keep the high volume of organic materials out of landfills and turns it into a product that is useful for soil restoration."

Environmental stories attract news coverage the way honey attracts bears. Watch local television news long enough, and you're bound to see a story about a beach cleanup, or a recycling drive for old electronics parts that can't be thrown way safely. Composting can get you coverage as well.

Consider Starbucks, which has been offering its customers used coffee beans for their own composting efforts. The program, "Grounds for Your Garden," began in 1995. Baristas scoop the used coffee beans into bags that originally carried espresso to the store, and give them to customers.

Jim Hanna, a director on the Starbucks Global Responsibility Team, said in 2015, "Grounds for Your Garden is a win-win for both Starbucks and our customers. We can keep valuable material out of landfills and put it to good use. Our vision is to recycle and reduce the waste in our stores as much as possible."

This initiative redirects waste to a socially responsible use and generates goodwill to customers by reinforcing the impression that a cup of coffee need not jolt one's conscience.

There is one caveat for businesses that want to tout their support for sustainability: make sure your "house" is in order, physically and professionally. In my book *Broken Windows, Broken Business*, I detail how overlooking details can create the impression among customers that you really don't care about your business, and that, by extension, you really don't care about them. I include a photo of a restroom at a Starbucks in Malibu. It showed a floor littered with toilet paper. Keep in mind that this establishment was located in a city where a no-limits credit card would seemingly not be out of place in any home. And yet, at least at the moment the photo was taken, the floor of the restroom was dotted with toilet paper sheets like so many snowflakes. As the title of my book suggests, a barista could remedy that "broken window" with a mop.

Some other points: Make sure you are using the most efficient energy systems available to heat and cool your establishment. All the better if they're certified by a professional ratings association, and consider using evaporative coolers, also known as swamp coolers. As the United States Department of Energy states, "In low humidity areas, evaporating water into the air provides a natural and energy-efficient means of cooling. Evaporative coolers, also called swamp coolers, rely on this principle by passing outdoor air over water-saturated pads." According to the department, that reduces the temperature by 15 to 40 degrees.

The point is: *Be consistent.*

The Cost: The outlay for the customized bags. For a business to succeed in the third decade of the 21st century, it must offer a unique experience. The purpose of this book is to show how to make the public aware of that unique experience without spending a fortune.

After all, a novel is nothing if it doesn't have readers, a Broadway show isn't much if it doesn't have an audience, and a scientific breakthrough is very little if other scientists aren't aware of it. A business that offers a unique experience, maintains its integrity about its mission, and strives to be transparent in all things will have the best shot possible at succeeding. Dreaming the vision is up to you. Showing you how to share that dream is up to us.

Chapter Nine

Gaining Visibility in the Age of Transparency

The Three Takeaways: This is not your father's marketing environment. In an earlier era, the product or the service sold itself. People used to choose cars because they were an efficient way to haul the family to school, to soccer practice or to Disneyland—and, yes, perhaps because they looked cool. People chose restaurants because they had great filet mignon, and commuters on-the-go patronized coffee shops to get a good cup of joe.

Today, consumers may buy aelectric cars because they don't want to jeopardize the planet with what comes out of their tailpipes. Before diners dig into that filet mignon, they might ask whether the cattle that produced the restaurant's meat stocks were ethically raised. And before socially conscious coffee drinkers savor that first morning sip, they might ask pointedly if the beans were ethically sourced.

In such an environment, honesty is the best policy when it comes to publicizing your business. Your customers are savvy, socially conscious, and selective. They will not accept anything short of the truth, the whole truth, and nothing but the truth. In many ways, you could call this the Jiminy Cricket business environment. So many customers believe what Jiminy articulated in *Pinocchio*: "Always let your conscience be your guide."

When customers demand candor, *Authentic PR* responds with candor: Mistakes are admitted, crises are handled immediately, and change is confronted and thoroughly explained.

Authentic PR has three takeaways:

First, Do No Harm
Tell the Truth
Get Real

These are not options. They're mandatory if you want to do business in a connected world. One misstep can ignite what will seem like a brush fire on social media that can consume your business.

You've probably heard it said that staying on top is tougher than getting to the top. Truer words were never spoken for businesses in the 2020s. Starting a business can be exciting. You're watching your ideas materialize into something that will have an impact, but once your business morphs from an idea to an ongoing enterprise, the real work begins. Employees, competitors, government regulations, economic conditions, technological advances, and unexpected change all claim your attention. (Just ask Eastman Kodak about how technological change can affect a business.)

Above all, you have to deal with customers and their comments, which can be amplified to the world on social media. That means you have two major challenges: gaining visibility in the age of transparency and achieving reputational advantage. When applied to businesses, reputational advantage is the assertion that, in a connected world, your reputation, and the reputation of your business, are equally important—so you, as a business owner, must do all you can not only to maintain good business and personal reputations, but also to develop a better reputation than your competitors.

Cunning will get you visibility. Conscientiousness will get you reputational advantage. How can these three takeaways send your business from plodding to soaring?

Chapter Ten

First, Do No Harm

The word "privacy" should probably be retired from the dictionary. At a time when companies like Apple, Google, and Microsoft can seemingly track every movement, purchase, and search request, privacy appears to be anachronistic. According to the United Nations, there were 8.27 billion people in the world as of February 2026, while according to the US Census Bureau, the number was 8.17 billion. According to the International Telecommunication Union, roughly 6 billion people (4 percent of the world's population were online as of 2025).

We are all increasingly connected, and our lives are becoming more and more transparent. In an age in which social media give all of us a global reach, our triumphs, our tribulations and our trip-ups can play out in front of a global audience.

If you run a business, that's concerning. All businesses have tribulations. The ones that achieve measures of success have triumphs. To survive in a connected age, the focus should be on the trip-ups.

As Michelle Cheng, editorial assistant for Inc.com, writes, "Nothing goes unseen on the internet. And as more entrepreneurs and brands are learning, a seemingly minor stumble on a social platform has the power to do everything from shake stock prices to inspire massive protests." In her article, "The 5 Biggest Social Media Fails of 2018," Cheng included a tweet from Jeff Bezos about going dog sledding in Norway. As Cheng put it. "People were quick to respond on Twitter that not everyone was out sledding in Norway. Comedian Sarah Silverman reminded Bezos about his employees who depend on food stamps and government assistance."

Want more? Cheng writes, "For International Women's Day, German appliances manufacturer Miele shared a photo on Facebook that reaffirmed a 1950s-era stereotype: four white women looking excited for a washer and dryer. The company deleted the post a few hours later."

And then there was the ad on Snapchat for a game called "Would You Rather?" According to Cheng, it was an ad "asking users whether they would want to slap Rihanna or punch Chris Brown, alluding to the 2009 incident when Brown physically assaulted then-girlfriend, Rihanna, to which he pleaded guilty." Cheng writes, "Rhianna called out Snapchat on her Instagram Stories, stating: 'Now, Snapchat, I know you already know that you ain't my fav app out there! But I'm just trying to figure out what the point was with this mess. I'd love to call it ignorance, but I know you ain't that dumb!" She also condemned Snapchat for being ignorant about victims of domestic abuse. The company lost $800 million in market value as a result.

You can make your own judgment about the intent of each post. The point is, they all had an impact, and the impact was swift, sharp, and sure. Never underestimate the power of an irate customer in the digital age. When the criticism begins to trend, hang on to your spreadsheets. There's trouble a-comin'.

Chapter Eleven

How to Do No Harm

The owner of a vegan restaurant who is caught on camera savoring a steak could literally be pelted with comments on social media, and those could wipe out business the way a prairie hailstorm wipes out a corn crop. But suppose that business is changing and is actually working to incorporate meat into its business model. In that case, the business owner has two choices: let it happen with no explanation and shock the customer base or prepare for the inevitable blow-back with a carefully considered strategy.

Just ask Matthew and Terces Engelhart, the owners of Gracias Madre, described by Wyatt Marshall, writing in *Vice*, as "a vegan Mexican spot with locations in San Francisco and Los Angeles," and Café Gratitude, which, according Marshall, had five locations in California. According to Marshall, the Engelharts "crossed over to the dark, omnivorous side and started raising their own animals for consumption, addressing the decision in a blog post that apparently no one read." But someone found it, and the Engelharts faced the threat of a boycott from former regulars.

When it comes to your brand, the aphorism *First, do no harm* should be your guiding principle. (Contrary to popular belief, *First, do no harm* is not part of the Hippocratic Oath, although it is traced to Hippocrates. As Robert H. Shmerling, MD, writes in *Harvard Health Blog*, "It is actually from another of his works called *Of the Epidemics*.") Little did Hippocrates know that in the 21st century, it would be applied to the health of a business.

There are times when businesses do harm, whether by accident or through avarice. What counts if that happens is contrition. CEOs, managers, and other responsible parties must step up, hold themselves accountable, and offer to implement measures that will mitigate the consequences of the mistake. Businesses are like a row of dominoes. If one piece topples, the entire row goes down. The vegan restaurant owner overheard practicing malevolence with meat is going to be hard pressed to run a credible café once word gets around on social media. Large companies aren't even immune to what might be called a "sudden image takedown."

Caught in the Tweet Trap (Now the X Files): Social media are like megaphones. They amplify everything that's put on them, and those who seek to "spread the word" could find it spread to the wrong places. In an article on *Business Insider*, "13 People Who Got Fired For Tweeting," Brian Love mentions what happened to Connor Riley, who, in Love's words, "had a job offer from Cisco on the table. She tweeted: "Cisco just offered me a job! Now I have to weigh the utility of a fatty paycheck against the daily commute to San Jose and hating the work."

Love writes, "Shortly after that there was a reply from Cisco employee Tim Levad: 'Who is the hiring manager? I'm sure they would love to know that you will hate the work. We here at Cisco are versed in the Web."

Then there's Nicole Crowther, who Love writes "was a recurring extra on *Glee* until she tweeted some plot spoilers she heard on set." Love continued, "She was more or less fired via Twitter by the show's producer, Brad Falchuk, who tweeted this response: 'Hope you're qualified to do something besides work in entertainment.'"

Case Study Twelve: X Success

The Challenge; An employee posts a message on X or an article on another social media site that thousands of your potential potential customers find offensive. Someone organizes a boycott, and begins to circulate a petition online asking people to pledge to join the boycotters.

The Strategy: Go online immediately, on the social media site where the offending message appeared, and post a video or print apology. Make it clear that the post was not authorized, and that it doesn't represent the views of the company. Highlight the company's email address, and reply personally to anyone who sends you a question or complaint.

The Rationale: A boycott can be triggered by an authorized post or an unauthorized post. Either way, the strategy is the same. Adam Fisher writes on *MediaFirst* in 2019, "Boycott has become an increasingly popular way of consumers showing their displeasure.

"It has become almost automatic for users to call for a boycott as soon as a brand does something they don't agree with. Nike, Heck, Paperchase, Pepsi, Starbucks, and Uber are just a small selection of brands that have been the subject of calls to be cold-shouldered and found themselves in crisis media management situations."

Anything that threatens to harm your business, your brand, or both should be addressed swiftly, candidly, and with humility. If you were at fault, admit it; if an employee was out of line, clarify that; and if it was beyond your control, explain why. Excuses could herald the beginning of the end for your business, while honesty could herald a new beginning.

The Cost: Zero.

Chapter 12

Tell the Truth

A company that specializes in manufacturing solar panels is caught polluting a waterway. The director of a drug rehabilitation center is caught with drugs in their car. An audit of the books of a financial institution reveals irregularities. All of these scenarios can cause a PR crisis. And in the era of *Authentic PR*, none of the solutions that were tried and true in the past will work. That's because you're no longer dealing with just the public; you're dealing with the visible public. They can review your strategies for dealing with a situation and talk back about them on social media. According to *The Bible*, Jesus proclaimed that "the truth will set you free." Nothing but the whole truth will do.

According to *PRLab*, "A crisis is anything that has the potential to destabilize an organization to any degree." Depending on your perspective, the Engelharts didn't necessarily do anything wrong in moving to meat, but they could have done irreparable harm to their brand if they hadn't adequately prepared for the inevitable fallout from their decision. Because, in a transparent age, anything you do can affect your brand. That doesn't mean you're doomed to inaction and paralysis. It simply means that if you take an action that could alter the character of your brand, you must have a comprehensive strategy to deal with the consequences, and that strategy must meet that change with candor, conscientiousness and credibility.

The Engelharts did two things definitively right: They told the truth, and they did their best to get ahead of the story. Instead of waiting for a die-hard diner to discover that they were covertly trafficking in meat, they disclosed their decision and explained why they did it.

They didn't follow the paths of some fossil fuel companies. Take BP. Before the blowout at the Deepwater Horizon Oil Rig in the Gulf of Mexico on April 20, 2010, BP PLC had positioned itself as a forward-looking energy company that was pinning its future on renewables. Fossil fuels didn't even get a mention in its advertising, which was geared toward giving the consumer the impression that it was multidimensional. Its slogan was, *Beyond Petroleum*. And it matched image with investment, spending billions of dollars. The blowout changed all that. Over the course of eighty-seven days, more than 200 million gallons of crude oil was pumped into the Gulf of Mexico, but it took far less time than that to reposition BP in consumers' minds as a fossil fuel conglomerate (and a flawed one at that.)

BP's handling of the blowout would later be characterized as an example of what *not* to do in a situation like that. Just ask Glenn DaGian, who had worked with BP and Amoco for decades and was retired at the time of the blowout. As Elizabeth Shogren of NPR put it, "DaGian watched from the sidelines as BP executives declared it was not their accident, blamed their contractors, and made the company look arrogant and callous." He was quoted as saying, "I was literally yelling at the TV set…I thought that the first reactions should have been more humble and more conciliatory. I was very upset that they didn't apologize. It sounded like they were hiding behind the lawyers' skirts."

When Da Gian was called out of retirement, his troubles became less academic, as BP CEO Tony Hayward, who had cut the company's public relations and government relations spending, came out with such comments as, "There's no one who wants this thing over more than I do. You know, I'd like my life back." Then BP created a video in which Heyward apologized, and said, "we'll make this right." So, in the words of *TechCrunch*, "it was mostly seen as a failed public relations stunt."

With comments like that, BP handled its public relations with one hand figuratively tied behind its back, and social media made its plight even more precarious. On *TechCrunch*, @BPGlobalPR had more than 175,000 followers, compared to 15,000 for BP's official account, @BP_America. Among the tweets from the parody site:

- "We are doing everything we can to stop the information leaks in the gulf: http://ow.ly/22XTw #bpcares"
- "Congrats to BP's Mother of the Year 2010! It's just oil people! Take the kids out and enjoy the beach! http://ow.ly/232ua"
- "Lightning struck one of our ships! Come on Planet Earth, what did we ever do to you?!?"
- "It's hurricane season now. Don't worry! We've planned for that just as well as we've planned for everything else!"

Social media is, overall, a conversation CEOs and other officials have to be ready to respond to when the public speaks out, not what they imagine the public to be thinking. In the era of three television channels, a well-crafted commercial might help turn public opinion in a company's direction. Today, a well-crafted commercial is just as likely to be lampooned as it is to be liked.

Mark Twain is quoted as saying, "Against the assault of laughter, nothing can stand." Given the right situation, and a bevy of clever content creators, much the same could be said about the "assault" of social media. The only antidote to this sort of caustic comedy is credibility. Before social media, practicing public relations was a matter of dealing with the "gatekeepers," and, by extension, the public. Today, members of the public *are* the "gatekeepers."

BP wasn't the first fossil fuel company to flounder. When the Exxon Valdez ran aground off Alaska and dumped hundreds of thousands of gallons of oil into Prince William Sound, Exxon violated the tenets of the then-developing field of "crisis management." In the words of John Horusha, writing in *The New York Times*, "[E]xperts in public relations say that Exxon seriously worsened the damage to its public standing by failing to seize control of developments after the spill and establish itself as a company concerned about the problems it had caused." Cases in point, as enumerated by Horusha:

- *Exxon's chairman, Lawrence G. Rawl, sent lower-level executives to the scene instead of taking charge himself;*
- *News was disseminated solely out of Valdez. Exxon's media relations people throughout the world were not updated;*
- *Exxon executives waited days before commenting;*
- *Public statements from Exxon at times contradicted information from other sources;*
- *Exxon apologized but did not take responsibility for the spill in an advertisement;*
- *Gerald C. Meyers, former Chairman of the American Motors Corporation, called it "an unmanaged crisis."*

The Exxon Valdez oil spill happened in 1989. The first step in twentieth century communications would have been to indicate quickly and honestly to the world what had happened and take responsibility where necessary. The rules of crisis communication are: clear, fast, humble, accountable, personally responsible, and fast. Today all those rules continue to exist, but there is now a greater need to know more about who's saying what and what will be done. There's now a much significantly higher level of cynicism and distrust. If you have in your company environmentalists who have been working alongside you, then that's something that consumers yearn to know about, where thirty years ago they only wanted to know what happened, what you are doing to fix it, and who should pay for it. There is a greater need to know more about not only the actions of the corporation, but also the *soul* of the corporation, the *heart* of the corporation, and the *conscience* of the corporation.

The trick is to get consumers to empathize with an entity that some regard as suspicious and evasive. First, as it relates to credibility, there's no way to really establish moral credibility unless you're willing to criticize yourself or your group. That's what I think *Authentic PR* calls for: responding quickly, humbly, and responsibly. It's good business compared to doing the opposite. Bad business involves taking a long time to respond, issuing denials, and passing the buck. That's a bad thing to do. You won't get away with it, so why do it?

Case Study Thirteen: Diamonds Are Forever

The Challenge: A jewelry store in a tiny part of an upscale city is caught sourcing diamonds from a conflict zone, prompting articles in some influential city publications. The store faces the threat of a boycott.

The Strategy: Without delay, second thoughts, or hesitation, the owner writes a letter of apology and posts it prominently on the store's website. The owner also offers to be interviewed by the publication(s), and promises that labels on every diamond in the store would identify their country of origin.

The Rationale: In a perfect world, a business would *do no harm* every time. Food and hot beverages would come from ethical sources, air and water would be pristine, and net-zero carbon emissions would be an immutable fact of life., but in a not-so-perfect world, things happen. *Your* job as an owner in those cases is to get out in front of the problem and have the backs of the people who are affected.

Conflict diamonds are precious gems that help fund civil wars, primarily in Africa. According to Beldiamond, "Diamonds have been found in more than thirty countries located in both the Northern and Southern Hemispheres, but only ten of these countries stand out for the volume of diamonds that they produce." Australia and Russia are on that list, but the rest are in Africa, where civil wars have taken a deadly toll. The same customers who would avoid drinking coffee from an unethical source would likely avoid cementing their love for each other with a diamond that had helped leave a nation divided and in ruins. Failing to deal with sourcing mistakes could cost a store dearly in a connected age. Stumbling on social media, where complaints about unethical businesses can spread around the world, can cost you your livelihood.

The Cost: Whatever it takes to research the origin of diamonds in the story, the cost (if needed) of revising your website to accommodate the apology; otherwise, nothing.

Change and its Consequences: Change comes hard to your customer base. Just think of how relationships with best friends deepen. It isn't through change; it's through familiarity. They get to know your quirks, foibles, eccentricities, habits, and overall patterns, and you get to know theirs. Business-customer relationships grow the same way, through familiarity. If customers sense disturbance in what Luke Skywalker would refer to as *The Force*, they're likely to react with bafflement at best, and anger at worst.

Take Bob Dylan, for example. It's difficult to fathom that the winner of the 2016 Nobel Prize in Literature was once booed at the Newport Folk Festival. He was, though, in 1965. Dylan initially made his name as a folk singer, writing and vocalizing songs that reflected the turbulence of the 1960s while accompanied only by an acoustic guitar and a harmonica. As Ryan Andrews put it on History.com, "By the summer of 1965, there were signs that Bob Dylan had entered a new phase of his career. The wild-haired troubadour had traded his everyman garb for sunglasses, trendy suit jackets, and pointy-toed boots, and he was beginning to distance himself from his reputation as a protest singer and folk balladeer. 'Like a Rolling Stone,' which, in Andrews' words, 'combined stream-of-consciousness lyrics with electric guitar and catchy organ riffs,' was released five days before the Newport Folk Festival, where Dylan performed the song for the first time in public." (He led off with a version of the song "Maggie's Farm" and then launched into "Like a Rolling Stone.") As Andrews put it, "This wasn't the Dylan the folk purists in audience had paid to see. To them, it was a musical betrayal—proof that he had abandoned the authenticity of folk for the glitz and glamor of rock 'n' roll."

It was up to Dylan to manage that change.

The point is, in addition to whatever title you hold, *you* need to be the perception manager of your own business. If you decide to change direction in a way that will affect your brand, you need to prepare your customer base for that change. Perhaps if "Like a Rolling Stone" had been out longer before the Newport Folk Festival, Bob Dylan might not have received the reception he did.

Ben Cohen and Jerry Greenfield, two school friends who founded Ben & Jerry's in 1978 in Vermont, understood the importance of perception when they sold their ice cream business to Unilever in 2001. Their business had been built on values with which the generation that came of age in the 1960s was familiar. As articulated on Unilever USA, "Ben & Jerry's was the first ice cream company to use Fairtrade-certified ingredients. It positions itself as unconventional and quirky, with its fun flavour names, and it has strong sustainability credentials."

Unilever owns hundreds of disparate brands, including Dove, Lipton, Lifebuoy, and Axe. One might wonder how a brand like Ben & Jerry's fits into that mix. In an interview with Katherine Klein, Vice Dean of the Wharton Social Impact initiative, Jostein Solheim, then-CEO of Ben & Jerry's, said, "I think the key thing in the whole transition to one shareholder from multiple shareholders was a governance structure that was put in place. Unilever was very visionary in recognizing that it says 'Ben & Jerry' on the packaging. If Ben & Jerry go out and say, 'Well, this is all not really true anymore and [social justice is] not a mission of the company anymore,' that would really undermine the value of the acquisition."

Case Study Fourteen: Flying the Coop

The Challenge: A chicken-themed restaurant in a gentrifying neighborhood faces dwindling sales because of a social media post asserting that all of the restaurant's chickens are raised in cages and are never free to roam.

The Strategy: Switch to an ethical source for the chicken. You can do the research through the ASPCA or the Certified Humane Program, which is run by Humane Farm Animal Care (HFAC). Then announce online that the restaurant will have a grand reopening from noon until 2:00 p.m. on a particular day. Hang certificates in the restaurant certifying that the chickens served there were raised and treated humanely. Announce that all the proceeds of the grand reopening, from noon until 2:00 p.m., will be donated to a local homeless shelter. At 2:00 p.m., put the servers in convertibles (loaned to the restaurant by an automobile dealer), and send them on a "chicken convoy" to the nearest homeless shelter to present the check for the proceeds.

The Rationale: A number of restaurant customers in the third decade of the 21st century are guided by conscience as well as culinary tastes. Advocacy groups and professional organizations have developed guidelines. Restaurant Brands International has identified five freedoms as their guiding principles in the treatment of animals:

- *Freedom from Hunger and Thirst*
- *Freedom from Discomfort*
- *Freedom from Pain, Injury or Disease*
- *Freedom to Express Normal Behaviour*
- *Freedom from Fear and Distress*

(Brambell FWR. (1965). *Report of the Technical Committee of Enquiry into the Welfare of Livestock Kept under Intensive Conditions*; HMSO: London, UK.)

The Cost: Costume rental, gasoline for the convertible, loss of income for one hour, and fees, if any, for certification.

The Chick-fil-A Effect: I go occasionally, not often, but occasionally to Chick-fil-A. They've got some friendly young kids working there, and the product is generally good. Now, I know people who are uncomfortable going to Chick-fil-A because the company was founded by a rather conservative Christian, and one of the decisions that Chick-fil-A made when they were formed is to not open on Sundays. This decision may even hurt their business, not just because of lack of revenue on Sundays, but because some customers are put off by the decision to be closed one day a week may refrain from going Monday through Saturday, even if the food is appealing.

On the other hand, if you're a conservative Christian, you may not have a problem with Chick-fil-A's position; in fact, it may induce you to be an even more avid patron. So, if you're a conservative Christian, you may be walking around the planet with a positive view of Chick-fil-A, and you may go there more often than you would if your sole motivation were to load up on calories. On the other hand, if you're discomforted by conservative Christians, not being open on Sundays, and those types of things, you may studiously avoid Chick-fil-A.

Whether you're a believer or a boycotter, you may stoke your opinion with information from the internet. This sort of cocooning can lead to insularity; and whether or not the information is credible, it's a factor that businesses must consider, particularly in the volatile restaurant industry.

In a polarized nation, restaurants and other businesses that are open about their values, and, in some cases, their politics, are bound to galvanize at least some of its customers to action, one way or another. Li Zhou writes on *Vox* in 2023, "Despite Republicans' longtime backing, the chain's decision to employ a vice president of DEI prompted backlash …" DEI, as you probably know, stands for diversity, equity, and inclusion. It is a way of promoting diversity and fairness in the workplace, from hiring practices to pay equity to making all employees feel welcome. According to Erica Foldy, a professor at NYU's Wagner Graduate School of Public Service, as cited on ABC7.com, "DEI initiatives focus on three main areas: training, organizational policies and practices as well as organizational culture." Tina Opie, a DEI consultant and professor at Babson College, continues that, "Initiatives focusing on policies, practices and culture are intended to correct inequities within an organization."

This is a cautionary tale, that your company's popularity could be broad but shallow. Anything that polarizes and politicizes personalizes your customers' decisions on whether to patronize.

Case Study Fifteen: On the Job

The Challenge: Entrepreneurs establish an advertising agency in a city, and want to demonstrate their public commitment to diversity in hiring.

The Strategy: Hold a job fair on premises over a weekend, inviting all comers who have reached maturity to apply for positions. Invite the media. If possible, get a local politician, such as the city councilperson for the district in which the business is located, to "welcome" the business the city.

The Rationale: Weekend stories about the economy resonate with radio and television stations, for four reasons: There's usually something going on with the economy, whether it's inflation (affecting consumer costs), recession (affecting job availability), or uncertainty (as pundits speculate about what's really going on). Producers are always on the lookout for stories that appeal to working people. More people are free to go to such events on weekends and the job seekers are a great source of sound bites. If the agency is already open, and there's ample space for parking, the job fair should be held on premises; and the premises should seemingly be overflowing with samples of the company's work. If the job fair is held as the business is being constructed, hold it in a public park, or ask a museum or historical society to host it. They should be more than happy about the prospect of boosting attendance.

The Cost: Refreshments for applicants, any permitting and fees, if the event is held off-site, and overtime if hourly employees staff the event.

Chapter 13

Get Real

Change can do harm to a business if it isn't managed correctly. Your job is to *do no harm*, to *tell the truth*, and to *get real.*

But what does it mean to get real?

It means to treat your customers as equals, as people with a discerning minds and steadfast values. Your job as an owner or a manager is to learn the values of your customers, then be frank with them about how your business is measuring up. Suppose you're in the apparel business and you discover that some of the clothes you've designed are being manufactured at a sweatshop in an impoverished region of the world. You would most likely move your business to another factory or invest in improvements at the one you are currently using. More than that, though, you need to be up front with your customers about making a mistake. That's the essence of *Authentic PR.*

In the article, "How to Admit to Your Customers That You Messed Up," by Stephanie Fisher, published on *Mojo Media Labs*, Fisher chronicles HubSpot's response to a mistake. In her words, "Recently, HubSpot issued a press release and email to customers with an update about a series of unfortunate events. There was an outage in service which affected many of their customers." Fisher's five pieces of advice based on HubSpot's response:

1. *Apologize.*
2. *Admit your mistake and take responsibility for it.*
3. *Empathize with your customer.*
4. *Explain in detail what went wrong.*

Anyone can make a mistake. Your customers will respect you if you own up to it. They will leave you if you don't. Even a brand-threatening mistake can be rectified with honesty. Your customers will reward candor with loyalty. It's that simple.

To illustrate, think of two politicians who each made career-threatening mistakes. One of them owned up to it, while the other tried to explain it away. *Which one do you think would have the better shot at retaining the office?*

Case Study Sixteen: Systems Down

The Challenge: A cybersecurity firm must work to restore its credibility after it installs an update that causes outages worldwide. (Perhaps you remember this incident, which took place on July 19, 2024.)

Reuters reported, "The CrowdStrike engineer who pushed through a seemingly harmless software update probably couldn't have imagined the global havoc it would cause. Nor, in all likelihood, could the $83 billion cybersecurity company's customers. The global meltdown that followed on Friday exposes the extreme fragility of a global IT network that prizes efficiency over stability.

"Widespread computer outages, characterised by the dreaded 'blue screen of death,' grounded US aircraft, stopped traders from settling positions, and kept broadcasters like Sky News off air."

The Strategy: It all started with what CrowdStrike CEO George Kurtz called a defect found in a single content update, "which went to customers using Microsoft's ubiquitous Windows operating system. The company deployed a fix, Kurtz also said." He went on CNBC and said, in response to a question, "Well, first, let me start with, I want to personally apologize to every organization, every group, and every person who's been impacted by this. And we understand the gravity of the situation." In other words, he obeyed the cardinal rule of crisis public relations: have the CEO, owner, or another person in charge take over the situation and apologize sincerely for any harm done. This is not the time for underlings to be in charge. The CEO or other responsible person needs to become, literally, the face of the situation, and take over the restoration personally.

The Rationale: Keep in mind that candor drives commerce. How you behave as an owner or CEO arguably has at least as much to do with sales as the product does. The product is no longer the center of gravity; the company or the entrepreneur is. Call it the center of gravitas. Intangibles like charisma and likability can boost revenue, but even if you're lacking in those qualities, honesty, integrity, and candor will keep your customers coming back for more.

George Kurtz did it right. He made the video apologizing for the outage, then he took responsibility.

The Cost: Zero for the video.

Case Study Seventeen: Food for Thought

The Challenge: Your grocery store or bodega stocks a food item that's recalled because of possible contamination.

The Strategy: Make your customers aware of the recall as soon as possible. Be candid and upfront about when you were notified and clear about the procedures customers should follow in disposing of the tainted food item and any health alerts that are linked to the product.

Information about the recall should be front and center on your web page as soon as the details are released. (Your job will be easier if you have a Facebook page, an X account, and a presence on Instagram. You can create a community of customers and communicate with them regularly.) Don't make it difficult for customers to get a refund or credit. Make it clear that you are not at fault, but at the same time, don't delay in getting customers refunds or credits. *Service delayed is service denied.*

The Rationale: With apologies to Nike, *just do it*. You don't need to take responsibility for a recall that wasn't your fault, but you do need to take appropriate responsibility for how efficiently customers re compensated for their inconvenience. If you have an internet presence (social media, website, or both), make sure you're up front and candid about the recall. Don't sensationalize it, but don't underplay it, either. Just write up a concise statement with easy-to-read instructions about how to get the tainted items replaced, then move on to your usual panoply of sales.

This sort of candor is not limited to food. Electronics, appliances, and children's toys are three other sectors in which vigilance to recalls is critical. Whatever the sector, be aware of what's going on in the market, and don't be afraid to be visible. Don't court coverage of the recall, but if media outlets want to interview you, be candid, and be forthright. Think of the media as bears that wandered into your neighborhood. They can be dangerous, but your chances of survival are better if you stand up to them more than if you run away, Above all, communicate with your customers. Mike Snider, writing in *USA Today*, cited a study in which, "[t]he US Public Interest Research Group queried twenty-six of the largest US grocers." He writes that according to the group's report, "[m]ost stores failed to respond to the survey. "A few stores answered 'a handful' of the survey questions about how they handle recalls including in-store and direct customer notifications. So researchers set out to check grocers' websites for store policies and ranked each chain on what they found.

"The findings: A vast majority of stores—84 percent—failed to adequately inform the public about recall notification efforts or how to sign up for notifications from a store, or where to find in-store postings about recalls, the researchers found."

You may not have a store or a chain that ranks in the top thirty, but the principle is the same: *communication*. Your customers don't like to be left out in the cold. Picture yourself on a commercial jetliner that's been moved away from the gate, but has stopped and isn't heading toward the direction of the runway. Wouldn't you be infuriated if the pilot, the first officer, and the flight attendants told you nothing about what was going on? Customers of grocery stores, electronics stores, and toy stores feel the same way when the owners of those stores fail to level with them about what's going on. They'll forgive any mistakes you made, but they won't forgive your silence.

The reason for their rage is well rooted in human psychology: *No one wants to be excluded or rejected*. If you leave your customers out of the communication chain, you effectively tell them that you find them unworthy of receiving the information, and that you don't want them inside what might be called a secret society of knowledge. If you're honest and open with your customers, they will bond with you. If you're secretive and exclusionary, they will abandon you. Think of yourself as the rush chair of a fraternity or a sorority. If you *don't* admit them, they're going to be bitter. If you *do* admit them, they're going to be brothers and sisters.

The Cost: Only expenditures associated directly with the recall. Honest, candor, and openness are free.

Truth is the Destination: Paul Simon got it so right years ago when he sang out poetically, "A man hears what he wants to hear and disregards the rest." People basically go on "scavenger hunts" online seeking evidence to support their views. Those who agree with them become part of a virtual posse. Those who do not get unfriended.

As Charles Dickens puts it, "It was the best of times, it was the worst of times." That could describe the communications climate of the world. Whether it's the age of foolishness or wisdom may be best left for history to decide, but it certainly isn't boring. The pressure to change the way you message is greater today than ever before, and that's what *Authentic PR* is.

I hope to lead a big and important conversation about how to do that more effectively. It's important to be *authentic*, and it is important to be *transparent*. Companies shouldn't pick fights unnecessarily, but they shouldn't shy away from who they are either. Companies will not prosper in this world if they try to disguise what they stand for. For all its faults, this is a world in which con artists have a short shelf life and conscience is a value added.

Authentic PR is truth on a fast track. Credibility is the driver. You need a toolkit to get started, and among the most powerful tools at your disposal are social media platforms. My advice? Keep in mind the words of Grail Knight in *Indiana Jones and the Last Crusade* when he was discussing the consequences of selecting the wrong cup as the Holy Grail: "Choose wisely."

Hit It Head-On: Do not attempt to hide or gloss over a change you're making. Change is tough. Some of your customers might not accept a change at first, but they can become former customers, even bitterly angry former customers, very quickly if you don't level with them from the outset. If you're candid with them and show respect, they will respond by giving you some latitude to transform your business.

Chapter Fourteen

Post It and Pitch It

If you want to reach your customers where they spend their time, you should already be visible on a number of social media sites. Deciding where to have a presence depends on the nature of your business and the demographic profiles of your customers. A hip sneaker outlet catering to young runners will have a far different social media strategy than a consulting business offering advice on income streams for retirement. Nevertheless, some social media spaces have a larger "footprint" than others, and all are worth considering to get the right mix for your business.

According to the 2026 Global Digital Report (Meltwater/We Are Social), and market analyses by Exploding Topics and DemandSage, the most popular social media platforms worldwide as of April, 2024, were:

- *Facebook*
- *Instagram*
- *WhatsApp*
- *YouTube*
- *TikTok*
- *WeChat*
- *Telegram*
- *Snapchat*

Just as you would logically want a mixed portfolio of stocks, bonds, mutual funds and ETFS for your retirement fund (along with some NFTs if you plan to spend your golden years in the Metaverse), you should also diversify the social media "portfolio" you create for your business. Each social media site has its strengths and its shortcomings, and how that plays out is unique for each business. A strength for one business may be a shortcoming for another, but some social media sites are *de rigueur* for all businesses.

Facebook: Think of it as the patriarch of social media sites. Its newsfeed should reflect the day-to-day growth and transformation of your business over time, with ample space for feedback from your customers. If you own a restaurant, Facebook is an ideal space in which to showcase your newest dishes and trace their journey from farm to table to demonstrate how they were ethically sourced. If you sell life insurance, Facebook is also a great platform on which to introduce new products and post articles of interest about trends in the industry. For those who are in sporting goods, Facebook is, as well, an excellent platform on which to post comments about the game, the playoffs, the Super Bowl, the World Series, and other major sporting events that may be engaging your city of operation. And, of course, sponsoring a local Little League team, and tracking its seasons on Facebook, is an excellent way to engage a community of family and boosters.

What It Is and What It's Not: Facebook is *not* a place for ten-percent-off-if-you-act-within-thirty-minutes hyperventilating. On the contrary, it is for humanizing your products or services and giving them new dimensions. To understand why, you need to be aware of why people spend time on Facebook.

In "Why do people use Facebook?," published in 2012, Ashwini Nadkarni and Stefan G. Hofmann "propose a model suggesting that Facebook use is motivated by two primary needs: (1) the need to belong; and (2) the need for self-presentation. Demographic and cultural factors contribute to the need to belong, whereas neuroticism, narcissism, shyness, self-esteem, and self-worth contribute to the need for presentation."

Because Facebook aims to fill the need to belong, the key in using this social media tool is to create a sense of belonging among your customers; specifically, a sense of belonging to a community. To create this community, you need to empower your customers and take the risk that the community you create will not always put you on a proverbial pedestal. It's risky, but it's healthy.

There are two types of communities you can create: a community of values; and a community of interests. Sometimes they overlap. A community of values brings together like-minded people who share a predisposition to deal with social issues or a particular social issue in the same way, while a community of interests brings together like-minded people who share a devotion to a common goal or pursuit. Ben & Jerry's created a community of values centered on the zeitgeist of the 1960s by never abandoning those values, even when Unilever took over. The community embraced the ethical sourcing of the ice cream and the hip names of its ice cream flavors. If you own a restaurant, you could create a community of values by posting articles about the farm-to-table journey of your food and invite your customers to comment.

A sporting goods store could create a community of interests by starting a fan page and forum and giving its customers an opportunity to open up about that controversial play in the third quarter. Automobile dealers could also start such a community. A General Motors dealer, for example, could start a forum, depending on the year, about an upcoming anniversary edition of the Corvette, while a Tesla dealership could start a forum about green energy and advances in autonomous vehicles. Electric vehicle manufacturers could even crowdsource ideas on how to increase battery charging speeds or how to reduce emissions even more from the vehicles they make. (This sort of community, from a manufacturer that pegs its hopes on green energy, could easily morph into a community of interests and a community of values.)

And the service department could post information about simple automobile repairs that can be done at home and create a forum in which it answers customers' questions about how to maintain a vehicle's warranty. (If it sounds counterintuitive that a dealer's service department would post information about do-it-yourself repairs or maintaining a warranty, that's precisely the point. This is *Authentic PR*. It should surprise and dazzle the customer with its seemingly self-defeating honesty.

Whether it's a community of values or a community of interests, remember that the keyword is community, and remember as well that it won't be much of a community unless you empower your customers to express themselves.

The Caveat: If your customer base skews younger, you should consider supplementing Facebook with additional social media sites, specifically ones that attract younger people. From an article by Henry Chandonnet published on *Fast Company*, "Facebook was born as a social networking tool exclusively for Harvard students. These days you'd be hard-pressed to find many US college students on the platform. Over the past decade, Facebook usership among US teens dropped from 71 percent to 33 percent."

It's easy to get the impression that Facebook has become a place for Baby Boomers to announce their retirement and show off their grandchildren. (Remember what Nadkarni and Hofmann wrote about "the need to belong" and "the need for self-presentation.") And that's not to say that you should abandon Facebook if your customer base is aged somewhere between zit cream and law school. Facebook is one of the essentials for business now, and likely in the future. Aging is the key driver here: Generation Z is growing up, and, as they do, some will join (or rejoin) Facebook. Baby Boomers are also growing older and growing out of social media.

Ultimately, younger people are more sensitive to trends, and because of that, you should be, too. Keeping track of the generations is like watching a parade. Some generations may be making more noise (or more music) within your earshot at any given time.

Instagram: There are a number of similarities between Facebook and Instagram. For one thing, they're owned by the same parent entity. But if you're searching for the defining characteristic of each social media site, think of the core of Facebook as the content and the core of Instagram as the image. In the words of a content writer identified as Diana on *SocialBee*, "Instagram is mostly limited to visual content. Facebook, on the other hand, combines visual content with text as well. "You've just tried imagining how adding just a block of text to Instagram (without the pictures) would be like, right?

"This can be considered the main difference between Instagram and Facebook. You can't post text on Instagram if you don't have a visual cue."

Ashley Galera of Chipotle put it, "Facebook is more for telling a story and actually writing out, and you can add pictures to it, whereas Instagram is more for video and photos telling a story and adding hashtags."

Jenn Chen writes on Sprout Social, "Instagram has over 2 billion monthly active users…59 percent of Instagram users log in daily."

Her "Key Takeaways: Instagram's app popularity is still on the rise, so remember to optimize your content for mobile use…The network's users are very active with a significant number who log in multiple times a day… While it is not the most preferred app for US teenagers, Gen Z and Millennials make up the majority of users."

What It Is, and What It's Not: Instagram is not a site on which to *tell* your story; it's a site on which to *illustrate* your story. If you're a furniture retailer, you may use Facebook to trace one of your products from inception to construction to showroom. Instagram would be an ideal place on which to post photos or videos of your manufacturing facilities, illustrating the measures taken to ensure worker safety. You could even post photos of employees captioned with their back stories to add a personal touch to the factory-to-showroom journey.

Testimonials from workers are fine, too, as long as they are demonstrably free of hype and hints of coercion. Similarly, a restaurant owner could post photos of new dishes, along with captions delineating how they were sourced. Photos of the Server of the Month, when coupled with a biographical caption, can personalize the dining experience, especially for a local community restaurant. Instagram is an excellent showcase for the Little League team that is sponsored by a sporting goods store or the youth symphony orchestra that is backed in part by a piano retailer. Automobile detailers can create catalogues of their best work on Instagram, where the picture tells the story. Domestic apparel manufacturers who want to tout that their products are made in the US can use photos and videos on Instagram to illustrate their entire in-country supply chains.

Hashtags are one major advantage of Instagram because they can position your business where you and your business want to be, and you will no doubt be tempted to sign up for Instagram Business. According to Dana Nicole, writing on DanaNicoleDesigns.com, being on Instagram Business will allow you to tap into Instagram Insights. At a time when data rules and technology can keep track of your customers' every move, such insight is invaluable.

And then there's the contact option, In Nicole's words, "You can make it super easy for your audience to figure out how to get in touch with you via phone, email or your physical address."

The Caveat: Even though an Instagram Business account has its analytical advantages, the site isn't a panacea for all your business challenges. According to Saritel Abbaszade, writing on FS Poster, an Instagram Business account may actually distance your business from your potential clientele. As Abbaszade put it, "Since social networks are all about connecting with others and engaging with them, an Instagram business profile may make followers less likely to engage with you than a personal profile. Because they perceive your account as promotional."

Abbaszade offers one way out: "Limiting promotional content and aiming for a genuine tone while partnering with an influencer that complements your brand will help you prevent this."

Instagram's photo-and-video-orientation presents a unique opportunity for you to tell the story of your business in a way that may engage and involve your customers in innovative ways. Max Freedman writes in *Business News Daily*, "Using Instagram for business can drive brand awareness, boost sales, and build and track audience engagement. It's an excellent way to find customers where they're already spending time. It can also provide valuable audience insight to use with all your marketing plan strategies."

Authentic PR is all about engagement. You don't want to do anything that will distance yourself and your business from your customers. On the contrary, you're aiming for a relationship akin to a personal friendship, not strictly a business association. As with personal friendships, you will develop a rapport that will enable you to be candid with your customers, share successes and, above all, admit mistakes. Keep your analytics close, but keep your customers closer.

TikTok: TikTok is another video-focused platform, but the videos are shorter: fifteen seconds to ten minutes. While Instagram is a place to find videos for the record, TikTok is the site for videos in the moment. That's an important distinction for your business. If you own a restaurant, you might use Instagram to showcase particular dishes in detail, while on TikTok you could send out a spontaneous message during peak dining hours about something your chef is cooking up at the moment. It's very much in the moment, and it gives your customers a sense that you are a personal friend and are eager to share something you are doing rather than a business trying to lighten their wallets.

Historically, TikTok has skewed toward shorter videos, even after longer content was allowed. It grew out of an app known as musical.ly, which was known for short-form videos and video streaming. Geyser writes that, "in August 2018, the app was taken over by a Chinese company ByteDance and its users were moved to Tik Tok. All of the content and accounts that were present on Musical.ly were automatically transferred to the new Tik Tok app." According to Geyser, "The key differentiating factor between Musical.ly and Tik Tok is that the latter has a much broader scope for video creation."

TikTok has created something of a community of users because of its focus on videos not exceeding ten minutes. It is a place for the short bursts of creativity that are especially popular among younger demographics. Take Jimmy Fallon. As Geyser writes, "In November 2018, Jimmy Fallon started a 'challenges' section on his show and used TikTok as a platform for the challenge. "He urged his viewers to take on the #Tumbleweed-Challenge and post videos on TikTok of themselves rolling like a tumbleweed. The TV host himself took the challenge, to kickstart this trend."

Think of TikTok as a sort of video X. It's a place for short bursts of creativity and insight. Much as a solar flare is occasionally ejected from the sun, disrupting communications on Earth, users of both TikTok and X bursts of insight and ingenuity out into cyberspace.

What It Is, and What It's Not: TikTok is a place for what I would call moment marketing. Ten minutes isn't long enough to tell the complete story of how you as, say, a footwear retailer ethically source your shoes, but it's long enough to showcase that award you received for sustainable marketing. Perhaps more importantly, it's an ideal place to involve your customers in fun and meaningful ways.

For example, you could post a challenge, as Jimmy Fallon did. Ask your customers to post videos of themselves using your product in very creative ways. Then, ask the community to vote on which video is the most ingenious. (Be sure to stay out of the judging yourself or you'll alienate every contestant except the winner.) The advantage of this sort of moment marketing is that it's ever-changing. It's always fresh. And you can come across as a CEO who doesn't take life or your company's product(s) too seriously.

There's another advantage to using TikTok. In Geyser's words, "Another key driving factor in TikTok app's popularity is the fact that despite being a global app, it has a strong focus on localised content. The app often runs local contests and challenges and captures on local trends through the use of localised hashtags."

This sort of flexibility can mesh well with your marketing goals as you grow. The ability to localize allows a company that is permanently tied to a specific geographic region to focus on its customers and potential customers in that region. Conversely, a company that's using its home base as a starting point to become a global presence can use hashtags to slowly expand its reach, and a company that's solely online can grow by networking with other communities online, using hashtags to reach out to them.

The Caveat: As of 2026, TikTok's US operation has transitioned to majority US-based ownership. ByteDance, the Chinese company that owns TikTok, has a 19.9 percent stake, but no longer has operational control of the US-based operation. The transition followed concerns that China could collect data on tens of millions of US users. Today, the data is stored on servers in Texas.

But, according to a CBS report and other legal analyses, TikTok's updated privacy policy in the US includes "precise location information…if a user enables location services," as well as citizenship, immigration status, racial or ethnic origin, religious beliefs, and sexual orientation. Some customers, once they're aware of this policy, may shy away from using social media sites that have these sorts of guidelines, whether or not they have to opt into having the information harvested. That said, a business that uses social media should not focus the majority of its outreach on any one platform.

As Devon Delfino and Dave Johnson note on *Business Insider*, "Safety is sort of relative when it comes to apps like TikTok. If your goal is to reach people ages eighteen to twenty-four, TikTok is a wise destination. But keep abreast of chatter and remember that younger people are more susceptible to trends. What ignites them today may fizzle tomorrow. Remember MySpace? It was at one time the largest social media site in the world. News Corporation bought it for hundreds of millions of dollars in 2005 and sold it for a fraction of that in 2011."

For the moment, though, TikTok offers the flexibility and creativity to be a significant marketing tool. Contests are particularly easy to pull off on this platform. If you sell sporting goods, for example, you can sponsor a contest asking customers to post videos of themselves using your products. Footwear companies can do the same. Restaurant owners may sponsor a contest challenging customers to come up with a new menu item and post videos of themselves with it. Hair salons may sponsor contests asking customers to come up with the most unusual hair styles (and possibly call it, "How Do You Do the 'Do?") Anything that lends itself to short-form video could easily dovetail with this app.

X: What TikTok is to video, X is to text: a space in which to share thoughts or activities of the moment. If your business aims to attract twenty-five to thirty-four-year-old customers, especially men, you're going to want to be on X. The social media site can be used directly, to promote products and services, and indirectly, to discuss ideas and developments of the moment that are related to your business. For example, an accountant could send out bursts of information about rising interest rates or little-known tax laws. The owner of a store that sells garden tools could offer advice about the ideal time to plant in a particular region. The owner of a hardware store could solicit do-it-yourself tips from customers and then showcase some of the best ones. And a clothing designer or retailer could publish information about trends in fashion.

X is possibly the most provocative of the social media sites because users aim to engage with opinions and insights. While you may share a milestone on Facebook and a snapshot on Instagram. X is the place where you share an aha moment. If Albert Einstein had been on social media, he might have posted on Facebook about his appointment to the faculty of the University of Zurich. On Instagram, he might have posted a photo of the ceremony at which he received the Nobel Prize in Physics. On X, he might have asked, in 280 characters or less, what it would be like to travel at the speed of light. (As a Premium user, he could have elaborated his description, up to 25,000 characters.)

Business is full of aha moments. Those moments spur the dreams of entrepreneurs and guide the preferences of customers. You may remember or have heard about a time when sugared cereals and white bread were the norm. The so-called Greatest Generation embraced that diet, still somewhat in awe of the idea that mass production of everything could make life easier and allow most people to work in specialized jobs rather than farm for a living. But their children, the Baby Boomers, grew up to be suspicious of corporations that mass-produced food and other commodities. Their preferences over the years have led to the popularity of organic food, ethically sourced products of all types, and a diet free of preservatives and chemicals. The businesses that took note of that are the ones that survived. Every trend begins with a vision.

What It Is, and What It's Not: It's easy to dismiss X as a haven for idea people. But as someone doing business in the 21st century, you *should* be an idea person. Keep in mind that in the experience economy, customers demand more than a good product. They want to know that it was ethically produced by a diversified, well-compensated workforce, and they will reward brands that assure them of that. In the experience economy, process is product. You can't separate what you're trying to sell from the way it was produced. A wise use of X can demonstrate to your customers that you have the planet in mind as well as their dollars.

What's important about X is that it personalizes the marketing experience and brings the business closer to its customers. A customer may express an idea on X, and the brand can respond directly and in a personable way. For example, who would think that bath tissue could prompt a conversation among users?

One user tweeted, "I HATE CHARMIN ULTRA SOFT TOILET PAPER!!!!!!"

Charmin responded, "We're beary sorry to hear this. We'd love to see how we may be able to help, and find the Charmin that's right for you. Could you roll us a quick DM?"

Charmin also used what was then Twitter to address a design issue: the wavy perforation of its bath tissue: "We appreciate your feedback, Jennifer. The wavy or scalloped perforation is a test that we're running in a few packs of Ultra Soft at the moment. We'll be sure to let our team know you prefer straight cut vs this wavy test. If you have any further feedback, feel free to DM us."

Think of it. If Charmin can host a dialogue about bath tissue, imagine what you can build around your business.

Charmin also used Twitter to promote its forestry practices. One tweet read, in part, "Charmin is committed to regrowing 2 trees for every one used, and pulp used in the products is @FSC US certified. #Charmin-Protect-Grow-Restore." (Note: Procter & Gamble, which makes Charmin, was the target of multiple greenwashing class action lawsuits regarding the Procter-Grow-Restore and "Keep forests as forests" marketing campaigns for Charmin and Puffs.)

Brands have been using X and Twitter in very creative and fun ways. A post by Tide, for example, reads, "Help clean the Cloak of Levitation before Doctor Strange finds out! Play for a chance to win free Tide PODS for a year!" This is a fun way to tie in to a film franchise.

Urth Caffé used Twitter to promote its engagement with law enforcement in the City of Pasadena (California). One tweet read, "Urth Caffé Pasadena showed its appreciation and gratitude to officers of the Pasadena Police Department with Urth Box Lunches as part of Urth's 'Feed Our First Responders' campaign."

The key to the successful use of all social media, X included, is community engagement. You want to make your customers feel like part of a family and a valued part of a community whose opinions matter. Since X is a medium of immediacy, it's ideal for promoting events that are designed to create immediate responses to immediate needs. A clothing retailer could invite the local community to buy blankets to send to a region of the world that was just hit by an earthquake and offer free merchandise in exchange. In other words, rather than buying or manufacturing the blankets themselves, the retailer engages the community in the effort and gives its customers the opportunity to feel that they are part of the team. No longer can businesses get away with simply marketing to consumers. Successful businesses engage their customers in a higher purpose, and X is an ideal place to promote this sort of effort, using hashtags to direct the message to the right consumers.

X is a great event magnet because it is a medium of the moment. In my earlier book, I discussed how KTWV, a radio station in Los Angeles that calls itself *The Wave*, garnered attention by placing trash bags with its logo on them in beach wastebaskets throughout Southern California as part of a beach cleanup campaign. It was cheap, it was impactful and it was ubiquitous. X is the ideal medium to use for promoting such an event.

X should be in the mix if a company makes a mistake and needs to apologize. Keep in mind that *Authentc PR* is all about candor. Admitting your mistakes is a powerful marketing tool because it shows consumers that you are honest and it demonstrates that you are strong enough to take your licks for a human error. Of course, you're going to post the apology on your company's website, but using X will transport the message to your customers in the moment and demonstrate that you are on top of things, and the apology must be sincere and not include denials. As Wesley Matthew noted in "How Brands Should Apologize," an article posted on *Meltwater*, "Denial can hurt subsequent apologies. Sincerely owning the mistake is at the heart of an effective apology."

Kate Kiefer Lee, in her article "The Art of the Corporate Apology" on the *Forbes* site, offered "tips:"

- Find out how people really feel. Keep an eye on Twitter and see how people are reacting to your screwup, and respond accordingly.
- Act fast. Don't wait a week to apologize when your customers are upset right now.
- Don't write a press release. This isn't the place to talk about how great you are at everything except the thing you're apologizing for.
- Actually say 'I'm sorry.' Don't forget the part where you say how sorry you are without finger pointing or justifying or nimblebragging."
- Say how you're going to fix it. Get specific.
- Watch your tone. In sensitive situations, the right tone of voice can go a long way.

"Use the platform that makes sense:" X is also possibly the best referral medium on the internet, a place where you can direct your customers (and the curious) to other sites for more information on your product(s) or service(s). For comprehensive information, X is more like the signpost than the destination. In other words, X can serve a dual role for your business: to pass along your thoughts of the moment and to direct the user to more comprehensive information about your business.

The Caveat: Posts can go viral on any social media platform, but if other sites are like dry kindling, X is like dry kindling drizzled with gasoline. With the correct use of X, your business could easily explode. With the incorrect use of X, your business could easily implode. As your business grows, you may need to hire people to manage your X account. Train them carefully.

When it comes to X, use wisely. And remember that you don't need a lot of words to make a loud noise. It took 272 words to complete The Gettysburg Address.

Case Study Eighteen: First Come, First Served

The Challenge: Owners of a coffee shop want to cause a bit of a stir.

The Strategy: Announce on X that the first three customers who show up on a particular day will get a free order, up to $100. (Limit the offer to walk-in customers. Invite the media to watch customers congregate as early as 4:00 a.m. for a free beverage. Suggested title: *Wake Up* [name of community].)

The Rationale: This strategy works best when the event is announced the day before it happens, then it takes on the characteristics of a sort of delayed flash mob. The aim is to give customers an incentive to gather at an odd hour and attract media coverage of this anomaly. For example, it's not unusual for a Starbucks to open at 4:30 a.m., which is precisely the time some television stations begin their local morning programming. At that hour, on a slow morning, stations are hungry to find a place to send their reporters, and your business can offer plenty of B-roll and sound bites to go.

The Cost: The beverages for the winner, and cost of security guard.

LinkedIn: LinkedIn is the place where social media users get down to business. According to industry reports from Martal Group and Sprout Social, LinkedIn has surpassed 1.3 billion registered members as of early 2026. According to Business of Apps and Martal Group, about 310 million to 600 million professionals engage with the platform monthly. And according to Social Shepherd, roughly 134.5 million users log in daily.

LinkedIn is essential for business-to-business enterprises, and it is a powerful tool for recruitment and hiring. If you engage in professional services, such as accounting, LinkedIn is one of the essentials. But any business can enhance its image and its profits with the careful use of this site.

The key to using LinkedIn wisely is professionalism. As an individual, you would not want to post cat videos and family hijinks here (unless you have somehow figured out how to market them). LinkedIn is a place to demonstrate your quality as a business, as a professional or as a potential recruit. It's a showcase for your business acumen.

Think of LinkedIn as a business retreat. While you're there, you want to make the best impression possible. At the conference, you dress according to the norms of your industry; on LinkedIn, you dress up your posts with professionalism. The three keys to the successful use of LinkedIn are presentation, presentation and presentation.

What It Is, and What It's Not: LinkedIn is a social media site on which your customers and your colleagues can engage with you on a professional level. In the words of Kiely Kuligowski, staff writer for *Business News Daily*, "A company page helps potential customers and job candidates learn more about your business, brand, products, services and job opportunities." In addition to the company page, Kuligowski recommends creating a "career page." In her words, "Finding an employee who fits with your company culture and has the right skill is a tough task for businesses of all sizes. LinkedIn career pages allow companies to tell their story, find the best talent and measure the impact of their goals."

While a company page and a career page might seem to encompass everything on LinkedIn, Kuligowski recommends the use of LinkedIn groups. She quoted Taylor Kincaid, social media director at Online Optimism, as saying, "A LinkedIn group is a great place to build an engaged community surrounding your business and to grow your online community." Once again, community is the key. Customers want the opportunity to engage with companies on an equal level. They want to be able to learn directly from the company why things are the way they are, and they want to be able to offer feedback. But make no mistake: The relationships you create with your customers on LinkedIn will differ from those you establish on other social media sites.

As Simone Johnson, staff writer for *Business News Daily*, put it, "From making connections and establishing partnerships to generating leads and boosting your brand awareness, you can do many things with LinkedIn that make it an invaluable addition to your digital marketing strategy. Unlike Facebook, Twitter, and Instagram, LinkedIn is a professional platform designed to help you establish and reinforce business relationships."

One of the primary benefits of using LinkedIn wisely is reputational advantage. LinkedIn is the site on which you can on which you can burnish your standing in professional circles and showcase your credibility. You can put up posts and you can write articles. Whereas a restaurant's Facebook page might include a blurb about a new dish or a video of Happy Hour, the owner might decide to post an article on LinkedIn about sustainable farming practices and the benefits of farm-to-table dining. Not to mention job postings.

The best way to look at LinkedIn is to think of it as a cover letter aimed at getting you a job interview. If you're a job applicant, it's a cover letter to a prospective employer. If you are a business owner or executive, the audience is your colleagues, your costumes, and your competitors. LinkedIn provides the opportunity for you to show them what you have.

The Caveat: There are a wealth of promotional tools available on LinkedIn. Articles published on the site can be valuable in giving more breadth to your brand and what you hope to accomplish by publicizing it. Make sure that what you write is on point and appropriate to your brand. That is not to say that you cannot express your own opinion or weave your own narrative in a LinkedIn post. In fact, that may be one of the most effective ways to give your brand dimension and fullness. But those posts won't work unless you're creative. Customers will recognize a blatant sales pitch, and they'll want something more.

What you write doesn't even have to mention the product as long as you establish the connection. With Ben & Jerry's Holdings Inc., they could publish a factual account of a social responsibility project, complete with statistics that illustrate how the project is improving the quality of life. On LinkedIn, the content should be a little more factual and businesslike than what you post on Facebook. Videos of the project could be posted elsewhere. In all cases, the product may not even be mentioned, but the link is clear.

You'll get points for posting information on LinkedIn and barely mentioning your product or service. People like to be informed, and your nine-minute read could be their intellectual jolt for the day. If your posts catch on, you could even start a series and focus on attracting followers. At some point, if your followers are well connected, your posts may reach critical mass and you may become an influencer.

Be creative, concise and consistent and you'll do well on LinkedIn.

Case Study Nineteen: The Brand-Boosting Virtual Job Fair

The Challenge: A chemicals business has been losing customers and potential recruits because of a toxic spill in a local river that's sickened some residents and tamped down tourism. The spill happened more than a year ago. The investigations are over, and the lawsuits have, for the most part, been settled; but recruiting is down more than 25 percent from the previous year. The owners feel like unwelcome neighbors, and they want to do something to burnish the brand and attract more potential employees.

The Strategy: Hold an on-site and virtual job fair using LinkedIn and Zoom. Publicize the event and the position(s) available on LinkedIn and include the formal job application, supporting information, and some videos of people who have held the job(s) before. While all of this is being posted on LinkedIn, offer local television stations interview opportunities with the CEO, an owner, or anyone else in a supervisory position. Nothing is off limits. This will give the company a way to publicize the breakthrough work it is doing in environmental responsibility, work that has been overshadowed by all the attention paid to the spill.

The Rationale: Dow Chemical became a target for protest during and after the Vietnam War because it produced Agent Orange, Agent Purple, and napalm, all of which were used in the conflict. In an article published on news.va.gov on March 10, 2015, Agent Orange was identified as "a blend of tactical herbicides the US government sprayed from 1962 to 1971 during the Vietnam War to remove the leaves of trees and other dense tropical foliage that provided enemy cover. The US Department of Defense developed tactical herbicides specifically to be used in 'combat operations.' They were not commercial grade herbicides purchased from chemical companies and sent to Vietnam." Dow says on its website, "During the war, Dow, Monsanto, and other companies were compelled by the US government to produce agent Orange under the US Defense Production Act of 1950. The government strictly controlled the transport, storage, use and the specifications to which Agent Orange was to be manufactured exclusively for the military." According to an article on ory.lsa.umich.edu, "Dow argued that according to military officials, napalm was only used on military targets. Dow also claimed they were not responsible for how the military was using their product."

Regardless, Dow Chemical Company became a target for protest. Its public image in the 1960s, 1970s, and 1980s had little to do with its household products, so much so that it launched an advertising campaign specifically aimed at recruiting, a campaign designed to make it easier for well qualified applicants to join the company's workforce without cringing. As Faye Rice noted in *Fortune* (as published on CNN in 1986), "THE ADS FEATURE misty-eyed college grads eager to save the world as employees of Dow Chemical."

They ended with a jingle:

You can make a difference in what tomorrow brings
Cause Dow lets you do great things.

Your company may operate on a smaller scale than Dow Chemical Company, but the principle is the same: engage your customers in a way they didn't expect. Showcase the work your business is doing that can help change the world. If your company is the target of protests and a boycott threat, start small. Don't create an easy target for demonstrators who will attract television coverage for the wrong reasons. Hold a few small-scale job fairs and then use your intuition to decide when it is time to scale up with this sort of outreach. Invite the media, and be transparent. Make your decision makers available for tough questioning, and create a counterpoint to the narrative that portrays you as a polluter. Reach out to environmental groups and engage them in town hall meetings. Over time you will be able change focus from pollution to production.

The Cost: Staffing of recruiters for the event, Zoom account, IT person to deal with technical issues, and ancillary record-keeping costs.

Chapter Fifteen

Television and Radio—
More Thoughts About the "Non-Social" Media

While it's true that they are not social, these media are still powerful forces in the US and around the world. Using television and radio wisely can be an excellent way of getting people to talk about your business rather than interacting with it. In that way, these media can heighten the visibility of your business. (That may sound ironic when it comes to radio, but the visual images generated by that medium are limited only to the imagination. Former CBS News journalist Charles Osgood once said, "Compared to a spoken word, a picture is a pitiful thing, indeed.")

The most accessible shows on television for businesses are local television news programs. According to the Pew Research Center in 2026, 70 percent of Americans trust local news organizations, a significantly higher rate than the 56 percent who trust national outlets. Evening and late-night shows tend to be more hard news-oriented, but it is not unusual for daytime news programs to set aside slots for lighter news features that could be a perfect fit for you as a guest.

The key to getting on television is to come up with an idea that will engage the viewer. It's not enough to tell producers that you own a restaurant. Suppose you own a restaurant that features a difficult-to-make gourmet dish. You could suggest to the producer of a television news program that they send a crew to Denny's so that you can teach one of the short-order cooks how to make it. If you sponsor a Little League Baseball team, does your roster include a girl? Suggest a feature about her to run on Major League Baseball's Opening Day. Tax tips are a perennial favorite. You could become the station's tax expert. Health segments are ubiquitous on local television. Some medical professionals have become highly visible in their communities through regular segments on health care. And then there are the cooking segments.

A Caveat: To reiterate, neither a guest slot on a radio talk show nor an appearance on local television is an opportunity to do an infomercial about your business. It's an opportunity for the talk show host or the anchor to tap your expertise. If you own a tour company, don't expect to have the opportunity to talk about the special deals you have on cruises to Alaska. Expect to talk about whether Alaska is a popular destination among Americans or Europeans and to back up your assertions with statistics. The host will measure your business in your introduction and at the end of the segment.

Some television and radio stations may have public affairs programs where you would be welcome as a guest. Stations would normally air these programs on Sunday mornings to satisfy Federal Communications Commission requirements for public affairs programming. You may wonder why you should waste your time with programs that have a smaller available audience. For one thing, an astute newsperson at the station may listen to the recording of the public affairs show, find something newsworthy, and use sound bites of you from the show, possibly in prime time. (Think of all the sound bites that get repeated exposure on Sundays from *Face the Nation*, *Meet the Press*, and *This Week*.) Also, the people who listen to the program on Sunday morning might be more focused on it and may want to contact you, engage you on social media, or both.

Never turn down an offer to be on a television or radio program, no matter when it airs. Producers are under such pressure to book guests for shows that they're likely to gravitate to the guests who always or almost always accept their invitations. The more invitations you turn down, the more likely producers at television stations or radio stations are likely to cross you off their call lists of reliable guests.

Chapter Sixteen

The Phone—The Forgotten Medium?

All your efforts on social media and all of your chutzpah in trying to become a television celebrity or a radio star will have been wasted if your customers are unable to reach you or your company quickly. They need to reach a human being when they are having the problem. Live chat falls flat if it's with an algorithm. Email pales in comparison to a phone conversation. I have a friend who tried to contact technical support for a medical website. He left an email message as instructed. Approximately five days later, someone called him. If that's the way you handle things, your business may face a reckoning and, possibly, a requiem. Stay in touch with your customers, and your company could experience a renaissance.

That means offering phone support even if you already have digital options. Frontier Airlines decided to offer real-time phone support for its passengers only if it's less than twenty-four hours before takeoff, twenty-four hours after landing, or if they have a frequent flier account with elite status. Frontier Airlines spokesperson Jennifer de la Cruz said in a statement quoted by Ramishah Maruf on CNN.com, "We have found that most customers prefer communication via digital channels." She said, as quoted by Maruf, "[T]hey can now receive information 'as expeditiously and efficiently as possible.'"

But speed and efficiency aren't the problem; comprehending a customer's dilemma and answering his or her questions are. According to Maruf, Breeze Airways "does not even have a call center phone number. Customers are advised to contact the carrier via Facebook Messenger, text, email, or they can make changes to their flights on its app and website." The human element is irreplaceable while building trust, understanding nuanced issues, and fostering genuine connections with customers."

Case in Point: a study conducted by Stanford University, which found that AI-powered customer systems, although efficient, often lack the empathetic understanding and personalized touch that human representatives provide. Another *Case in Point*: a Massachusetts Institute of Technology Report that found that while AI can handle basic inquiries, it struggles with complex problem-solving and emotional intelligence.

A good customer service representative should be an advocate and a problem solver. At its best, the relationship is somewhat ironic, because when customers perceive that customer service representatives are acting as advocates for them by knowing and using the shortcuts and loopholes that are available, those customers develop more loyalty to the company. The company's challenge is to make the customer feel like an insider who "knows the ropes." When customer service representatives act more like they're representing the company, the relationship becomes more adversarial.

Case Study Twenty: The Human Factor

The Challenge: A small business or hotel that has invested in phone support hopes to win new customers and solidify its relationships with existing customers by touting the fact that it offers phone customer service with real human beings.

The Strategy: Draw attention to people's nightmarish experiences with companies that do not offer phone customer service with real human beings. Invite people to email or text accounts of their worst experiences with companies that offer digital-only or zero phone support. Post them on your website. Keep it light. If you decide to name the companies mentioned in the complaints, make sure the complaints are accurate. Then, ask visitors to your website to vote on which was the worst "nightmare." All the while, reinforce the fact that companies can reach a live human being when they call your company.

Don't limit entries to your sector of the business ecosystem. The idea is to make fun of businesses in every sector that maintain that they can do full customer service without paying for full customer service.

The Rationale: Phone support is the foundation of customer service, since only direct personal contact or a direct phone conversation can communicate the subtleties of a customer's request. A friend of mine who didn't know that an airline had curtailed phone support called the airline with a request to move a flight from Tuesday morning to the following day. The airline's AI customer service bot didn't understand his request and kept kicking him back to the main menu. Eventually, my friend texted his request and was connected to what purported to be a live agent. It took hours to resolve a simple change in dates.

That kind of customer service is bound to backfire because it deprives the customer, and the company, of the opportunity to create a relationship that can literally bond the customer to the company. Only direct conversations can convey the subtleties that enrich human communication. Artificial intelligence may be able to understand those subtleties in the future, but the future is not now.

That's not to say that companies shouldn't take advantage of advances in technology, but if a company gives AI a task that was previously performed by human beings, AI had better be up to the task with improved results.

Another friend of mine recalls trying to call Verizon for technical support. On a number of occasions, the music on hold was interrupted by a reminder that Verizon offered a digital option. In my friend's opinion, the reminder had all the dexterity of a piledriver. He felt he was being guided like a bull in a rodeo chute to use the digital option. He felt that Verizon hoped to push enough customers into the digital "chute" so that the company could whittle down its workforce.

Verizon had a number of options to help my friend, and he said the tech coach was very pleasant and helpful...and at least Verizon *offered* phone support.

Public-facing companies that don't offer phone support are making a mistake, and companies that make changes (such as adding meat to the menu at a vegetarian restaurant without adequately notifying and preparing their customers for what could be a tumultuous transition period) are making a second mistake. *Two strikes and you're out!*

Remember Albert Einstein's equation $E=mc^2$? It describes the relationship between energy and matter. Given that c stands for the speed of light, which is more than 186,000 miles per second, it's easy to understand the enormous amounts of energy in matter. And then there is another equation that has to do with the effectiveness of customer service: $Cl=Cs^2$, where Cl stands for customer loyalty and Cs stands for customer service. Developing customer loyalty takes energy and a commitment to customer service.

Holding a contest to find the worst customer service story will illustrate the contrast between your business, with its personal service, and competitors who value efficiency over excellence.

The Cost: Zero.

Chapter Seventeen

When Is a Phone Not a Phone? When It Is a Camera.

A smartphone is a medium of the moment. It can capture a phone call or a text at any time, and it allows people to capture an image in the moment. It allows anyone with access to it to stop the world for a split-second and capture an image that could endure a lifetime or more. *Baby's first step. Mom's prize-winning rhubarb pie. Dad's first tax audit.* All of them can be captured on a smartphone. Not to mention the guy with the fruit stand down the street. The library festooned for Independence Day and other bits of local color. On a good day, a smartphone could capture the image that was described in print by William Carlos Williams when he writes "The Red Wheelbarrow":

so much depends
upon
A red wheel barrow
with rain water
Beside the white chickens.

Smartphones are simultaneously global and personal.

According to data from Statista and BankMyCell, as of 2026, there are approximately 7.58 billion smartphones in use globally. Savvy public relations firms have learned that knowing the best practices of smartphone use can transform their clients into wireless PR strategists. And an important part of that strategy is knowing how to capture the moment on a smartphone camera. After all, any business is a business of moment: the moment a customer sees a store with an attractive exterior and decides to enter, the moment a customer is approached by a friendly salesperson who asks if they can help, the moment of indecision when the customer weighs whether to purchase and the turning point when the customer decides to buy.

Think of the camera on a smartphone as a paintbrush that can render the narrative of a moment. If you're a business owner, you can use that paintbrush to a create a fresh and enduring image of your enterprise.

Case Study Twenty-One: Twenty-Four Hours of Moments

The Challenge: To create or strengthen an affinity between a business and its community and, by extension, its customers.

The Strategy: Choose an upcoming day and enlist your customers and anyone else who may want to participate to use their smartphone cameras to capture photos of the community and people in it between 12:00 a.m. and 11:59 p.m. on that day. Publicize the effort on your website, through television and radio interviews and in your business. Then, on the appointed day, spring smartphone photographers on the community, with instructions to take only in public places. Invite reporters to tag along with one or more of the photographers. Television stations and local newspapers may want to display the photos.

The Rationale: Are you familiar with Rick Smolan? His work is the inspiration for a public relations campaign that can create a strong bond between a business and a community. He is a professional photographer who had the idea to have people all over the US take photos on one particular day. The day was May 2, 1986, and the book that resulted from that effort was titled *A Day in the Life of America*. He was also behind *A Day in the Life of Canada*, *A Day in the Life of Japan*, and *A Day in the Life of Spain*, to name a few of his thirty-nine books.

According to his biography on thephotosociety.org, "Rick Smolan, CEO of Against All Odds Productions is a *New York Times*–bestselling author with more than five million copies of his books in print. A former *Time*, *Life*, and *National Geographic* photographer, Smolan is best known as the co-creator of the *Day in the Life* book series. His global photography projects, which feature the work of hundreds of the world's leading photographers and combine creative storytelling with state-of-the-art technology, are regularly featured on the covers of prestigious publications around the globe including *Fortune*, *Time*, and *GEO*.

Fortune describes Against All Odds as "One of the 25 Coolest Companies in America." His concept has inspired an entire genre that focuses on the capturing as many moments as possible within the confines of one time period, such as a day.

A business can use that same approach to bond with a community: send photographers out to find out what's going on in different lives during the same twenty-four-hour period. The mention of the business or brand need only be in the title; for example, "Johnson Home Repair Presents 24 Hours in Houston," "Randy's Rotisserie Presents Minute By Minute in Minneapolis" and "The Grande Hotel Presents One Day in Denver."

The Cost: Admittedly, this strategy may be a little pricier, since you may want to hire an attorney to make sure the participants play by the roles, but once any legal costs are met, the only calculus is any overtime for employees who are involved with the project.

Chapter Eighteen

Prankster Public Relations

Do you remember Alan Abel? Perhaps you read his obituary, which was published in *The New York Times* on January 2, 1980, when Abel was still alive. (He died decades later, on September 14, 2018.) After his actual death, *The New York Times* published an article headlined, "Alan Abel, Hoaxer Extraordinaire, Is (on Good Authority) Dead at 94." The article, written by Marshall Fine, went on to state, "His daughter, Jenny Abel, said the cause was complications of cancer and heart failure.

"Mr. Abel's putative 1980 death, orchestrated with his characteristic military precision and involving a dozen accomplices, had been confirmed to *The Times* by several rigorously rehearsed confederates. One masqueraded as the grieving widow. Another posed as an undertaker, answering fact-checking calls from the newspaper on a dedicated phone line that Mr. Abel had installed, complete with its own directory-information business listing." The obituary was published, and Abel held a news conference. *The New York Times* published a retraction.

Abel's pranks over the years went beyond the staging of his own death. As Fine noted, "Mr. Abel's first major hoax, the Society for Indecency to Naked Animals, or SINA—began in 1959. He sought to clothe all naked animals that appear in public, namely horses, cows, dogs, and cats, including any animal that stands higher than four inches or is longer than six inches. It starred his friend Buck Henry, then an unknown actor, and later a well-known actor and screenwriter, as the group's puritanical president, G. Clifford Prout." He called the Pennsylvania Turnpike, which is lined with farms where hooved animals graze "a moral disaster area."

As Fine notes, Abel also organized a demonstration in front of The White House, calling on then First Lady Jacqueline Kennedy to clothe her horses. He was also behind a campaign to run a purported Jewish grandmother, Yetta Bronstein (played by his wife), for president in 1964. ("Vote for Yetta, and things will get betta.")

Hoaxes and absurd publicity campaigns, when artfully done, can engage audiences because they step outside boundaries. Morning radio personalities have used satire, hoaxes, and pranks to good effect for decades. My friend Jerry Edling, who for years was part of a number of morning teams in Pennsylvania (using the air name The Captain), was a participant in a number of these. One prank took place on an FM contemporary hit radio station that was upstairs from an AM country station. The premise of the prank was that Jerry's on-air partner, Jim Cooke, was stuck in an elevator between the first and second floors with a cow that was being used for a promotion on the AM station. Jim was allegedly talking on the air through the elevator's emergency telephone. In the background, listeners could hear the cow mooing and the canned music playing. (In reality, Jim was in the production studio next door, and the moos and elevator music were sound effects.) It worked. The audience was never the wiser, and Jim, of course, was able to get out of the elevator at the end.

That morning team was also involved in a prank that involved two radio stations in two states. They told their audience that they were being transferred to a radio station in Rochester, New York. The morning team in Rochester told their audience that they were being transferred to the station in Pennsylvania where Jerry and Jim worked. The "transfer" was to happen on April 1. People sent letters asking the station to reconsider, but on March 31, Jerry and Jim flew to Rochester, and the morning team from Rochester flew to Pennsylvania. Each morning team did the other team's show on April Fool's day. At some point that morning, the hoax was revealed: no one was *actually* moving.

The memory of a well-executed prank may linger for years or longer in the minds of the audience. Everyone loves to laugh, and if you pull off a joke like this artfully, they're likely to repay you with loyalty. It's extremely important to know your audience if you're going to try to pull a prank such as this one. If people feel they're being duped, they can vocally step away from your business. The key is to develop an affinity to your brand. Once you do that, your audience may be more willing to take a joke.

If you're in the shoe business, customers may also be willing to try on your footwear. *Case in Point*: Payless and Palessi. In the words of Brady Werkheimer, a marketing manager, "Payless staged their shoes in a fake, high-end storefront called 'Palessi' and charged customers $400–500 for a pair of shoes that normally retail for $50. It wasn't a shameless money grab; Payless gave the customers their money back after the prank was over."

Then there's American Greetings, which, Werkheiser writes, "pranked twenty-four unsuspecting job applicants who were interviewing for a 'Director of Operations' position over Skype for their 'World's Toughest Job' campaign. The position had a nearly impossible list of responsibilities and paid absolutely nothing. The position was actually describing the role of a mother. This heartwarming prank generated over 27 million views on YouTube and boosted sales for American Greetings Cardstore's make-your-own card orders by 20 percent."

IHOP pulled off a prank that generated anger against the brand, and that was the whole point. Werkheiser calls it "outrage marketing." In his words, "Outrage marketing is the attempt to create brand awareness by intentionally sparking a powerful reaction of shock, anger or indignation." IHOP announced that it was changing its name to IHOB (International House of Burgers instead of International House of Pancakes). In the words of Jeanine Girn, writing on *Narcity*, "Yes, they stated that they were done with pancakes and were going to become the International House of Burgers.

"Naturally, customers were pissed. No one could understand why IHOP would change their entire branding just for some silly burgers. The chain restaurant has always been known for their fluffy pancakes, why would they change the identity now?" Brady Werkheiser writes, "In the first day IHOP recorded 614,000 tweets. In the first ten days there were over 2.1 million social media conversations. In the first three weeks they sold 400 percent more burgers."

You might think that pranks and hoaxes could provoke a backlash from the audience, and you might be surprised at how receptive audiences are if the prank or hoax is unique, intellectually engaging, and well executed. Employing this sort of thing as a form of public relations for your business can be done, but it must be meticulously planned, well thought out, and seamlessly executed. Take the April Fools' Day joke. Four days before April Fools' Day in 2023, Lauren Hovey writes on *PR Newswire*, "April Fools' Day is just around the corner, which means the internet will be inundated with companies releasing mock headlines, parody videos and joke press releases to raise their brand awareness."

Along with these practical jokes "inevitably come the naysayers who insist that consumers are sick of the gags, and that the effort brands put in are not worth the potential blowback of their stunts. Others argue that a well-executed April Fools Day joke is a simple, lighthearted way to interact with the public, elevate visibility, and show their sense of humor and relatability." April Fools' Day jokes are somewhat like competitive gymnastics: in each performance lurks the potential to triumph or tumble. In Hovey's words, "Done correctly, it is an effective tool to increase positive brand sentiment. If not, it could cost the brand its reputation or financial loss."

So, do the risk-reward analysis, and if you're ready, take a step forward. Hovey suggests:

- **Do:** Make it simple and (Actually) funny. She cites Taco Bell's announcement that it was going to buy the Liberty Bell and rename it the Taco Liberty Bell in an effort to help lower the national debt. Taco Bell placed an advertisement in newspapers around the country, stating, "In an effort to help the national debt, Taco Bell is pleased to announce that we have agreed to purchase the Liberty Bell, one of our country's most historic treasures." The advertisement states, "It will now be called 'The Taco Liberty Bell' and will still be accessible to the American public for viewing. While some may find this controversial, we hope our move will prompt other corporations to take similar action to do their part to reduce the country's debt.
- **Don't:** Lie About Your Products and Services. Hovey cites an announcement by Volkswagen that it was changing its name to Voltswagen "to show its commitment to electric vehicles." Volkswagen later admitted that the name change was not real. In a statement sent to CNN Business at the time, the company said, "The renaming was designed to be an announcement in the spirit of April Fool's Day, highlighting the launch of the all-electric ID.4 SUV and signaling our commitment to bringing electric mobilit to all.
- **Do:** Stick to April 1. According to Hovey, Scope announced a week before April Fool's Day that it was intruding a bacon-flavored mouthwash.
- **Don't:** Upset or offend your audience.

Case in Point: Google, which created an April Fools' Day send button on Gmail that would send a meme known as a mic drop, featuring some minions from the *Despicable Me* movies. BBC.com reported, "Google has removed an April Fool's Gmail button, which sent a comical animation to recipients, after reports of people getting into trouble at work.

"The button appeared beside Gmail's normal send button and allowed users to shut down an email thread by sending a gif of a Minion dropping a microphone." But users accidentally sent business emails and other formal correspondence that ended up depositing the mic drop where it shouldn't have been seen on screen. That resulted in firings, misunderstandings and other consternation.

Google apologized.

Pranking is a powerful tool to build brand awareness. Just play nice with your brand as you're making the audience laugh.

Case Study Twenty-Two: Sundaes Will Never Be the Same:

The Challenge: To pull off an April Fools' Day prank that will endear customers to an ice cream business and transform them into repeat customers.

The Strategy: Announce that, on April 1, you will be introducing a new menu item for a limited time. That "menu item" should be improbable, perhaps shocking, and definitely witty. An example for an ice cream store: a chili sauce sundae (served mild, medium, or hot); an example for a restaurant: a peanut butter and tuna salad sandwich; and for a coffee shop: a cinnamon and liverwurst croissant with whipped cream. When customers arrive, they should be greeted with a sign explaining that the special items are for that day only. (*Happy April Fools' Day!*)

It should also explain that anyone who finishes one of the special menu items will not only get it for free, but will also receive a $10 coupon for items off the establishment's regular menu if they agree to have themselves recorded on video while eating and reacting to the one-day-only culinary items. Then, post those videos on YouTube, your website, your X account, LinkedIn, Instagram, TikToK, and your Facebook page.

Of course, the media should be alerted. Imagine watching television and seeing your customer try to chow down on that chili sundae.

The Rationale: Historically, college students have congregated at hangouts that serve hamburgers and hot dogs laced with chili sauce, layered with cheese, and sprinkled with onions. Such a place stands at the intersection of High Street and Hanover Street in Carlisle, Pennsylvania, within a block of Dickinson College. The Hamilton Restaurant's variant of this concept is called the Hot-Chee Dog, and its contributions to cuisine in Carlisle have been recognized in a historical marker. On one evening, some students at the college dared another student to eat an entire Hot-Chee Sundae. That's right, a bowl of ice cream festooned with the ingredients that normally serve as accoutrements to the Hot-Chee Dog and the Hot-Chee Burger. If he made it through the entire serving, he was to be given a bottle of Chivas Regal.

He made it. He said, "The killer was the onions."

Pairing odd food combinations for laughs is a perennial gag for pranking. Comedian James Corden once had a feature titled, "Spill Your Guts or Fill Your Guts" on his television program. People were asked questions with no-win answers designed to reveal their real feelings. If they didn't metaphorically "spill their guts," they were forced to dine on food combinations that were designed to repel them. If you're in food service, you could put some of these concepts to work. Just make sure you don't mislead the customer into thinking that the added menu item will be a permanent fixture at the eatery. You never know. Someone may like that chili sundae.

The Cost: The cost of the added menu items, and potential overtime for crew members who need to retool the supply chain and signage.

Case Study Twenty-Three: By Comparison

The Challenge: Differentiating a company from a competitor.

The Strategy: Take aim at a competitor directly by comparing its product to yours.

The Rationale: This was inspired by a stunt Burger King pulled off in 2019. Imogen Watson writes on *The Drum*, "Burger King's Whopper is positioned as a heftier option for fast food lovers getting their fix. Seeing this as a differentiating benefit against its rival burger, Burger King endeavoured to find a way to prove it on a massive scale:

"It hid a Big Mac behind every Whopper ad that its creative agency BBH made this year. Within every piece of print, TV, OOH, and in-store advertising, Burger King placed a Big Mac behind every Whopper photographed, but due to the size of its own burger, the rival was often eclipsed from sight." Watson quotes Ian Heartfield, chief creative officer at BBH

London, as saying, "Placing our competitor's product in our own ads throughout 2019 without anyone knowing has been one of the most fun ideas we have ever executed. It is, of course, just a good old-fashioned product comparison, but it's been brought up to date by some lateral thinking and rebellious media behaviour. We're loving it."

Good old-fashioned product comparisons can be fun, and it can jump-start your revenue streams by showing publicly how your product overshadows another. Burger King's core advantages over McDonald's are flame broiling and size. This is an example of how one competitor took advantage of what was perceived as another's soft spot and barreled in with a direct comparison.

Restaurants can use variants of this idea to gain visibility and, perhaps, a bit of notoriety. One possibility is a social media campaign comparing the size of its top-of-the-line steak with the size of its competitor's. One photo of the two steaks together should do it. (One caveat: make sure you're comparing apples to apples. Don't compare your full cut round to a competitor's petite sirloin.)

This comparative photography works well with all sorts of dishes. If you find that a competitor's Cobb salad is aesthetically less pleasing than yours, point it out in a photo. Same with roasted Brussels sprouts, medallions of beef, and shrimp with lobster sauce. Not to mention apple pie. Food comparisons are reminiscent of a campaign launched in 1975 by Pepsico. The Pepsi Challenge sought to create the impression that Pepsi Cola was a superior, more palatable product even though Coca-Cola was the clear leader in the cola beverage sector.

As an article in Juicebox Interactive put it, "The Pepsi Challenge signaled a major shift in the winds of the cola landscape. In 1975, Coke was the 800 lb. gorilla in the cola market, holding the #1 position for decades. A superior distribution system, effective marketing (before it was called marketing), and incredible brand loyalty created legions of happy customers.

"Pepsi was the new kid on the block looking to prove something. They were hungry and willing to mix it up. A savvy exec at Pepsi came up with a bold, revolutionary strategy to do just that. That idea was the Pepsi Challenge. Pepsi went inside malls around the country and invited people to do a blind taste test between Coke and Pepsi. The results were remarkable; people picked Pepsi over Coke significantly. Pepsi happily touted the results in a TV campaign showing people, much to their own surprise, picking Pepsi."

Your taste test can accomplish the same objective as the Pepsi taste test, especially if your business is the upstart going up against a more well-established competitor. It could take you from "go past" to "go to" in a very short period of time.

Cost: The cost of the food from your competitor. This strategy generally works best when the business conducting the campaign is the runner-up in the race for revenue and wants to increase visibility by taking some potshots at its better-known competitor. If a business is the runner-up, there's no harm in saying so. Decades ago, Avis, which was running a consistent number two compared to Hertz in the vehicle rental sector, decided to embrace its runner-up status. As Marie Page put it on *CareLineLive*, "In the early sixties the car rental company Avis launched an ad campaign with the slogan 'We try harder.' It was created to differentiate Avis from its main competitor, Hertz, and to convey the message that Avis was willing to go the extra mile to provide excellent service to its customers." Avis embraced its status as number two but made it clear that it was not an also-ran, but rather an ambitious competitor that was willing to go out of its way to attract and keep customers,

You need to know your brand. *Authentic PR* is the process of embracing who you are and what your brand is and building from there. Because your audience will see through any attempt by you to portray your brand as something that just does not fit, and they'll spread that skepticism quickly and relentlessly on social media.

Volkswagen embraced what it was in a campaign titled "Think Small," which was aimed at selling the Volkswagen Beetle. If the Corvette was the Afghan Hound of 1959, the Volkswagen Beetle was its basset hound. Basset means "low" in French, so you get the picture. This breed is low-hanging, sad-faced, and plodding. There's nothing flashy about this doughboy look, just a dour invitation to take it for what it is. That was exactly the perception the "Think Small" ads tried to perpetrate. It was an invitation to think different, to go with the practical over the pompous. Keep in mind that the economy was booming in the 1950s, and suburbanites in their tract homes were flouting the fallout from World War II and displaying cars that resembled tanks in the driveway. Volkswagen's message resonated.

The message should be clear: *Be yourself. Be authentic.* Don't leverage your customers; level *with* them. Whenever you practice prankster PR, make it funny and make it real. Make it true to your brand. Comedians know this. No successful comedian tries to do everything. One may do topical humor, another may do deadpan observations, and another may do show business impressions. Don't try to live somebody else's dream. Turn your dream into a reality.

Humor is one of the tools you can use to be authentic. And publicity stunts can be timeless, memorable, and true to the zeitgeist; or they can be ill-timed, forgettable, and way out of tune. It depends on your situation and approach, but remember: the pranks have to be funny.

An article on *PRLab* states, "Publicity stunts are a double-edged sword for a startup. Stunts can enhance a company's financial stability and visibility. Poorly organized PR stunts can negatively impact the brand's image." Anything novel, colorful, or extraordinary jolts the intellect—and humor, when well done, can create impressions that last a lifetime. Take Diesel. And *Deisel.* You may recognize Diesel as a fashion brand, but it was also the creative force behind *Deisel.* What is *Deisel*?

As the article on *PRLab* puts it, "In early 2018, a store named Deisel popped up on Canal Street in New York City. Appearing to sell counterfeit clothes from the popular fashion brand Diesel. As part of Diesel's clever PR stunt, the bootleg store was opened just before New York Fashion Week. All the items, including Deisel-branded T-shirts, sweatshirts, hats and lifestyle products, were crafted by Diesel's design team and featured a misspelled logo. The store quickly became an event when rapper Gucci Mane invited his Instagram followers to meet him there, resulting in a massive line outside."

Diesel's publicity stunt worked because it was true to the brand. It was authentic. Diesel's image is hip, snarky, live-and-let-live, rugged individualism. It originated at a time (the 1970s) when denim was undergoing a transformation, going from work clothes to fashion fabric. As an article on *Bang & Strike* put it, "When founder, Renzo Rosso, rebranded the denim manufacturer 'Moltex' to Diesel in 1978, his goal was to create a truly authentic brand. At the time, fashion and technology were evolving rapidly. Whilst other brands chased the next trend, Rosso wanted Diesel's denim to stay true to its roots. Diesel jeans were distressed and vintage—they looked 'worn' from the moment of purchase. It was an innovative but retrospective approach and it catapulted the brand to success in Italy and, later, worldwide.

"The history of Diesel is a history of going against the grain—and the brand continues to raise eyebrows today. Diesel is a brand for rebels—ignoring the highly-strung world of trend forecasts and coming up with unique ranges from their designers' own creativity and tastes. They have a purposefully multi-national team who travel the globe up to four times a year to get inspiration. International fashion, Made in Italy. And it works."

A good public relations event can only resonate with customers if you put them in a familiar place. Whether it's a publicity stunt, a poster campaign or an online thread, be mindful of who your audience is. Tailor it to their sensibilities. Make sure they "get the joke," and make sure they get the point.

Chapter Nineteen

The Campaign

Whether they're for political, philanthropic, or pop culture causes, campaigns evoke deep emotions. Straw hats, patriotic bunting, sawdust, and a whiff of summer are all part of campaigns, if only in the mind. But campaigns aren't just about nostalgia for a simpler time. They're about taking part in a cause and becoming part of a movement. In short, they're about belonging. The yearn to belong is one of the most basic drives in the human experience. *And rejection?*

In the words of Nicole Roberts, writing in *Forbes*, "We all know that rejection hurts, but neuroscience has confirmed that it does, in fact, liteally, hurt. While the brain does not process emotional pain and physical pain identically, the reaction and cascading events are very similar, and a natural chemical (painkiller mu-opioid) is released during both events." A business owner can make a customer feel accepted through good customer service, but it isn't enough to establish a firm one-to-one relationship. That still implies that the customer is an outsider. The best way to make the customer feel like one of the group is to enlist that customer in a common cause.

Ben & Jerry's Homemade Ice Cream Holdings achieved that by enlisting its customers to preserve protect and defend the values associated with the 1960s. You can accomplish the same goals by enlisting your customers in common causes. As I mentioned in my book *Guerrilla PR*, an improv comedy venue in Los Angeles started a petition drive asking the Academy of Motion Picture Arts and Sciences to add Best Comedy and Best Comic Acting categories to the Academy Awards.

The most basic advocacy technique is the petition drive. It's a no-frills technique, and it cuts right to the heart of the matter. This is something business owners can use only if they are sure their customer bases are completely aligned with the aim of the petition. It wouldn't be a good idea for a business to display a petition for a presidential candidate, although it *would* be a good idea for a business to conduct a voter registration drive. And a business that lists ecologically sound practices among its core values should be safe in sharing petitions advocating measures aimed at fostering sustainability.

With this, there are some basic rules to keep in mind when offering customers an opportunity to join the group and participate in a petition drive. David Fouse offered some recommendations in an article on *PR News*:

- Make sure your petition has a concrete and specific goal. Vague wishes or emotional diatribes rarely result in action.
- Target petitions to the people or groups that actually has power to effect the change you seek.
- Manage expectations. Setting petition signature goal levels too high in the beginning can stall momentum before it has a chance to build. So, start with reasonable expectations.
- Before or shortly after you release the petition, identify key influencers who can identify with your cause and will use their network(s) to raise awareness.
- Share, and ask others to share, your petition over social media. Use the petition as a call-to-action through Facebook and organization newsletters.
- Celebrate your successes (signature-target levels, petition success) by pitching stories to traditional earned media—radio, newspapers, TV—for an even wider reach.

Don't let your customers enlist in common causes against you, such as boycotts, unless your brand is rebellious and thrives on controversy.

Chapter Twenty

To Your Health

Case Study Twenty-Four: Healing the Community

The Challenge: Owners of a privately owned pharmacy in a medium-sized city want to appeal to Millennial and Generation Z consumers by proving their commitment to sustainability.

The Strategy: Conduct a drive for unused prescriptions and invite customers to stop by and dispose of them safely. At the collection point, have petitions available that call on the state legislature or Congress to enact laws that include stricter regulations regarding disposal of medical waste. The aim would be to keep prescription medicine out of storm water drains, where they can cause a health hazard at local bodies of water. Invite local politicians to participate, and invite local media to cover.

The Rationale: At a time when *Authentic PR* is a must, businesses need to tackle the issues that touch them directly. While pharmacies are charged with filling prescriptions, not emptying them, their packaging, their approach to the distribution of pharmaceuticals and their attention to sustainability can make the difference between an environmental win and an environmental woe. The event should be held at an environmentally safe disposal site that is convenient to the pharmacy's customers.

The Cost: Disposal bins, site permitting, if necessary, and personnel to monitor the site and bins for disposal. Best done as a partnership.

Local-only and privately owned pharmacies face a number of challenges in gaining visibility in the presence of national chains that have the advantages of quick access to pharmaceuticals and efficient delivery. But pharmacy chains largely do not necessarily command brand loyalty. They're perceived in the same way a supermarket is: a convenient way to purchase essentials. It's safe to say that most customers of chain pharmacies will let proximity be their guide on where to shop. There's little differentiation in stocking as well. Most pharmacies have the same liquid soap, bandages, over-the-counter pain medication, shaving cream, razors, toothpaste, and shampoo. Aesthetically, grocery stores and pharmacies can be unappealing places to shop, with all the attraction of an industrial warehouse. Pharmacies survive, either as stand-alone businesses or as parts of supermarkets, because they have what people need to buy to survive, not necessarily because they have what people want to buy to live.

Three things can make pharmacies stand out: good customer service that begins with a smile and a greeting, good community service that makes the store and its employees appear to be caring caring people, and a design that makes the store look cutting edge. A new design ean be expensive to pull off, but a community service drive can be organized and finessed for less than you might expect.

Pulling off good public relations for pharmacutical companies can be challenging but rewarding. David Ingram writes on *Chron*, "Public relations is the branch of marketing concerned with building brand equity, enhancing relationships with consumers, and building influence in communities outside of the context of advertising. Public relations activities include participating in charitable events, informing the press about upcoming product releases, and finding ways to give back to the communities that support a business. All business types can benefit from a clear PR strategy, including pharmacy companies. Because of their focus on healthcare products, pharmacies are uniquely positioned to make meaningful impacts in the public health of their communities as part of a comprehensive PR strategy."

Ingram's recommendations for pharmacy public relations: "Offer Free or Discounted Vaccinations, Donate Time and Resources, Inform the Public, and Keep an Open Line to the Press."

It may seem counterintuitive to pin your public relations hopes on a topic like unused prescription, but if you couple good community service with good customer service and are perceived as a good corporate service, the gains can be substantial.

Doctors face special challenges in what Manuel Castells called "The network society," where everything is connected. Gone are the days when medical professionals could be aloof and analytical. Today, doctors are beholden to the connected age just as businesses are. Patients can fight back after an unpleasant experience in the clinic. They can yelp loudly enough about a physician to scare away potential patients. Whether or not they want to, doctors are forced to treat their patients as customers as well as patients. They must be credible and caring. They must cater to patients, listen to them and empathize with them, and they have to market to them. *Authentic* public relations offers a powerful tool with which to accomplish that.

An article, "The Importance of Public Relations in the Health Care Industry: A Comprehensive Guide," published on *Real News PR*, states, "Public relations in healthcare is crucial for building trust with patients, managing crises, promoting health education, and enhancing the institution's reputation. It also aids in patient satisfaction and community engagement, making it a vital part of healthcare management. To effectively serve their patients and communities, healthcare organizations must not only provide excellent medical care but also establish strong connections with their patients.This is where the power of public relations comes in."

If a healthcare institution is remote and aloof, patients are left to wonder whether it will provide excellent care in the event that it's needed. If an institution establishes strong, empathetic ties with the people it serves, patients will assume that it provides excellent care. That's why it's essential that all healthcare institutions, from the doctor's office to the elite teaching hospital, invest in authentic public relations. Candor creates confidence, and healthcare professionals who establish strong relationships with patients will reap rewards.

Case Study Twenty-Five: A Shot in the Arm

The Challenge: Create a high-visibility community project that will enhance the image of a clinic that opened within the last month and help its owners gain a foothold in the community.

The Strategy: Offer free or low-cost flu vaccinations either at the clinic or in a low-income area in the community in which the clinic is located. To gain highest visibility, it may be a good idea to give out the vaccinations at a higher-profile location—such as a school, church, or community center—and couple it with a health fair where students display their health-care projects. The additional planning involved in situating the event at a remote location can pay off handsomely in television news coverage and community awareness.

Remember that, for the most part, television news operations are more receptive to event pitches on weekends because they have a smaller amount of stories to cover. It's not a stretch to say that on a slow weekend, television news coverage consists primarily of crime, crashes, and local events.

The Rationale: An event coupling health care and education is likely to have universal appeal, but if you're appealing to a media outlet for news coverage, it's best to hone your pitch to the type of media you are targeting. As an article on TicketSpice puts it, "When reaching out to different types of media, tailoring your approach to each one will increase your likelihood of responses." According to the article, the way to pitch to newspapers and magazines is to "[s]tart by researching journalists who cover topics related to your event. Craft personalized pitches highlighting why your event would interest their readership. Consider offering exclusive content or interviews to increase the appeal."

With television and radio, "Pitch your event as a visual or auditory story. Highlight elements that make for compelling footage or soundbites. To make their job easier, offer to provide visuals, such as pre-recorded interviews or B-roll footage."

With social media: "Leverage social media platforms to engage with journalists and media outlets. Follow them, interact with their content, and share relevant updates about your event."

With online media: "Identify bloggers and online influencers whose audience aligns with your event. Reach out with personalized messages emphasizing how their platform can benefit from covering your event. Offer incentives such as VIP access or exclusive content for their followers."

By all means, mention whether there's going to be food at the event. Journalists are drawn to food like flies to a porchlight. Having a deli spread at your event is not likely to affect the assignment editor's willingness to commit a crew to a story, but it's likely to increase the reporter's enthusiasm for it.

Of course, never offer any sort of remuneration for news coverage, even a dinner. You're likely be viewed as desperate for news coverage and someone to be avoided when it comes time to choose what stories to cover.

In short, make a good impression. If you succeed in getting a television station to cover an event, you want them to keep coming back for more. Exchange contract information, get personal cell phone numbers if possible, and establish a rapport.

By the way, if a television station decides to cover the event, it's possible that the only person who stops by is the videographer. If your event is conveniently located en route to other stories, the assignment editor may decide to have the videographer stop by and "spray" the event. He or she may be gone in ten minutes. Don't be offended that you didn't get a reporter. The number of reporters available on the weekend may tend to be smaller, and they're going to be preoccupied with other stories, but the videographer who covers your event is just as capable of getting interviews as the reporter is.

When the video arrives at the station, a writer or producer will take care of the narrative. To help the producer or writer articulate the point of the event, make sure you have plenty of background material for the videographer to take back to the station. Otherwise, it will be very difficult for the writer or producer to tell your story. That means it's even more vulnerable to being bumped by another story. In fact, you shouldn't have to create a press kit for this event. Creating a professionally designed press kit should be one of your first priorities when you open a business. Ideally, it should be an amendable press kit that can be topped with information about your event and have background information already included. (This is how journalists in some cases write their stories. They write up background information that's already known and then "top" it with the development(s) of the day.)

One other possibility is that the reporter may also be the videographer and may be swamped with stories. To make the reporter's job easier, line up interviews in advance—*and don't let interviewees wander off!* You don't want to have to search for them when the television news van arrives. If you're well organized, that reporter is likely to want to come back and cover another event. If there are multiple news outlets at your event, make sure all of them get the interview(s) they need. If you let an interviewee wander off after an interview with network affiliate A, the videographer from network affiliate B is going to be angered if her or she has to go back to the station with video but no sound bites.

The Cost: For the vaccine, it depends on the partnership. The cost may be zero if the vaccine is donated, or a price may be negotiated with the help of a government or NGO partner. Otherwise, permits, security, the news release, background package, and (optional) the deli spread.

Chapter Twenty-One

Influencers, Influencing and the Internet

Influencers have always been important. In an earlier time, the primary influencers were business leaders, politicians and public intellectuals. For them, ink was a catalyst and a weapon. They could be found very easily, in their offices, in Congress and in the pages of some of the more erudite publications. Today, influencers are more elusive because there are more of them and because the dynamics are constantly changing. Anyone with enough clout and connections can be an influencer. One gauge of how powerful they are might be the number of followers they have on X or the number of friends on Facebook, but that isn't really the definitive litmus test. Because then the question becomes, how influential are their followers?

Think of the internet as a form of options trading. You have almost limitless options for entertainment, education, research and connecting. In exchange for those options, you trade your personal information. You even get cookies with the deal. As you familiarize yourself with some of those options, you may notice familiar names and familiar faces popping up. These may be influencers.

Jesse Relkin writes on *Wix Studio* in 2023, "The last few years have seen a seismic shift in the social media landscape, thanks to the rise of TikTok, Facebook's massive rebrand initiative as Meta and Elon Musk's rocky acquisition of Twitter."

Social media is, by definition, volatile. Keeping up with the trends that seem to shape social media constantly is a tough job, but tapping into those trends can be rewarding in more ways than monetary. When social media first came into the public realm, there was great optimism that they would cross borders seamlessly and unite the world. They may have crossed borders initially, but they also encouraged people (without saying so) to stop crossing the street, to spend time online and not with their neighbors. Today, they're chided for being the instruments of what Shoshana Zuboff has called "surveillance capitalism," and the ability of people to speak freely across borders has been hampered by some governments that do not value free speech and free association. Companies are under pressure to moderate their content. For example, Facebook suspended the account of Donald Trump in 2021, only to reinstate it in 2024. Social media companies, as private entities, have the right to exercise editorial control over their sites, but a court case allowing the State of California to compel a shopping center to allow petitioners to gather signatures may be applicable to social media. According to the Los Angeles County Sheriff's Department, in the case of "*Pruneyard Shopping Center v. Robins*, the US Supreme Court held that the California Constitution protects 'speech and petitioning, reasonably exercised, in shopping centers, even when the centers are privately owned.' The central theme of the court's ruling was that Pruneyard Shopping Center, because of its open public gathering areas, had become the modern equivalent of the 'Town Square.'" (Shopping centers were free to establish regulations for such activity, and smaller stores not having the "town square" characteristics of shopping centers could prohibit petitioning on premises.)

This ruling could arguably apply to social media, which are the digital "town squares" of our time. Communities are no longer exclusively organized around physical spaces.

As people seek out closer relationships, community has become the organizing principle of business and creating community has become the mission of marketing and public relations.

Case Study Twenty-Six: Building a Better Business

The Challenge: Owners of a hardware store that opened within the previous three months seek to establish themselves and their business as active members of the community.

The Strategy: Partner with a non-profit organization that paints the houses of low-income and disabled residents for free. Use your app to take applications from people who want to have their houses painted but lack the means to pay for it. Announce the winner in a news release and follow up with local media, giving the date and time. Donate tools and volunteers, including you and your employees.

Any interviews with local media should include you and the project organizer(s). Don't spend your interview time thanking the project organizers, that sound bite won't be used. Journalists are under a deadline. They want you to get to the point. The same rule applies to any remarks you deliver from the podium. Journalists are somewhat jaded after sitting through news conferences about drug busts and other crimes in which the public officials on hand spend time thanking each other and don't get around to talking about the incident until minutes have passed.

If you want to be really ambitious, partner with a restaurant and bring food to the site at lunchtime.

The Rationale: Independent hardware store owners "look over their shoulders" time and time again to see if corporate chains are searching for opportunity in their communities. Helping to spruce up on a blighted area of the city is one way to brand your business as civic-minded and community-spirited. In my book *Broken Windows, Broken Business*, I discussed the broken windows theory of policing, which argues that crime goes down in neighborhoods that appear to be maintained well, while neighborhoods that appear to be blighted may be vulnerable to a rise in crime. I drew an analogy to businesses, arguing that the success of a business can decline if owners don't pay attention to things like peeling paint, dirty restrooms and broken windows. Any business should follow this rule to be successful. But businesses that go "beyond the call of duty" and help spruce up part of a city are doing themselves a favor as well as the community. Once the community looks well maintained, crime may decline, and people may tend to patronize local businesses more because they feel safer.

The Cost: Paint, tools, and insurance. Also may include labor costs if your employees are paid to volunteer on-site for the day.

Chapter Twenty-Two

To Be Real

Has anyone ever told you to be yourself? Shakespeare wrote a famous line, "This above all: to thine own self be true, And it must follow, as the night the day, Thou canst not be false to any man."

Part of your makeup is intrinsic, but part is shaped by your environment and how you interact with people. Two identical twins, one of whom grew up in Tennessee, the other in Brooklyn, are likely to present themselves somewhat differently.

Then there's a third determinant of who *you* are: the culture around you. Compare and contrast what it was like for some to grow up in the 1950s with the milieu in the 2020s. In the 1950s, television and other cultural clearinghouses stipulated that family life consisted of a man in a fedora and a well-tailored suit who came home to his suburban tract home, where his loving family awaited. He would read the newspaper and have dinner with the family, tell his son to sit up to the table. Shows like *Father Knows Best* and *Leave It to Beaver* were like meat loaf, comfort food for a lily-white generation of family members who fought a war and created a heavy-lifting economy. Contrast the gray-suited breadwinner of the 1950s with the work-at-home, AI-reliant, sustainability-focused assistant DEI officer of the 2020s, who tells his son to stop texting at the dinner table.

To be authentic in your public outreach, you must first and foremost be yourself. That's because there are two types of transparency. One type, the one you get by being yourself, could catapult your business to the next level. The other type, the one you get by putting on a persona that is not you, can expose you to ridicule by a knowing customer base.

But you must also be sensitive to the culture of the moment. That isn't to say that you can't tweak the culture, or even blaze a trail to a new culture with your business, but you must be sensitive to the culture. An automobile dealership that gives away a fossil-fuel-powered automobile instead of an electric vehicle runs the risk of running afoul of climate-change-conscious consumers. An insensitive comment on your website can morph into a viral attack on your business. If you're in retail or any other business that deals directly with the public, get advice from people of all generations on how to design the business to attract the widest range of customers—and pay attention to language. Anachronisms can cast you as out of touch, and insensitivity can leave you out of the conversation.

If you're not familiar with the conventions of a particular generation, the first thing you should do is hire at least one member of that generation so that your business's grand ideas can be vetted for appeal and accuracy.

Case Study Twenty-Seven: Knowing the Lingo

The Challenge: Owners of a clothing store catering to teenagers and young adults want to increase their visibility and burnish the store's image as a fun place to shop.

The Strategy: Recruit a team of four members of Generation Z (or whatever generation is just entering the workforce), and another team of four Baby Boomers (or the current generation of senior citizens), then hold a generational competition in which the two teams try to stump each other with questions about the lingo, mores and culture of their respective peer groups. Offer a suitable prize to the winning team and a consolation prize to the other team. Have refreshments on hand for spectators, and hold the competition at a peak shopping time. Stream it online, and, of course, invite the media.

The Rationale: This is a fun way either to introduce or re-introduce a business to the community and to bring generations together in a spirited but friendly competition. This is an ideal event for media coverage, since there are opportunities for sound bites form the panelists and the management and staff of the store.

The Cost: The price of refreshments and the cost of prize(s). Insurance, if not covered by the existing store policy.

If you have a toy store, the people to whom you are marketing may seem inaccessible, but it's possible to infiltrate them and find out how the trends that drive their tastes develop.

Hasbro did that openly when it was trying to put its toys in the hands of the coolest kids in school. The key to toy marketing is reaching what's known as the "alpha pup." Simply put, the "alpha pup" is the coolest kid in school, the kid everyone wants to emulate. As Professor Swati Soni and Professor Makard Upadhyaya put it in their paper, "Pester Power Effect of Advertising," alpha pup is the child who is armed with the latest, coolest, and hippest brands. Tracking this alpha pup is critical for marketers because peer groups have a very strong and vital power and influence in the kids' community. Unraveling the psyche of the alpha pup helps creating a buzz or street marketing effect with the little pup as a cool trendsetter and leader in his own way." Hasbro went about finding the ultimate alpha pup. According to an account by John Tierney in *The New York Times Magazine*, market researchers went to playgrounds, video arcades, and skate parks around Chicago and asked boys between the ages of eight and thirteen for the name of the coolest kid they knew. When they obtained a name, they would find that kid and ask the same question, repeating the process until the answer was, "Me." Then they offered to pay those kids $30 to learn a video game. The alpha pups were assembled at an office building for a training session at which they learned a game called Pox, named after a race of extraterrestrials who had escaped from a laboratory. Mankind's only hope was, in the words of the narrator, "to enlist a secret army of the world's most skilled hand-held-game players. Their mission is to use advanced RF containment units to create a race of new, more powerful hybrid warriors and test them in battle against these alien infectors." The games were equipped with radio transmitters that enabled players to battle any other player within thirty feet. That meant, conceivably, that two players could be playing each other in separate classrooms. (Not that they were supposed to be engaging in this activity at school.) At the end of the training session, the alpha pups were given ten units to distribute. Thus began the process of "infecting" hundreds of schools with Pox.

Alpha pups today have considerably more clout than those of past generations. Real-time texting and networks of friends can make or break a game within hours or days, and it's not just the "pups" who are wielding clout. According to Pew Research Center, approximately "seven-in-ten Americans use social media to connect with one another, engage with news content, share information, and entertain themselves." Adults wield as much clout from behind the walls of their urban townhouses and suburban Colonials as alpha pups do from the playground and public intellectuals once did from the newsroom. To reach these influencers, even *Guerrilla PR* is insufficient. Only *Authentic PR* can do the job. And technology notwithstanding, it's still possible to mount an effective public relations campaign without going broke.

Espionage is good business. It doesn't mean spying or surveillance. It means engaging and influencing. Megan Morris writes on *WordStream*, "When the classic strategies aren't delivering, you send in the guerrillas. They're the extra-special forces—the ones that implement killer strategies to turn the tide and defeat the enemy." She continues, "Guerrilla marketing is a great alternative to traditional marketing. It thrives on original thinking and creativity, where imagination and ingenuity beat out big budgets." Morris cites the example of a Sony campaign "in which actors were hired to wander about cities, asking strangers to take a photo of them. During the interaction, actors would rave of their cool new phone, boastng of its features and capabilities."

Case Study Twenty-Eight: The Play's the Thing

The Challenge: An independent toy retailer is trying to survive the downturn in the genre and attract new customers.

The Strategy: Have demonstration model toys available in the store with which kids can play. There are a number of ways to accomplish this. One is to cordon off an area of the store where the kids can play under the supervision of a parent or guardian. Another is to provide supervision and allow parents to shop while the kids are playing. A third option is to have parents reserve thirty minutes or one hour of play space in advance, either in person or online.

The Rationale: The best way to market to children and their parents is by allowing the kids to play with the products. Just ask Toys R Us, which was founded in 1948 and had a profitable run for a number of years. But it moved from buoyancy to bankruptcy by failing to keep up with the times. Tzvi Koegel writes an article, "You won't 'B' Missed: How Toys R Us Brought About Its Own Downfall," originally published in *Nightcall*, the *Brooklyn College Evening News* in 2018: "An easy argument to make to explain Toys R Us" failure is to point towards its online store and say Toys R Us should have had a more robust marketplace online. This may have helped it compete, but it wouldn't have been enough against the juggernaut Amazon had become. Compared to Amazon, Toys R Us was a relatively small company, so directly challenging it in its own space would be unwise and ultimately lead to failure.

"However, if Toys R Us had focused efforts on physical locations, it could have challenged Amazon in an area where the online retailer had no advantage, thus giving itself an edge."

But maintaining a physical presence in the community isn't enough. The interior of the store is just as important as the exterior, perhaps more so. Because the interior is the heart of the business. In the case of Toys R Us, the pre-bankruptcy time could have been a beating heart, filled with the happy sounds of children playing with demonstration model toys. Instead, it had the feeling of a warehouse, with all the toys locked up, not unlike a supply depot from *The Terminator*. What a way to welcome families to the unique experience of play. Kroegel states, "Toys R Us' layout resembles a warehouse: tall shelves packed with boxes, each aisle practically indiscernible from the next. Shopping becomes a chore of wandering the store, trying to find the item you want." Kroegel writes, "With no competitive tactics against online retailers, unfair prices and no way to interact with the product, it becomes obvious why Toys R Us had to declare bankruptcy."

Toys R Us tried to rekindle the wonder in kids' eyes after bankruptcy by establishing play labs at dozens of locations, places where kids could play with toys. It was experiential shopping taken to its logical extreme for both children and their parents, a place to recreate Christmas morning at home, with kids running around the floor in erratic patterns mimicking the sounds of the toys and letting their imaginations run free while retailers watched to see which toys expanded the kids' attention spans.

All Toys R Us stores closed in 2018.

This is the essence of *Authentic PR*: give kids the toys and see what stretches their imaginations. Toy retailers don't need to invest in a smiling clown and hundreds-of-dollars worth of flashing lights and gaudy decorations to pull off a promotion that keeps kids engaged and parents happy. Just let the kids play with the toys. It could feel like Christmas morning in the store, and it could be a good way to generate sales and goodwill and lasting customer loyalty.

The Cost: Demonstration model toys.

Chapter Twenty-Three

Seasoned Public Relations

In the words of a notable country music song, "Time changes everything." Some of the changes are irreversible: kids grow up, they go to school, they annoy their parents, they go to college, they move into their parents' basement, they leave home, they never call, they have families, and they annoy their kids. But some of the changes are cyclical and happen every year: baseball yields to football, which yields to basketball, which leads to holiday shopping, which yields to maxed-out credit cards, which yields to complete personal bankruptcy by the time spring training starts.

All right, maybe not. But the seasons are real, and your customers' summertime selves may be strikingly different from their fall-and-winter-holiday selves. Part of the trick to authentic public relations is to tailor the message not only to the customer, but also to the seasonal version of that customer, because seasons can have enormous impact on peoples' moods, energy levels, focus, and well-being.

An article on embeddedlivng.co.uk cited a study that states, "The time of the year in which most people are happiest is summer, because of the brighter blue skies, warmer temperatures and longer days." It cited a study involving nearly 150 adults aged to seventy-four that "asked them to reflect on their own personal happiness over the course of the seasons and looked at times of the year when they were happier. Results showed that January and February were the least happy whilst summer months shot straight to the top of the scale."

The article continues, "Just over half of all respondents identified the clocks going forward as a factor in their experience of happiness, whilst two thirds identified brighter skies."

Think of your own summers past. Perhaps there was one particular languid summer night when you watched from the porch swing as sunlight skimmed the water in a last benediction before it set. Or perhaps it was the tennis game when you left your friends trailing in a doubles match. Summer is about drinking it in, and a business can help refresh those memories with the right promotion.

Some people have difficulty functioning in the winter months. They may suffer from Seasonal Affective Disorder. According to the National Institute of Mental Health, "Many people go through short periods when they feel sad or unlike their normal selves. Sometimes these mood changes begin and end when the seasons change." Seasons can have a measurable effect on your customers, and since your goal is to develop a rapport with them, it's wise to know what they may be enjoying and enduring at any given moment. Your summer promotions, which emphasize relaxation and savoring life, may be totally different from the ones you do in the fall, not just because the holidays and the weather may be different, but also because your customers may be different.

Maddie Neugent, writing on woodnews.org, "According to experts, Fall is our most productive time of the year! The temperature is still warm, our leaves are beautiful and most importantly our sun is still shining most days! The best month for human productivity is October!" Neugent continued later, "Between back to school and the approaching holidays, it tends to be a productive time of year for people."

"But as the energy of the holiday season fades, the next cycle of the seasons brings us the cold, dreary, cloudy weather of the winter season. As the days are shorter with longer stretches of darkness and the sun shines less as the weather is often cold and dreary we experience drops in our serotonin levels and a rise in melatonin."

My friend Jerry Edling recalls taking his son to a Cub Scout event in Florida that brought together packs from around the region. Each pack brought its own projects. One year, it was held in November. Jerry recalls that the event was well attended and the energy level was up. The next school year it was held in May. To the best of Jerry's recollection, the energy level was down, and it was less well attended. Jerry's cousin, Ron Kenney, once attended the Pig Bowl, an annual flag football game between the Sacramento Police Department and the Sacramento County Sheriff's Office. Normally, it's held the day before the Super Bowl was played—which is to say that it's played at a time when football was on peoples' minds. However, it was decided to move the game to the spring. *Baseball season. Picnics.* How many people were thinking about football then? As Kenney put it, "The Pig Bowl was a phenomenon, the likes of which I had never seen. It was held on Saturday, the day before the Super Bowl; so everybody was just football-crazy. I didn't understand why it would draw so well. I walked out there and the stadium was packed. I was shocked. I am from Los Angeles, so I understood rivalry.

When USC plays UCLA, the Coliseum is packed. For the Notre Dame game, the Coliseum is packed. I was at the first Super Bowl, and the Coliseum was packed. The Pig Bowl turned into a phenom, then someone got the great idea to have it in May. I told my buddy that it was the stupidest idea in the history of the world. I said, "*Idiots!* You've been to the Rose Bowl. It's *always* played on January first. They don't move it to the summer in order to accommodate with warming weather. That's pathetic. It's like, as soon as you have a phenomenal idea, somebody has to pee on the fire hydrant and mess it up."

The point is, target your promotions to the seasonable mindsets of the people you are trying to attract. You can find a number of opportunities for *Authentic PR* in any season. Just make sure your promotion is in sync with the season, and if you have an annual event that's successful, remember the Pig Bowl if you decide to change it.

Case Study Twenty-Nine: Batter Up

The Challenge: Owners of a sporting goods store, facing increased competition from a chain store in a local mall, want to increase their visibility as a member of the community and create a reputation as an active participant.

The Strategy: Sponsor a Little League team, then recruit politicians (such as the mayor and members of the city council) to compete in a home run derby, with the kids pitching and the adults hitting. Then, have an adults-versus-kids baseball game in which the adults are required to hit and throw with their non-dominant arms. If no politicians are available, the adult players can be drawn from the local Senior League.

The Rationale: As the fringes of ice melt away and suburban lawns turn muddy, thoughts turn to Major League Baseball and the thrill of paying eight dollars for a tube of pork while being entertained by nine players and an organist. Major League Baseball today is a mixture of nostalgia and technology: nostalgia for the image of kids looking through a knothole to see a perfect pitch and the technology of an animated shell game on the Jumbotron. Professional baseball may be the pinnacle of a player's aspiration, but you don't have to make $40 million a year to enjoy the game.

In its purest form, when it's played in a park, baseball is authentic: a carefree way to celebrate the season of renewal. Most communities have some kind of baseball league for adults, and the teams generally include some movers and shakers, including, possibly, the adult version of the alpha pup. Playing the season with these seasoned community veterans is one way to learn what makes the community "tick." Supplying athletic equipment to the league helps to show commitment to the community. And holding the home run derby with the mayor, city legislators, television anchors, radio personalities and others can raise a business's visibility in a fun and inexpensive way.

The Cost: Ongoing costs include equipment, insurance and uniforms for the team. Costs for the event should be nominal.

Chapter Twenty-Four

Pop-Up Events

It's a pop-up world. Retailers of the moment flicker to life like fireflies, then disappear. Tastes can change in a matter of moments if an idea goes viral, so it behooves businesses to bring those ideas to life as quickly as possible: hence, the pop-up event.

Case in Point: Anthropologie, held its Holiday House in New York on September 17, 2024, in a brownstone in New York and limited access to its AntroPerks members. Anthropologie Group CMO Elizabeth Preis is quoted on PYMNTS.com as saying, "This holiday season, we are thrilled to expand our holiday house experience, presenting it on a larger scale than ever before…This year's showhouse boasts more spaces, an expanded product range, and enhanced design elements."

An article on InEvent.com states, "These unique, temporary experiences are becoming increasingly popular for businesses looking to connect with their target audience and create awareness for their brand. They can range from temporary online stores to unexpected storefronts promoting newly launched products or simple booths at fairs. The possibilities are endless. Experiential events," such as "escape rooms for a puzzle game or a virtual reality adventure for a VR headset"; "engagement and social media," such as, "a fun photo booth with branded backdrops and props"; and "Interactive Games," that are "related to the product."

"Pop-Up Restaurants" get a mention. In the words of the article, "Food fairs are popular worldwide, and pop-up restaurants or food trucks can be a great addition to such events. They provide an opportunity to attract new customers while keeping operational costs low."

Pop-up activities need not be costly. To find your ideal pop-up event, do some thought association. How could people have fun with your product? Whatever comes to mind is likely to be your best idea. In the words of John Hunter, writing on Cvent.com, "Remember flash mobs, a huge trend of the last decade? Remember how a droning humdrum space, like the outside of a mall or shopping center, would suddenly erupt into a choreographed frenzy of excitement and dance for bystanders to witness? These impromptu performances became a buzzing viral trend that people tried to replicate all over the world."

Pop-up events will carry the message of the moment to your customers. And they will create a moment that endures. That is the heart of experimental marketing. Think of pop-up events or stores as a form of animation. Each frame, event or pop-up store can stand alone, but put them together in sequence and they can create a narrative.

Case Study Thirty: A Winter Wonderland in July

The Challenge: Owners of a coffee house hope to increase customer loyalty with a surprise event that is completely out of context.

The Strategy: Pick a weekend that is likely to be degrees above normal in July, a time when customers are craving a cooldown, and hold a winter wonderland event. Celebrate a time of merriment and apple cider. Serve drinks analogous to Starbucks' holiday servings, such as the ones in an article in *The Foreword* titled "Ranking Starbucks' Holiday Drinks: *The Foreword*," written by Sophia Hadi and Abigail Naveh: Sugar Cookie Home Brew (7), Peppermint Mocha (6), Caramel Brulee Latte (5), Sugar Cookie Almond Milk Latte (4), Chestnut Praline Latte (3), Peppermint Hot Chocolate (2) and Gingerbread Oatmeal Chai Latte (1). Decorate the store in the trappings of the winter holiday.

Rationale: Out-of-season promotions are attention getters, and they're a natural for media coverage. Schedule the event for Saturday, and alert the media well in advance with news releases and calls to the assignment desk or editor.

People enjoy the unexpected because it's a refreshing change, if only for a day. Some people love the change of seasons, while others would rather languish in a tropical paradise or ski all year down a frosted mountain. But when the temperature rises to uncomfortable levels during the summer or dips below zero after a whistling blizzard, even the diehard one-season afficianados may tend to crave the polar opposite. Transforming a business into a wintry mode in July could spike day-of sales and position the business as a go-to innovator that understands the customer.

Valerie Santalla wrote in an article, "10 Christmas in July Ideas to Promote Your Brand This Summer" on *Placei by Envato Blog*, "'Christmas in July' is not just a quaint notion from old movies; it's a fantastic marketing opportunity for brands to capitalize on the holiday spirit during the summertime. Whether you're a retail store, an online business, or a service provider, embracing the festive cheer of Christmas in July can inject new life into your marketing efforts and attract customers during a typically slow season."

The Cost: Decorations, possible overtime to decorate the coffee shop during off hours and the cost, if any, of making non-seasonal drinks available in the off season, theoretically offset by sales.

Case Study Thirty-One: Spring Cleaning

The Challenge: Owners of a business specializing in scuba diving equipment hope to position themselves as good stewards of the beach and the ocean to attract environmentally conscious customers to their enterprise.

The Strategy: Organize a beach cleanup day on a weekend in spring. Print up enough recycling bags to accommodate all volunteers. Hand out the bags, rubber gloves, and masks to volunteers at the start of the event. Set a definitive cutoff time for registration so that the demand for cleanup gear does not exceed the supply of volunteers. Conduct a contest to see who can bring back the most trash in a specified period. Give the winner a series of free scuba diving lessons.

A beach cleanup should be planned as a strictly weekend event, since more volunteers are available and television producers are more receptive to event coverage on Saturdays and Sundays.

The Rationale: This type of promotion is a natural for television, with opportunities for oceanfront visuals, and sound bites from organizers, volunteers and residents. There is an aura connected to the beach that is present nowhere else. In a sense, the beach is a prize. If you win an academy award, you may want to dust it off occasionally so that it appears shiny and new on the mantel. Same with the beach. It's the pride of any community that happens to be located next to a body of water. Even people who do not live at the beach take pride in it. That may explain attendance at beach cleanups, and the assignment editors and producers who populate the newsrooms on weekends are going to want to find the events that resonate with the market. What better way to do that than by going to the beach?

The Cost: Free scuba diving lessons for the winner, protective gloves, and recycling bags with the business' logo.

Chapter Twenty-Five

Adrenaline Public Relations

Imagine jumping out of a perfectly good airplane at an altitude of about five miles and plummeting to Earth. Imagination is a powerful, too, and it's especially potent when it is fed by actual events.

In 2012, Red Bull appealed to peoples' sense of adventure with a skydiving stunt in which a man jumped out of a capsule that had been carried up to the stratosphere, broke the sound barrier on the way down and survived. The stunt was dubbed *Stratos*. Felix Baumgartner became the first human being to break the sound barrier in Earth's atmosphere without the aid of an aircraft. In the words of an article published by the Federation Aeronautique Internationale (World Air Sports Federation), "At 38,969.4m altitude above Roswell, New Mexico, Baumgartner stepped out of the pressurized capsule, which was suspended from a gas balloon. Wearing a specially designed suit, he made a freefall of 36,529m, some of it in a 'violent spin' until he pulled his parachute, stabilised and floated safely to earth."

Who can truly quantify the experience of watching a human being jump from a record height and make it safely to the ground? It gives people who are used to warnings about human fragility the sense that they can evade mortality, if only for a number of minutes. It was a feeling of exhilaration that was well suited to a brand that portrays itself as the beverage of risk and perseverance.

One could argue that Red Bull's entire public relations strategy is fueled by adrenaline. Every year it holds a mountain-biking competition. For years, the event was for men only; but in 2024, women were admitted. In the words of John Branch, "The women were competing, finally, at Red Bull Rampage, the biggest and gnarliest mountain bike competition in the world." Branch writes, "The goal is to impress a panel of five judges with creativity, daring and fluidity. It is also to survive. No one has died at Rampage, but at least one competitor has been paralyzed. Helicopters are on hand to fly the injured to an area hospital, if needed." Not an event for the timid; but, as of 2024, an event for women as well as men. As Branch put it, "Danger did not stop women from wanting to participate. Just the opposite."

The foundations of a good public relations stunt are attention and impression. It gains attention by being outrageous, audacious, or both. The audience simply can't ignore it. Then, it creates an impression that will linger and associate brand and the stunt in the minds of the audience. In the words of Kris Gia Escueta, "A well-executed PR stunt can skyrocket a brand's presence in the market. Think of it as a high-impact performance that creates a lasting impression on the audience. These stunts often involve a blend of creativity, timing, and a deep understanding of the target audience to maximize their effect."

She continued later, explaining that, for a PR stunt to be effective, it must be well-timed, relevant, and highly engaging. Here are the key elements that contribute to the success of a PR stunt:

- ***Creativity:*** *The stunt must be original and innovative. It should stand out and be something that people haven't seen before.*
- ***Timing:*** *The event should be planned to coincide with relevant dates or current events to maximize its impact.*
- ***Audience Engagement:*** *The stunt should resonate with the target audience and encourage them to share and discuss it.*

Brady Werkheiser, on his blog, "Outrage Marketing is More Than Publicity Stunts and Pranks," cites both Stratos and a stunt that took "Starman," a mannequin in the driver's seat of a Tesla roadster, into space aboard Falcon 9 heavy rocket. In his words, "SpaceX's launch of a Tesla roadster might have seemed a bit cartoonish to some, but having a payload the size of a car on board made perfect sense as a test of the rocket's ability to carry a payload beyond low Earth orbit."

Werkheiser continued, "Both of these publicity stunts captured the nation's attention, earned positive media coverage, and supported the brand's primary business objective."

Case Study Thirty-Two: Summer Surprise

The Challenge: Owners of a surf shop that does mainly seasonal business in a beach community want to burnish their image as the go-to spot for gear.

The Strategy: Announce ahead of time on social media that on a given Saturday, the surf shop, in cooperation with a local restaurant, will cater a beach with free food (while supplies last). Do not reveal the name of the beach ahead of time. Those who are interested can sign up on a website, entering their names, email addresses and phone numbers. Inform them that they will receive an email one hour before the event announcing the name of the beach where the free food will be available. (Media can be alerted ahead of time to the location of the event with a press release that's embargoed until the information is disclosed to those who registered.)

Ideally, the visual would be a rush to the beach for free food. In the meantime, beachgoers would be treated to the sight of paragliders sailing in the breeze with the surf shop's logo prominently displayed.

But don't hesitate to ask the media to observe your embargo and help preserve the surprise element of the promotion. Media organizations take thos requests as seriously as a request to be "off the record" or "on background." Just be sure to specify that you're asking for coverage, but prefer not to have the details of the story released until the end of the embargo. (Actually, in a sense, adding an embargo can also whet a producer's appetite by making it appear more exclusive.)

The Rationale: While costs involved in this kind of event may be somewhat higher, both the expense and the payoff are shared between the restaurant and the surf shop. It's a partnership. Business owners who want to have an impact should remember this model. The key is to search for the synergies that will create a perception of exclusivity for both brands (together and separately) in the audience's minds. The goal is to create places where the "cool kids" hang out. A restaurant and a surf shop are natural partners on a beach.

In adopting this sort of strategy, business owners, along with marketers and brand executives, make use of brand synergy. According to Faster Capital, brand synergy "refers to the idea that, when two or more brands work together in a coordinated way, they can create a more powerful and effective message than they would be able to on their own." Before diving into co-branding, partnerships and extensions, set the scene by saying examples of brand synergy include:

- Co-branding: This is when two brands come together to create a new product or service that combines their respective strengths. For example, Nike and Apple teamed up to create the Nike + iPod Sport Kit, which allowed runners to track their progress using their iPods.
- Brand partnerships: This is when two brands work together on a marketing campaign or event. For example, Coca Cola and McDonald's have a long-standing partnership, with Coca Cola products being sold exclusively at McDonald's restaurants.
- Brand extensions: This is when a brand creates a new product or service that is related to their existing offerings.

The Cost: Food, brand-imprinted paragliders, permits, and labor costs (possible overtime).

It's been said that the whole is greater than the sum of its parts. That is certainly the case with brand synergy. In fact, when two or more brands remain separate but work together, the audience sees one powerful partnership, not two separate brands. Think of the difference between talking to two random people and speaking with two close friends or a married couple. The chemistry is subtly different, and there's a reason for that. When you speak with a married couple or two close friends, you're speaking with two people who not only know each other, but have accepted each other. It's as if they rushed a fraternity or sorority and were chosen to pledge. They *endorsed* each other.

A couple or two close friends are part of a team, not two separate individuals, and that means they have more credibility. When it comes to two or more brands partnering, that sort of credibility sends a powerful message to the consumer. When McDonald's chooses Coca Cola products as their exclusive soft drinks, Coca Cola gains credibility, and when Coca Cola chooses to showcase its soft drinks at McDonald's, the restaurant brand gains credibility with customers. The article on FasterCapital states, "By working together, brands can create a more powerful message and reach a wider audience than they would be able to do on their own."

Case Study Thirty-Three: Peak Performance

The Challenge: Owners of a bicycle shop that's been open for a month want to seal their relationship with mountain bikers in the region.

The Strategy: Create a makeshift pop-up store on a mountain where two-wheel enthusiasts congregate. Stock it with tools, biking gear, shirts, jackets, socks, water bottles, replacement parts, sunscreen, first-aid kits, energy drinks, and Gatorade. Also, partner with an optical retailer to offer high-end sunglasses. Depending on the owners' level of ambition, they may want to partner with a restaurant to bring food to the peak.

The Rationale: This is a surprise event that could become a tradition: a pop-up store on a mountain. The wilderness. When you think of pop-up stores, you may think of urban retail space where the hippest of the hip go to buy French mascara and sip on mimosas. Not in this case. To be practical, this would be more like a stand than a store: a mobile merchandise mart with enough supplies to get mountain bikers in gear. No mall kiosks, no high-end clothing stores, no food court, and no electric vehicle dealerships next to the giant aquarium. Just a bird-chirping wilderness filled with wildlife and chief diversity officers who load up the water bottle and take to the trails every weekend.

An event like this is one way to form and sustain brand partnerships. It may sound counterintuitive that a bicycle shop would partner with a restaurant, but on a mountain, where people are getting the kinds of workouts for which they bought a bicycle in the first place, a partnership with a restaurant is a natural. Down below, it could lead to all sorts of synergies, such as discount coupons the bicycle shop could give customers to encourage them to go to the restaurant while their bicycles are being assembled.

The best public relations will leave the audience regarding you and your brand as good neighbors. *Authentic PR* takes down the wall that separates the audience from the brand and integrates it into the audience's way of thinking. Once that affinity is established, it becomes second nature. That's how members of the audience become customers.

The Cost: Mobile cart that will serve as the pop-up store, permits, and transportation. Items for sale would be from existing stock.

Authentic PR should be aspirational. It should transport the audience to where their dreams live. Red Bull's Stratos event allowed everyone's spirit of adventure to live vicariously through one human being's record-breaking trip from the sky to the surface of Earth, and it associated that feeling of exhilaration with the brand, creating the sense that drinking a can of Red Bull could in part mimic that faster-than-the-speed-of-sound experience. Similarly, positioning a pop-up store or stand at a place where adventurous people congregate can associate a brand with the exhilaration people feel when they push the limits in any field.

It's always a good strategy to go where people live, work, and play.

In a sense, *Authentic PR* has two definitions. One is the moral obligation to do the right thing: to meet mistakes and successes alike with honesty, not hype. The other is to meet the audience where they are and take them where they want to be. That's what Stratos did in the stratosphere, and what you can do at your business.

Chapter Twenty-Six

Restoring Reputations

We live in what one might call the age of global visibility. Nothing is private in a connected world, and everything ever posted online about anyone is in full view of anyone with an internet connection. Some have more prominent footprints online than others. But anyone can be a star in the cloud.

That wasn't always the case. Decades ago, in what has been called the Golden Age of Hollywood, celebrities were shielded by a publicity industry that portrayed them as near-perfect superhumans. If you believed the publicity, you thought that actors in Westerns were pillars of character and were so coordinated they could twirl a lariat with their feet. Screen actresses were the epitome of glamor: showboats of style who could dazzle the planet with a perfect smile. As for politicians, Franklin D. Roosevelt's disability was unknown to some, and John Kennedy's philandering was known to The White House press corps but never reported. Watergate changed the relationship between politicians and the press. Every move by the president is scrutinized, and rumors of scandals are checked out by relentless reporters who refuse to take anything at face value. News reports covere peccadillos as well as policy. As for the entertainment industry, the decline of the studio system has left actors as free agents who can chart their own courses with the help of public relations firms and agencies. Their mission, like that of their predecessors in the 1930s, is to tell a story; but the story must be *authentic*, and they must deal with crises without covering up.

The stories of celebrities' and politicians' falls are unscripted drama, ironic counterpoints to the wealth and power these prominent individuals derive from "sticking to the script." They're probably, in many cases, examples of *schadenfreude*, as the eight-to-fivers gloat at the human frailty of the one percent, but there's almost certainly more to the phenomenon than that. Perhaps for that reason, much has been said and written about it. Tony Sciafani of MSNBC even suggests that, "with our 24/7 news cycle, the public's fascination with falling (or fallen) stars has become all the more obvious. And let's admit it: networks are all about ratings, so if we didn't watch it, they wouldn't show it."

"Over the past few decades," he continues, "a star sytem has gradually evolved that's the opposite of a meritocracy. Call it a 'trashocracy.' We offer stars polite applause when they make a great CD or film, but if they want our undivided attention, they'd better do something really crazy—like wear a surgical mask in public or buy up the remains of the Elephant Man." He quotes C. David Marshall, author of the book *Celebrity and Power* and chair of the New Media and Cultural Studies Department at the University of Wollongong in Australia, as saying, "One reason we're drawn to 'human train wrecks,' as they've come to be known, is people are instinctively drawn to tragedy."

He continues, "The same impulse that draws us to soap operas manifests itself when we watch people like Michael Jackson fall from grace." Marshall believes that "[o]ur desire to bring down celebrities can also be considered part of the democratic process. Like political leaders," he says, "celebrities embody power given to them by the public. When that relationship breaks down, the public is, in essence, not letting the celebrity 'represent' them anymore."

Business owners may or may not be celebrities, but in an age of global visibility they are inseparable from their businesses.

Case Study Thirty-Four: Under the Influence

The Challenge: The CEO of a business, who is also running for mayor of the city, is driving home from a social event when he's pulled over on suspicion of driving while under the influence of alcohol. He fails a sobriety test and is arrested. Since the arrest occurred at night, he's able to bail out of jail before dawn and return home before anyone other than law enforcement is aware of what's happened.

The Strategy: When it comes to crisis public relations, the best offense is a quick defense. Whether in politics or business, it's best to get out in front of the story, to go public with it before the news media become aware of it.

If the plan is to plead guilty or no contest and if there is no way that candor can jeopardize the case, the first step is to record a video explaining what happened and apologize to customers, the city and potential constituents. The apology should be sincere without being maudlin and should never portray the offender as the victim. Taking responsibility for the offense is critical, and it should be coupled with a promise to do better and to learn from the mistake.

This all assumes that the case against the CEO is pretty solid. If there are questions as to whether the CEO is guilty, the video should still be made, but the CEO shouldn't admit guilt. Instead, he should acknowledge that the arrest was made, praise members of law enforcement for their professionalism, and conclude with a vow to cooperate with law enforcement in arriving at the truth. Unless there's reason not to speak openly about certain aspects of the case, he should consent to interviews for radio, television, newspapers, and podcasts.

Is all of this easy? *Of course not!* It's difficult, but the payoff is credibility—and the public tends to respect a sincere apology.

The Rationale: A conviction for driving under the influence of alcohol or drugs can have a disastrous effect on a career or a business, but it doesn't have to. The difference between successful crisis management and *un*successful crisis management lies in the strategy used to deal with it. That strategy should incorporate accountability, apology, and *authenticity*. Accountability means taking responsibility for whatever happened. Don't try to deflect responsibility, and don't try to delay taking responsibility. (In other words, don't say or write that the matter is under review and you'll have a complete statement later.) Apology means saying you're sorry. *Period.* Any statement or interview that doesn't include saying you're sorry or that you apologize is *not* an apology. One or the other has to be stated explicitly, and never issue a conditional apology, saying you're sorry if anyone was offended by what you did or if anyone thought you meant.... *You'll* be very sorry you did that.

The Cost: Zero. And the cost of not doing it may be your reputation. Mel Gibson's career was damaged by his arrest for driving under the influence in 2006. Earlier in the decade, Gibson had directed the movie *The Passion of the Christ*, which some interpreted as anti-Semitic. Abraham Foxman of the Anti-Defamation League was not one of them, but according to an article on *Decent Films*, "Foxman has been one of the film's most outspoken critics; he's described the film's portrayal of Jews as 'painful to watch,' and expresses that while [he doesn't think the film itself is] antisemitic, it may fuel antisemitic sentiments among some audience members."

Leslie A. Miller-Dancy, Editorial Assistant with *Religion in the News*, writes, "... LA. County Deputy James Mee pulled over Mel Gibson driving his Lexus at eighty-five mph in a forty-five mph zone on the Pacific Coast Highway in Malibu. After smelling alcohol on Gibson's breath and spotting an open bottle of Tequila riding shotgun, Mee administered a Breathalyzer test, which showed the actor to have a blood alcohol level of 12 percent, well above the legal limit of .08 percent. Gibson proceeded to ask Deputy Mee, 'Are you a Jew?' and launched into a barrage of antisemitic invective, during which he blamed Jews for 'all the wars in the world.' Throwing in a sexist comment about a female officer on the scene, he continued to mutter remarks from the back seat of the squad car taking him to the police station."

According to Miller-Dancy, Gibson issued an apology that same day, writing, "in part, 'I have battled the disease of alcoholism all for all of my adult life and profoundly regret my horrific relapse. I apologize for any behavior unbecoming of me in my inebriated state and have already taken necessary steps to ensure my return to health.'

"To which Foxman responded, 'Mel Gibson's apology is unremorseful and insufficient... It does not go to to the essence of his bigotry and his antisemitism. His tirade finally reveals his true self and shows that his protestations during the debate over his film *The Passsion of the Christ*, that he is such a tolerant, loving person were a sham.'" Miller-Dancy quoted a story in the *San Francisco Chronicle* as saying, "By now, Mel Gibson is a public relations train wreck."

Gibson issued another apology, saying, "I want to apologize specifically to everyone in the Jewish community for the words that I said to a law enforcement officer the night I was arrested on a DUI charge." According to Miller-Dancy, "Foxman declared himself satisfied. 'This is the apology we have sought and requested,' he said. 'We are glad that Mel Gibson has finally owned up to the fact that he made antisemitic remarks, and his apology sounds sincere.'"

Gibson's two apologies, taken together and separately, provide a lesson in the nuances of good crisis public relations. In his first apology, Gibson acknowledged his alcoholism and vowed to get help and to get better. While this may seem like a noble gesture, Gibson could be seen as shifting the burden of responsibility from himself to a disease. In other words, he didn't take responsibility for what he said and did. Gibson directed his second apology at the Jewish community and took responsibility.

That is the essence of *authentic* public relations.

For George Kurtz, the aforementioned CEO of CrowdStrike, the first priority was to get on the air and apologize while the internet was still out. Others in the company followed with their own apologies. That is the natural order of crisis communication. In the case of CrowdStrike, Kurtz could have sent out some other managers to explain the outage while he remained cocooned at home or in his office. That would have backfired, since the public would have been clamoring for accountability from the CEO.

He would have been very sorry.

United Airlines found itself in a changing public relations environment when, in 2017, four passengers were removed involuntarily from a flight so that some crew members could be seated. Three of the passengers went voluntarily. The other passenger, Dr. David Dao, did not. Needless to say, in this connected age, the incident was caught on video and spread through social media.

Julie Creswell and Sapna Maheshwarl writes in *The New York Times*, "By the afternoon, after more than a day of changing statements, United's chief executive apologized and promised a review of its policies.

"'No one should ever be mistreated this way,' Oscar Munoz, the company's chief executive, said in a statement, but on social media, videos and invective flourished. In the words of Creswell and Maheshwarl, "social media has proved to be a powerful outlet for complaints. United drew quick criticism for its initial response to the Sunday evening incident, with many people calling it tone deaf. On Monday, when Mr. Munoz apologized for having to re-accommodate these customers, the internet saw it as a joke. Nice to know 're-accommodate' on United now means 'drag you violently out of your seat,' one woman posted on Twitter."

"A few hours later, United seemed to go on the offensive to blame Dr. Dao, saying he 'defied' the officers. Finally, on Tuesday afternoon, the airline changed course again, with Mr. Munoz saying that United would take 'full responsibility for the situation.'"

The lesson here is that when a business responds to a crisis, the response should be decisive, unwavering, and contrite. The *first* time. Not after two other tries, and above all, that response should take into consideration what the audience's reaction is likely to be. Issuing a statement with the wrong wording is like tossing a lit match out the car window during the dry season in California. In both cases, you risk starting something that will spread.

Chapter Twenty-Seven

AI PR

In an era of deepfakes, *authentic* public relations becomes critical. People are unbalanced and disoriented. Because trusted sources of information have become scarce, there's no easy way to vet a story for accuracy. That presents an additional challenge to public relations, which is perennially regarded as news for hire, but that belies the fact that public relations historically has been a business-to-business operation: a PR firm working with the media to engage the public.

Responding to a question on *Quora* as to whether public relations is "essentially a dishonest profession," Sheila Gardezi, SEO at Words Plus Design, writes, "Although there have been cases of public relations representatives acting in a dishonest ways, the profession itself is not dishonest. Tactics that employ dishonesty can easily be caught by anyone doing a little bit of research, especially in this internet age. The purpose of public relations is to build engagement between the public and the company or organization. In order to do this, the company must be perceived as genuine and authentic."

Enter AI, which can manipulate words and images on its own. Now, everything is under scrutiny, but there's promise, as well. An article on Microsoft.com, "AI in Marketing and PR: How Professionals are Reimagining Communication with Technology," states:

"In the world of PR and marketing, innovation and following new trends are the key for remaining competitive. So, it's no surprise that AI has become a powerful partner for professionals working in these sectors." It helps them stay ahead and adapt. Develop strategies and brainstorm. AI can automate their monotonous everyday tasks, create data-driven insights, and personalize communication, while leading to more efficient and impactful PR and marketing campaigns." This can work for business at any level.

One of the primary advances of artificial intelligence is the ability to detect patterns that human beings might take years, decades, centuries, or millenia to figure out, if they can discern them at all. Retail businesses may be able to project store traffic, inventory levels, and sales volumes far into the future. There's evidence that AI can generate weather forecasts that are more accurate than the ones human beings can develop. That can help as well in predicting store traffic, sales volumes, and staffing needs. Then there's sentiment analysis, in which AI can analyze text to get a sense of where public opinion is and where it's headed. "People's desire to engage with businesses and the overall brand perception depend heavily on public opinion. According to a survey by Podium, 93 percent of consumers say that online reviews influence their buying decisions. Users may not give you a chance once they've read a few bad reviews. They won't research whether feedback is fake or not. They'll choose another option." Rather than looking at online reviews haphazardly or undertaking a laborious manual search, businesses can rely on sentiment analysis to collect and analyze public opinion.

AI is the ability of machines to perform tasks and learn skills. There are three levels: narrow AI or weak AI (ANI), in which machines will perform tasks to which they are assigned; artificial general intelligence (AGI), in which machines will equal humans in their abilities to perform tasks; and artificial superintelligence, in which machines will generate and perform tasks at a level beyond human capability. Within the realm of AI is ChatGPT, which can understand questions and comments, and respond to them in conversational language. Ryan Chacon, in his article "What Does GPT Stand For?" writes, "GPT stands for Generative Pre-training Transformer. In essence, GPT is a kind of artificial intelligence (AI). When we talk about AI, we might think of sci-fi movies or robots, but AI is much more mundane and user-friendly. If you've ever asked a question to Siri or Alexa or used predictive text on Google, you've already used AI."

For public relations professionals, and for businesses of any size, AI can write news releases, draw up event calendars, keep track of analytics, and search keywords for leads to story ideas. It can also keep track of the preferences of television producers in the local market and match them to story ideas. It can help develop and organize press kits and pitch decks.

It can also deceive. All it takes is a prompt to generate a story that isn't true, produce a "photo" that isn't real, or start a rumor that isn't substantiated.

Case Study Thirty-Five: Faking It

The Challenge: Owners of an electronics store hope to raise the store's profile while at the same time calling attention to what they perceive as the hazards of deepfakes.

The Strategies: There are a number of ways to tackle this topic, some of them potentially controversial. For example, one option is to hold a deepfake contest, using specified photographs or paintings that are all in the public domain and available for anyone to use. The contest would begin online, with contestants being given a list of rules and restrictions. Then, a group of finalists would be chosen and the altered images displayed at an event held on a Saturday (in conjunction with a sale) at the computer store. Winners would be chosen in a number of categories, including most creative, most believable, and most humorous. Food would be provided by a concession partner who would pay related expenses and receive all the profit from food sales. The broadcast media would be invited, and video of the event would be archived for later display on YouTube, X, and Facebook.

Another option is to stage a march from the store or some other location to city hall, calling for human control of artificial intelligence. The event would be publicized ahead of time, and everyone would be welcome to join. Before the march, a contest would be held on Zoom to choose the speaker for the event. Each contestant would give a three-minute speech, and participants in the Zoom meeting would vote for the best speaker on the chat function on the day of the march. The public would be encouraged to get creative and come in costume (perhaps a robot), if they so desire. Food would be provided by a concession partner. After the march, and a speech by the winner of the contest, there would be a separate contest to choose the best costume and the best picket sign. Those two winners and the speaker would get a free computer.

The Rationale: Deepfakes are of concern because it can be a challenge to discern what is real and what is not. Used with malice, they are like a shot over the bow. It may seem like a stretch to use deepfakes as fodder for a contest on a Saturday, but, as Mark Twain once observed, "Against the assault of laughter nothing can stand." And so a contest becomes not only a way to spend an afternoon, but a way to spoof the "art" of faking it.

As for the march, the idea of machines taking over has been fodder for science fiction for decades. The word "robot" first appeared in the play *R.U.R.*, an acronym for *Rossumovi Univerzální Roboti* (Rossum's Universal Robots), by Czech writer, Karel Čapek, which premiered on January 2, 1921. But the advent of artificial intelligence and, specifically, the development of the large language model and generative AI, have prompted warnings that the day could come when machines exceed the capabilities of human beings. The use of artificial intelligence in entertainment was the focus of two strikes: one by the Writers Guild of America, and another by SAG/AFTRA, both in 2023. That's because artificial intelligence is capable of writing a screenplay and using the likeness of a human being to create a character and generate publicity shots. The march, done in the spirit of fun, would nevertheless have an element of urgency to it that Karl Čapek might have only imagined.

The Cost: The cost of the prizes, and permits, if held in a public area. Security. No cost for food, since that would be the responsibility of the concession partner.

Case Study Thirty-Six: The Newsletter

The Challenge: The founders of a startup that aggregates news want their website to become the most influential news source on the internet.

The Strategy: Create an AI-generated news briefing that comes out twice a day automatically. It would include a digest of the news of the day, perhaps a point-counterpoint commentary, weather information, a preview or review of the markets (depending on the time of day), and sports. The fact that it was all written and produced by AI would be clearly disclosed. The newsletter would be interactive so that those who view or listen to it could ask questions and AI would respond. The user could also ask for transcripts of the digest to be emailed for later use, and each digest would be archived temporarily.

Alternatively, the news digests could be delivered by one or more avatar anchors. Ideally, the anchors would deliver the news and the point-counterpoint, while other avatars would cover weather and sports. This technology is being refined, but it's being deployed around the world. Making it interactive would eliminate the "fourth wall" that excludes the user and provide a fully integrated experience that would be entertaining, educational, and informative, with the goal being to make the site the go-to point for news, a news "publication" that is interactive.

The Rationale: At this point in time, anything that showcases the capabilities of artificial intelligence to the fullest is likely to draw a loyal audience (as long as it changes with advances in technology). Ask Sana, an avatar anchor that's been on the air in India. In the words of Faraz Sayyad, writing in the article, "AI Anchor Sana: The Modern News Broadcasting Era," Sana "is a remarkable artificial intelligence news anchor, making her debut on the Aaj Tak News Channel's Black & White program alongside journalist Sudhir Chaudhary. With a human-like appearance, she exudes confidence and delivers her speeches flawlessly."

But does AI have a future in news broadcasting, given the resistance of human anchors, writers, and producers? An article from AI Studios, "AI News Anchors: The Future of News Broadcasting" says, "The rapid evolution of artificial intelligence (AI) is reshaping industries worldwide, and news broadcasting is no exception. The advent of AI news anchors is poised to revolutionize how news is produced, consumed, and perceived. Coupled with custom avatars and AI video generation, these intelligent systems are set to transform the news landscape dramatically." *Possibly.*

Entertainment is also a sector that's grappling with the questions posed by artificial intelligence. There are questions as to who or what is actually the source of AI-written screenplays. In an article titled "WGA Sends Letters to Studios Urging Lawsuits Against AI Plagiarism: 'Inaction has Harmed WGA Members,'" published in *Variety*, Michael Schneider states, "The Writers Guild of America's east and west chapters have sent a strongly-worded letter to the heads of the major Hollywood studios criticizing them for inaction as artificial intelligence appears to be taking copy-written scripts and using it to 'plagiarize stolen works.'"

Schneider continues later on in the article, "In the letter, the WGAW and WGAE officers cite a Nov. 18 article in *The Atlantic* noting that 'tech companies have looted the studios' intellectual property—a vast reserve of works created by generations of union labor—to train their artificial intelligence systems.'" This is a legitimate concern, one that prompted strikes by writers and performers. It's up to you whether to employ artificial intelligence to creative works, keeping in mind that AI learns how to create content from works that were written by human beings. That includes same-day news copy."

The Cost: Since it's a startup, the equipment to produce the news briefings is probably on premises and the programmers are on staff. Other costs are likely to be in line with normal daily operations.

Case Study Thirty-Seven: The Cyber Comic

The Challenge: An artist who dreams of creating comic books online hopes to become the next Stan Lee.

The Strategy: Stan Lee was an editor, producer, and writer of comic books who worked in a family business called Timely Comics, which later became Marvel Comics. To aspire to the success level of Stan Lee with an AI assist, you would still need imagination. In fact, if you want to feel truly alive, you need imagination. It's the bridge between you and reality.

A number of strategies could be used, all of which employ artificial intelligence and human beings. In one scenario, the artist would create a group of superheroes (comparable to, say, the Fantastic Four) as a basis for a series of comics that would be created by artificial intelligence. It would be publicized as the world's first automated comic book or comic strip series. Given the fact that artificial intelligence can produce a full creative work in seconds, a new comic strip or comic book could be generated frequently. Perhaps the ideal frequency would be about once every two days. (Every day might be too much, but if it were updated weekly or monthly, readers might get distracted by something else.) Since it would be an online creation, there would be no printing or distribution costs.

Again, the superhero(es) would be human-created, but the story line and the execution would come from artificial intelligence. That way, both the audience and the artist would watch together and comment as the plot unfolded. For the artist, this could ultimately lead to a lucrative arrangement with a newspaper site or entertainment periodical. It could also lead to a movie or television deal.

A second strategy would be to create the superheroes or the comic strip, then have AI generate a number of possible storylines and ask viewers to vote for one. AI would proceed with the winning plot, and the process would repeat *ad infinitum*. People could both vote and comment, and the goal would be to create a community around these characters, much as there is a community centered on *Star Wars*. In this case, the creator of the comic trip or comic book would face an additional copyright challenge. There would have to be a disclaimer at the outset stating that even though viewers were voting on the storyline, the copyright for the characters belonged to the creator. That's because, under current law, only human-created intellectual property is eligible for copyright. An AI-generated storyline would not qualify for copyright protection. Conversely, the creator could decide not to pursue television or movie rights to the characters, and instead use them to create a following, after which they create another set of characters and sell them to the studios, armed with a formidable following online.

Another option would be to leave it all up to artificial intelligence, put it on the internet, and let audiences watch the process unfold and comment on the direction of the plot. In this case, it would be an experiment in human-machine communication rather than a vehicle to a deal. But it would increase the name recognition of the artist for future projects.

The Rationale: Artificial intelligence is a tool that isn't, at least at the moment, fully understood, not even by those who invented it. No one really knows how AI solves the problems with which it is presented. That's because AI is given both the tools with which to solve problems and the latitude to do it on its own. Because of that latitude, there have been times when scientists and engineers have been surprised at how AI developed a solution. For both the scientist and the non-scientist, there's both a sense of wonder and a sense of caution over AI's improving capabilities. The risks of artificial intelligence *are* real, but its rewards are equally real. It isn't going away, and it can be dangerous, but when it's used safely, it can be of enormous benefit.

For the most part, the artist will be using generative artificial intelligence, which produces text and video using generative language models. According to Amazon Web Services, "Large language models, also known as LLMs, are very large deep learning models that are pre-trained on vast amounts of data. The underlying transformer is a set of neural networks that consist of an encoder and a decoder with self-attention capabilities." GPT is an LLM.

Artificial intelligence can measure the reaction to a creation such as a comic book series while it is creating it. Using sentiment analysis, it could troll not only the comments on the artist's website, but also comments around the internet. (It might be interesting to ask AI to write its own review of the comic book series.) This sort of project could take AI beyond its current uses. The article "PR and AI: 21 ways artificial intelligence is changing the PR game," published on *PRLab*, states, "We've all seen the impressive things AI can do. We're at peak hype where AI is concerned. Everybody seems to be talking about it, but while many are scared of missing out, they don't quite know what to do with it yet," AI has been successful at organizing, interpreting, and analyzing; essentially, as a means of freeing up the office or virtual collaboration for creative tasks. But why not allow AI to participate, share its views and come up wth its content? If you tell someone AI made the office more efficient and then tell that same person that it created a new generation of superheroes, which activity is going to intrigue him or her the most?

The Cost: All it would take to start is an AI account. Presumably, income, whether through monetization or deals with entertainment companies, would offset any higher expenses as the project grows more complex.

AI has a low barrier to entry and a high potential for growth. Anyone can use it, but only the bold will take the risks necessary to use it powerfully. Budding artists and musicians living in the proverbial studio apartment, entrepreneurs living in the proverbial garage and scientists living in the proverbial college town have the potential to change the culture by creating new hybrid forms that involve people and machines and the potential to change the world by detecting the patterns of growth that have eluded people until now. Only the bold will have the chutzpah to go where no one has gone before.

Chapter Twenty-Eight

The Quest for Influence

Influencers have been around ever since humankind began to populate the Earth. There's always a dominant personality in any group of two or more people. Charisma can carry the day in social situations and in the media. But as technologies have changed, so have the strategies for gaining influence.

There was once a time when people respected the media. Baby Boomers had Walter Cronkite, and a bevy of other trusted anchors and reporters to deliver the news of the day. People railed at the media, but for the most part the anchor was an authority figure: trusted, truthful, and tenacious.

National news anchors were some of the influencers of their time.

And the news was highly regulated on the basis of the assumption that the frequencies that carried the stories were a limited resource. The rise of cable television and the demise of the Fairness Doctrine changed all that. They left the media free to engage in what was called niche casting: directing their programming at specific audiences—and they didn't have to play fair with controversial topics. Both their audiences and the media became more fragmented, and broadcast and cable outlets became more cost-conscious.

This is vastly different from the 1950s, when media organizations were expected to be loss leaders. As Marc Gunther writes in "The Transformation of Network News," published in *Nieman Reports*, "The Big Three broadcast television networks—ABC, CBS, and NBC—all covered news, but they generally didn't make money, nor did they expect to turn profits from news programming. They presented news programming for the prestige it would bring to the network and to satisfy the licensing requirements imposed on their affiliates. They wanted to be accepted by the public as good corporate citizens and responsible journalists. Then cable television began the process of fragmentation. The establishment of CNN in 1980 made the concept of cable news credible, but broadcast news still dominated cable as an information source. Rush Limbaugh's talk radio show debuted in 1984, turning radio into a sort of political rodeo."

In 1995, Republicans took control of the House of Representatives and the Senate for the first time since the 1950s, MSNBC debuted in June of that year, and Fox News started reaching the public in October. The internet had become something of a public pastime, as had gaming with people thousands of miles away. It had become possible to reach out to people in social media while at the same time cocooning in a realm that represented a limited number of interests and a limited amount of face-to-face contact. Television news fragmented into a cacophony of commentary. Listening to commentators reinforcing points of view arguably became the rule, while listening to others' points of view arguably became the exception.

The advent of artificial intelligence made machine-to-machine communication possible, made ubiquitous human-to-machine communication, and seemingly made obsolete human-to-human communication.

As technology became more sophisticated, public relations became more challenging, because the core principle of PR is credibility. And when the institutions that safeguard credibility erode and fragment, there are no authoritative sources to cite. If you lose sight, you can't cite.

But each of the transformations in the media has presented its own opportunities. The repeal of the Fairness Doctrine made possible talk shows with a point of view. *Case in Point*: Rush Limbaugh, According to Ray Thomas, an AM radio programmer at WIOO in Carlisle, Pennsylvania, Limbaugh was not a conservative commentator; he was a "shock jock." He was a radio guy, not a journalist or a political commentator. And he took advantage of public relations to do his core job: build an audience.

On one occasion, he celebrated a day when people were asked to go meatless by eating a steak on the air. (The steak was furnished by a meat producers' organization.) It was an effective counterpoint, and it cost nothing.

Case Study Thirty-Eight: See You on the Radio

The Challenge: Increase the visibility of an anti-smoking non-profit organization.

The Strategy: Work with a radio station to recruit a heavy smoker to go on the air and try to last twenty-four hours without smoking. The volunteer could be a member of the audience or someone known to the non-profit or the station. (Whoever is chosen would have to be vetted to ensure that he or she actually has a smoking addiction.) Start the no-smoking challenge at 6:00 a.m. or whenever the morning drive show begins. The smoker would be in the studio, where the morning personality or team could ask him or her questions periodically and keep the audience aware of how they are doing.

Serve a meal with juice (but no coffee) to help keep the smoker's mind off the addiction and (in the case of the juice) flush out nicotine and stabilize blood sugar. (The meal and drinks could be catered by a local restaurant, which would get hours of attendant publicity.) If the smoker makes it through the morning drive show, invite him or her to remain on the air. If the smoker makes it through the midday show, challenge them to try and stick it out through afternoon drive—and so on, all through the night (with time allotted for sleep).

The goal is to keep the smoker awake and smoke-free for twenty-four hours. Throughout the promotion, on-air personalities could ask questions and invite audience members to call in with questions or advice. If the smoker lights up, the promotion ends. If he or she makes it to the start of the morning show, a prize would await. (One option: a gift certificate good for two months of free meals at the restaurant. This would help the smoker adjust to a nicotine-free life while providing the restaurant with good will for doing a good deed.)

The goal of the promotion would be to show the smoker that he or she could make it through a full day without lighting up, on the theory that if you can make it through one day, you can make it through permanently.

The Rationale: Ira Glass said, "Radio is your most visual medium." In listening to the journey of a smoker trying to quit, audience members can easily get caught up in memories of their own struggles in life. Plus, radio programming is continuous, whether it's talk programming or music programming, so it's easily adaptable to a long-form struggle, such as listening to whether a smoker can make it through twenty-four hours without lighting up—and radio is *interactive*. The audience can become part of the play.

The Cost: Zero if sponsors or other businesses provide the food and juice.

After repeal of the Fairness Doctrine and the development of cable television, the internet became the focus of media, first, through email, as a way to communicate person to person, then, through social media, as a way to develop entire communities that could influence popular culture and politics. Influencers on social media now rival and, sometimes, surpass those on radio, on television and in print. Gitti Malinsky states on CNBC.com, "More than half of young people want to be influencers—57 percent to be exact. That's according to a 2023 Morning Consult survey of 1,000 GenZers. And they're not alone. Nearly half, 41 percent of adults overall, would choose the career as well, according to a similar Morning Consult Survey of 2,204 adults."

An article on IZEA, "Impact and Influence: the Effects of Influence Culture on Society," states that, "Influencers are an integral part of the online space, creating communities, working with brands to showcase products and forming human connections online. Influencer culture shapes our everyday norms, from shopping habits to trends to beliefs to lifestyles.

"In our 2025 Trust in Influencer Marketing report, we surveyed 1,200 American consumers to see how impactful influencer marketing was in their daily purchases. The give-and-take between influencers and their followers is stronger than ever. Influencers shape what people buy and the trends they follow, and people turn to influencers for recommendations and lifestyle tips. This has a big impact on what people buy; 79 percent of people said they had bought a product after seeing an influencer use it. This proves how important influencers are in any solid marketing strategy."

According to the report, 77 percent of those surveyed "find influencer content more scripted than your regular, scripted ads. Plus, 85 percent of people trust posts m influencers more than those from famous TV, film or sports stars, up from 61 percent in 2024."

What's more, influencers are technically accessible through social media sites such as Facebook and LinkedIn, although getting their attention may be more difficult than getting a photo with a head of state. As the article states, "Influencers have become digital celebrities but differ quite a bit from TV, film and other celebrities. Because influencers have grown their audiences, creating connections and trust, their followers more apt to purchase a product based on what an influencer recommends versus a Big Celebrity."

Case Study Thirty-Nine: Influencer 101

The Challenge: Owners of a computer retailer hope to become the "go to" source for computers and cyberware in the community.

The Strategy: Create a *Survivor*-type competition online by recruiting four would-be influencers and challenging them to grow their audiences with posts that mention the computer store. The contestants can use any strategy they want. They don't have to make their posts oriented toward the computer store, but there must be a tie-in of some sort that promotes the store. Every week, the administrators of the contest would check the analytics. The contestant whose audience had grown the least would be eliminated until there was one left. The winner would get a free computer.

This type of contest could also be conducted using four teams rather than four individuals. The structure would be the same, with one team eliminated each week. This would create a larger brain trust for innovation, but it would also increase the cost of the grand prize(s). The choice would depend on how much the owners of the computer store want to spend. The eliminations could be announced online or cybercast on either Zoom or YouTube. One other possibility would be to give each team a coach who is a major influencer. Then there would be two competitions: the one involving the contestants and the prestige match between the influencers.

The Rationale: Reality shows have become popular over the years, and voting someone "off the island" has become something of a catch phrase. Combine that with the power of online influencing, and you have the prescription for an all-out brawl backed by ingenuity. In the midst of it all, the computer store gets oodles of free publicity and, possibly, more of a following.

There are a number of ways to enhance this following. The ultimate way to grow an audience is to develop and cultivate an influencer who can charismatically lead a following. It shouldn't take long to find a wanna-be. There aren't age limits to being an influencer. Kaye Tsakis, in the *New York Times* article, "How Being an Influencer Became a New American Dream," writes, "Capitalism and modern technology have mixed to create an internet world where users are transformed into brands." *Case in Point*: Peyton and Lyla, two preteen sisters from Alabama. Tsakis writes, "From their rural Alabama home under their mother's watchful gaze, they hawk fashion and beauty products to tens of thousands of online fans around the world. Every day, packages arrive at their doorstep for them to unbox and try out—deluxe makeup sets, floral dresses, exercise bikes—all free, as if delivered by a shopping mall Santa." Influencing can work in a number of ways. A computer store could find users to hawk its brands, or it can become a clearinghouse of its own, inviting its customer base to test and rate products and develop a formidable online presence.

The Cost: Prizes for the contest, sound system, setup, and refreshments for the event. Zero for the clearinghouse.

Case Study Thirty-Nine A: Influencer 102

The Challenge: Same challenge, but in this case, the competition would be different.

The Strategy: Instead of becoming influencers, the contestants would try to reach influencers. Each team or individual would create a product, send it to any or all of a number of influencers and attempt to get it endorsed. The contest would culminate in a *Shark Tank*-like event to which the media would be invited and at which the finalists (those who had their products endorsed by an influencer) would present their creations to a panel of judges.

Getting media coverage is the whole point. But this may also be an opportunity to create a YouTube channel that will develop a loyal following all its own. *Shark Tank*–type encounters are unscripted, raw, and compelling, like life itself. But there are a number of follow-up YouTube type programs that could also help boost visibility. How-to videos on topics such as navigating the latest generation of Windows populate the internet in general and YouTube in particular.

The Rationale: Perhaps the reason the show *Shark Tank* is so popular is that it's *authentic*. A perfect tonic for the authentic age. In a world in which technology can change the rules and the culture in a matter of weeks or months, people search for programming that gets to the point, and the drama of the encounter between entrepreneurs and venture capitalists isn't scripted. That's appealing at a time when seemingly everyone has an idea. Eighty years ago, the dream may have been to get a job in the mailroom of a corporation and then go from there. Today, the dream is to start a corporation that will have some staying power. In such a volatile environment, in which today's top Super Bowl advertiser may be tomorrow's memory, the audience doesn't have the time or the inclination to put up with anything but the real thing. A real-life pitch fest is real, it's entertaining and it's inexpensive.

And it works. According to to Cecily Mauron, writing on *Mashable*, "Appearing on *Shark Tank* isn't just a way to raise capital, it gives entrepreneurs free national publicity. Many entrepreneurs that appeared on *Shark Tank* saw huge boosts in traffic, revenue, and customers—even if they didn't get a deal with one of the Sharks." Mauron states, "In fact, the national exposure is arguably the biggest benefit of the show. Entrepreneurs are given the chance to tell their story and showcase their product and service in ways that a straightforward advertisement could never accomplish. Often, the entrepreneurs have amazing stories of overcoming hardships and risking everything because of the businesses they fiercely believe in. That passion and tenacity has a persuasive effect of connecting to the audience on an emotional level, which, in turn, makes us root for them and want to support them (*i.e.* buy their product). It can also be a chance for the entrepreneurs to receive valuable feedback."

Influencing creates centers of gravity and authority, rare commodities in a fragmented world, but there are also forces that still draw people together even as technology pulls them apart. Commenting on an Amazon Ads study, "From Ads to Zeitgeist," Kate Scott-Dawkins, Global President, Group M, writes, "There has been increasing atomization of culture—everyone is getting a more fragmented, personalized feed. In response to that, what we are seeing is the outsize importance of things like sports, the draw of the Barbie movie or Taylor Swift's *Eras* concert tour—the few places now where people can feel like they're doing, seeing and feeling something together. For brands, tapping into those places where people are still engaging with the same cultural moment is increasingly important." Bringing people together may sound like a tiresome cliché, but it is a vital way to reach customers in a connected but fragmented world.

The Cost: The grand prize, setup and refreshments for the event, sound system. Zero for the YouTube channel. You may be wondering how to attract followers on YouTube and on social media in general. That's like asking how you yell for help in space, where there are no sound waves to carry your voice. When you are starting out, trying to attract a crowd is easier if you already have a social network of friends who are influential online and if you are naturally outgoing. But even if you're more the "still waters run deep" type, don't be afraid to share your thoughts with the world, especially if your personality is a little off the beaten path.

The internet craves three qualities from would-be influencers: authenticity, credibility and a touch of eccentricity (ACE). The girls from Alabama who receive packages on their doorsteps have what you call the authority of demographics; that is, they are part of the target age group for the products they vet. The "alpha pup" whom Hasbro asked to use a product had the credibility to talk to his peers, and how-to hosts attract viewers by talking about topics such as how to tie a tie or how to back up your data on a personal computer. Some of these use a combination of expert timing, visual effects, and graphics—some may be talking heads in front of a wall. Most have interesting forms of presentation, but the key to their success is invariably authenticity. No one accepts the varnished truth anymore; only the unvarnished truth—raw and un-sanded, a diamond in the rough.

Julie Tyler Ruiz, in her article, "How to Become an Influencer in 11 Steps, Your 2024 Guide," writes, "Successful influencers typically offer value on social media with quality content in the form of:

- Specialized knowledge
- 'Edu-tainment'
- Insight into a niche topic

Influencers are also known for their ability to foster relationships with an audience to build an engaged and loyal follower base."

Becoming an influencer is like starting a fire in the fireplace. It can take a number of tries to go from igniting kindling to enjoying a roaring, hand-warming blaze. You just have to position the kindling very carefully so that it hits the logs at a point or points of vulnerability and, voila, a crackling masterpiece. Your goal is to reach critical mass, or what author Malcolm Gladwell calls the "tipping point." You would think that to accomplish this, you should cast as broad a "net" as possible, but the truth is the opposite. Don't broadcast. *Niche-cast.* It's one thing to plan to become an influencer among baseball enthusiasts, and it's another to focus on baseball cards. The smaller the niche, the more likely you are to cut through the clutter and find a fiercely devoted following. There may be millions of sites devoted to baseball, but baseball card enthusiasts may have fewer options. If you "play your cards right," you may become the pied piper of the Mickey Mantle rookie card owners.

How broadly you "cast your net" depends on the topic(s) or brand(s) on which you plan to focus. For example, fashion is trendy. If you're a fashion influencer, your job is either to spot the oncoming trends before anyone else notices them or to create those trends. Keep in mind that if you're a successful influencer, you *are* one of the trendsetters. Don't hesitate to speak your mind. If you don't, someone else will beat you to the opportunity. Go into every day as if you were just launching a startup.

It's important to identify your ideal social media. You may notice that each social medium has its own niche. The reach may be broad, but the niche is narrow. If Facebook is the family room of social media, where people go to tout their social successes, LinkedIn is the office (or the office space in the home), a place where people announce their professional successes. Facebook is a place where people showcase soccer trophies, family vacations, weddings, passings, and personal milestones. Businesses have a presence on Facebook because they want to create a sense of family around their brands. Facebook is their direct-to-consumer social medium. LinkedIn is a place to tout promotions, promote business ventures and show off expertise in current topics. LinkedIn is the business-to-business social medium (and, for those who aspire to start or become part of a venture, it is a direct-to-business channel). Facebook and LinkedIn emphasize text and multimedia, while Instagram is all about photos and video. There is certainly no law against using multiple sites, but you have to tailor your strategy to each one.

Leverage successful influencers. Find out which of your friends and acquaintances have the largest followings and ask them to help promote you. You may go viral, but don't be disappointed if your initial promotional efforts don't light the proverbial fire immediately. Your goal at this point is to attract the attention of other influencers and build a network. Pay close attention to who seeks you out and who compliments you. That may help to define who you really are and where you should devote your efforts. Indeed, that's the purpose of life, isn't it? To find out who we are? The only difference today is that we have millions, perhaps billions more people who are unknown to us but who are accessible through social media and can help us learn what's working and what's not working. My friend Jerry Edling has been an editor and writer for television and radio news for years, but he's also a futurist, a published author on the future, a speaker, and a former radio show co-host. That means he has friends in comedy and entertainment, as well as journalism and strategic foresight. These are diverse pursuits that in some ways have little to do with each other. Whenever he posts something, especially on Facebook or LinkedIn, he tracks the responses to find out in which sector the post has resonated most. To do that, he tracks likes, comments and new connection or friend requests.

Speak. In person. If you're truly an authority on something, even if you aren't an influencer, leverage your expertise to get speaking engagements. It may be easier than you think. Joining Toastmasters International, or a similar group, can help you overcome any fear of public speaking by giving you constructive criticism in a non-threatening environment, and they can also provide you with networking opportunities. Through those groups you may be able to qualify as a professional speaker and get booked for speeches to other groups. Service organizations typically have lunch or dinner meetings, and they may be clamoring for guest speakers. If you get paid, great, but the purpose of getting these gigs is to network. If members are interested in your topic to the point at which they want to book you with something else, they're likely to know other people who are also interested and who may have followings of their own. Don't limit your proposed topic to your area of expertise.

If you're interested in artificial intelligence, go to small business groups and talk about the impact of AI on their businesses. One particularly active area of interest now is the use of AI to create new drugs in a shorter period of time. Talk about the patterns that artificial intelligence can discern and that human beings may not. Again, the point is to *network*, to meet other people and to grow your circle of friends, acquaintances, followers, and associates to the point at which they reach critical mass and send members of the electronic community to your door and to your sites. Set your sights high.

Case Study Forty: Passion to Profession

The Challenge: A baseball card enthusiast and collector hopes to transform their passion into a business.

The Strategy: Transform the enthusiast into an entrepreneur by establishing him or her as an influencer. Begin by taking advantage of every networking opportunity and building a base of contacts in the community and online. Then, pursue aggressively a presence online, in this case choosing Facebook (for the community), Instagram (for visual appeal), LinkedIn (for the business advice and potential investors), and Medium (for the opportunity to display expertise and develop a following).

Also useful: Substack, which allows users to publish and manage digital newsletters. These subscription publications are powerful media not only for developing a following, but also for getting paid by subscribers. Speak at every opportunity and collect contact numbers. (Try to collect contact numbers with a text, email, or card, then follow up with a text or email.) Thank contacts for their time and add a quick question to show interest in what they had to say. (It's wise to invest in QR Code business cards. Traditional business cards are easily thrown away or ignored, and texts and emails can fade from memory with time.) QR Code business cards can be photographed over and over, saving paper and eliminating the need to carry a pile of business cards at all times. Go to conferences, perhaps combining the trips with vacations, and *post*, *post*, and *post again*.

The next step is to determine goals. Is the goal of the baseball card enthusiast to establish themself as the go-to person for information and generate Zoom meetings and speaking opportunities? Or is the goal to create a clearinghouse to attract traders from around the world? They're two distinct types of influencers: one is the expert who draws an audience by supplying knowledgeable insights into new developments and trends; the other is the entrepreneur who attracts an audience by offering a business opportunity. For the expert, the challenge is to establish a presence on social media and set up a YouTube channel. Creating a channel is critical even if you are already a YouTube fan. YouTube Help states, "You can watch and like videos and subscribe to channels if you have a Google account, but without a YouTube channel, you have no public presence on YouTube. Even if you *have* a Google account, you need to create a YouTube channel to upload videos, comment, or make playlists."

A next step for the expert is to decide on a format for the YouTube videos. Some of the ones you'll encounter online are crackling with special effects and in-your-face graphics, but you can be equally successful by just being a talking head in an empty room (as long as your fund of knowledge isn't empty). If you're going to create a series of videos, you need to establish a format for the entire series that the audience will recognize. When it comes to formatting, familiarity doesn't breed contempt; it breeds comfort.

Don't forget the podcast. Creating one will enhance your online presence even more. In some ways, the podcast offers more opportunities for programming because, like radio, it's a "theater of the mind." It can be time-intensive to produce, as can YouTube videos, but it's essential if you want to create an audience. In an article, "The Simple Guide to Valuing Your Podcast: From Mic to Millions," Mark deGrasse writes, "They're intimate, engaging and have a knack for turning listeners into loyal fans faster than you can say, 'Don't forget to subscribe!'" He called them "the perfect storm of accessibility, authenticity and monetization potential. In a world where everyone is fighting for eyeballs, podcasts fight for eardrums—and they're winning."

The next step on the expert track is to bring it all home. At this point, the baseball card collector presumably has established a formidable presence on all key media, has spoken widely, has gone to meetings populated by experts and influencers and is becoming a known quantity online. Now is the time to integrate all social media and cross-promote. Mention the website on the podcast and the YouTube video, put links on the website to the YouTube channel and the podcast, and add content, such as videos from speeches and interviews.

A next step for the entrepreneur is the same as for the expert: establish a presence on all appropriate social media. Keep in mind how each of them excels and what their weaknesses are. If the goal is to create a clearinghouse where baseball cards can be viewed, discussed, and sold, the first task is to create a community around that business. If you get people talking about it, they'll get involved, and they'll get their friends and acquaintances involved. Facebook is a place to create community, to introduce people to each other, and to create a sense of familiarity. Ideally, even though it is open to the public, it should have the feel of a fraternity, where people congregate for a common aim. Facebook is a little jumbled, a place where talk is informal and fun. LinkedIn is like a business, a place where the presentation is more formal and professionalism reigns. On Facebook, the object is to get acquainted with potential investors and sort out the business of creating a business. Facebook is the preview, while LinkedIn is the prospectus. Instagram is a must because it is a photo and video sharing service, perfect for sharing images of baseball cards and, potentially, getting them graded.

The budding baseball entrepreneur could stop there and be content with establishing a "home plate" for baseball card collectors. Or the community could get together and create a clearinghouse where the products are bought and sold. That's a business decision. Formalizing a new venture will involve higher costs, but it carries the potential for larger rewards. Whether the collector seeks to become a go-to expert or a go-for-it entrepreneur, the requirement is the same: Get known.

The Rationale: The equation for becoming an influencer is $I=p^n$. I = the goal of becoming and an influencer, p equals the number of posts, and n illustrates how the impact of those posts can increase geometrically, depending on how often and how strategically they are published. Becoming an influencer is a matter of going viral and going exponential. Anything that can increase the visibility of the prospective influencer is good (provided that it's within the law.) Just keep in mind that there are two kinds of influencers: the arbiter of taste and trends (such as the sisters in Alabama); and the teacher of fields of knowledge (such as the lecturers on the economy and quantum reality). For the former, you need to be creative and credible. For the latter, you need to be knowledgeable and credible.

If you're credible, you can expect incredible results.

This is especially important if your aim is to be an expert. You may have a new idea that confounds the law of physics. By all means bring it up, but be prepared to back it up with solid and evidence. You may get pushback, since new ideas can be counterintuitive (just ask Albert Einstein), but if you choose not to share your idea, remember some key words of Mark Twain: "We regret the things we don't do more than the things we do."

Whether you aspire to be an expert or an entrepreneur, watch your step. The trap of obsolescence may be lurking where you least expect it. It's impossible to be invulnerable to changing trends, but you can take steps to protect yourself. Read widely online. Look for patterns that suggest a cultural shift. Follow strategic foresight professionals in your area of interest. Most of all, though, follow your hunches. People are following you because of your intuition. They want a glimpse of the future that only you can provide. They want to see the world through your lenses, and they secretly hope that your ability to set trends will somehow rub off on them.

The Cost: Enough for equipment to record and refine the video or podcast. Production costs can range from zero if a friend produces it to hundreds of dollars if you have to hire on the open market. That's why it is so important to put together a tight-knit community whether your goal is becoming an expert or becoming an entrepreneur.

Chapter Twenty-Nine

Marketing Your Product or Service—What Could Possibly Go Right?

Perhaps you're familiar with the situation comedy *WKRP in Cincinnati*, which premiered in 1978, and aired for four seasons on CBS. The show was about a radio station in its namesake city in Ohio that's populated by some of the sorts of characters you might imagine working at a sixteenthth-in-the-market radio station in Cincinnati.

As stated on *Rotten Tomatoes*. "When a Cincinnati radio station switches from sedate music to rock 'n' roll, the staff of oddball characters has to switch gears quickly. New program director Andy Travis brings in a DJ named Venus Flytrap to work with the station's burned out veteran, Dr. Johnny Fever. Neurotic newsman Les Nessman, eager beaver Bailey Quarters, sleazy salesman Herb Tarlek, blonde bombshell Jennifer Marlowe—who serves as the station's ultracapable receptionist—and station manager Arthur Carlson, whose domineering mother owns WKRP, round out the eccentric bunch."

In one episode, the station decides to do a promotional Thanksgiving turkey drop, which will involve dropping live turkeys out of a helicopter. Les Nessman is on the scene to cover it, and he becomes the eyewitness to the turkeys plummeting to the ground. At one point, Nessman chronicles the scene with a parody of the on-scene report about the crash of the Hindenburg ("Oh, the humanity").

Now that you've learned from this fictional PR stunt (which was based on a real incident), you're probably unlikely to repeat that mistake as you conduct your public relations. But you should be aware that even the slightest miscalculation can send your soaring aspirations into a tailspin.

An article on *PRLab*, "PR Nightmares Revealed: 13 Unimaginable Crisis Moments," states, "Navigating a Public Relations disaster is a nightmare for any brand, capable of inflicting irreplaceable damage to its image. "This underscores the challenge brands face and the importance of crisis communication in the era of online virality."

When Jacques says, "All the world's a stage" in Shakespeare's *As You Like It*, you might wonder whether he is referring to the internet and modern connectedness. A misstep at the Globe Theater, Shakespeare's venue, in the 16th or 17th century might have been observed only by the audience. A misstep today might be observed by people around the entire planet within seconds and for years to come. Kristen Harris of *BuzzFeed*, in an article, "Worst Corporate Blunders in History, And It's Honestly Shocking," writes: "In 1981, the Osborne Computer Corporation had one of the first home computers on the market. At the launch, the CEO said the next version will be so much better , so everyone decided, 'Why buy this version if the next version will be better. We'll wait for V2.' So V1 sold terribly, the company folded, and there was no V2."

Comparatively, an article, "15 Worst Marketing Blunders of All Time," posted on US Data Corporation, cites New Coke as number one, stating, "New Coke tampered with a century-old formula that, despite falling market shares, still resonated soundly with the public. What made New Coke a bad marketing idea is that it essentially celebrated one hundred years of a popular product by throwing out the formula people had grown to love and replacing it with something unproven. Its creation was an inadvertent admission that its primary competitor Pepsi had won the 'cola wars.'" According to the article, second place belongs to Honda Asimo, a robot created in 2000. The article states, "The approximately four-foot-tall, 119-pound astronaut child is capable of a wide range of movements, endangering the butler profession if not for tiny little setback; it was clumsy."

Then there's Circuit City DIVX (Digital Video Express). According to the article, it was a video format designed to compete with DVDs. Did it work? As the article states, "[Y]ou had to buy the disc for around four bucks. It would be playable for forty-eight hours after the first watch. From there you had to purchase additional play time. And the machine itself tied up your phone line, which, at the time, was the only way you hadof logging on the internet"—and customers had to use a proprietary player to view the content. New Coke, Honda Asimo and Circuit City DIVX should be cautionary tales of the importance of developing high quality products as well as brainstorming public relations campaigns to endear them to the public.

What happened when New Coke was introduced should be a reminder that people like familiarity. Despite their protests that they are adventurous and that change is in their genes, people want a sense of stability. They get that through familiarity. That's how fast-food and fast-casual restaurants survive (even though they have adjustment problems of their own). Some innovations are embraced with ease, and others are embraced over time, but innovations that are most vulnerable are the ones that tamper with products and institutions that are regarded as immutable, such as the World Series and the Super Bowl. Not to mention New Coke.

Honda Asimo was a product before its time. A nice gimmick for display, but not ready for the living room. The lesson for smaller businesses here is, if you're going to create a product, make sure your customers will be comfortable with it. If not, allow enough time to familiarize themselves with it.

Circuit City DIVX didn't resonate with the audience because it was limited, complex, and time-sensitive. With Netflix, you could keep the DVD as long as you wanted, though you couldn't see another movie until you returned the DVD. With Circuit City DIVX, you had forty-eight hours to play it after the initial watch. Then you had to pay again.

Authentic PR brings together marketing and public relations to create and promote a brand. The product or service itself must be fashioned with integrity. A well promoted but shoddy product isn't going to succeed in a connected world. There's too much information available, and consumers are savvy, but if you take the time to build a brand with honesty and foundation, potential customers are likely to welcome your idea.

Perhaps what's needed is a new tactic that is both marketing and public relations. Call it *authentic storytelling*. An article published by St. Bonaventure University in 2022, "The Ten Most Successful Marketing Campaigns of All Time," quotes writer Richard Powers as saying, "The best arguments in the world won't change a single person's mind. The only thing that can do that is a good story." The article cites Nike's "Just Do It" marketing campaign as number one. According to the article, "One of the first television advertisements for the campaign featured an eighty-year-old marathoner named Will Stack, who runs seventeen miles every morning. After the campaign went live, thousands of people submitted personal stories about how times when they decided to take the leap and 'just do it.'"

The article goes on to state that the "Key Takeaway for Marketers" is "Outline your value propositions and connect your audience emotionally so they feel aligned with your brand."

A key to success is developing an affinity for your audience and your customer base. If you can find out what resonates with their values, you can reach them where they live. Anyone can identify with an eighty-year-old marathoner. The runner's story speaks to living boldly and never giving up, to acting as if you were guaranteed tomorrow, to just doing it. It's safe to assume that everyone has at least one dream. Everyone wants to take a dip in the sunrise, to seize life and never let it go. Tapping into that kind of story and associating your business with it can only help draw your customer base close or closer.

There are also things you need to remember. Be careful how you nurture your image. All the public relations in the world isn't going to help you if you aren't a careful custodian of how your business is perceived. (Just ask whoever thought up New Coke.) But, if you're sure you have a handle on what your customer base can take, the sky's the limit. Just ask whoever thought up Red Bull Stratos.

The purpose of PR is to enhance or repair image. If you take care of your core business, the rest will come naturally.

Case Study Forty-One: Cars on Parade

The Challenge: Owners of an automobile dealership want to soften their image and dilute the stereotype of the flashy, gold-cufflinked, fast-talking car dealer to make people comfortable buying a vehicle at their business.

The Strategy: Offer automobile buyers discounts if they will shoot video of their families in the car during a summer or winter vacation. The video would then be sent back to the dealership to be used in a local commercial. The commercial would show a happy family and their real adventures in the vehicle.

The Rationale: The road trip is an enduring part of American folklore. It's a time when family dramas, sibling rivalry, laughter, and slapstick play out as the wheels spin down the highway. According to Lacey Pfalz, writing on *TravelPulse*, "Road trips have always been an American pastime, but the nation set a new national record for road trips in 2023, with Americans driving 3.263 trillion miles."

The Transportation Department and *Reuters* report that the record is the first time the level has increased since before the pandemic era. It rose 2.1 percent from 2019, the first time the level has increased since before the pandemic era." According to Pfalz, people were also going back to the office "more regularly" and gas prices were down.

Anyone who has had a great vacation, a nightmare vacation, or both, can identify with this adventure on the road. The family vacation has been celebrated and satirized, but it's never been forgotten. Automobile commercials have traditionally focused on the vehicle, which is generally depicted as a waxed-to-the-max, sleek, roomy-but-fuel-efficient comet whipping down the highway. Why not make local dealership commercials more customer friendly by spotlighting families in the community? Members of the families could conceivably become local celebrities. (Why watch *The Real Housewives of Orange County* when you can see real families from your county enjoying their summer vacations?)

The Cost: The cost of the discounts. That could be lowered by staging the promotion during a slow time of year, when dealers use every incentives they can find to bring in customers. (Note: Costs of the commercial are not included because it is assumed that the dealership will produce an advertisement of some sort, using their annual budget for advertising. The idea of using a family as the focus of the commercial would be a way of supplying content for a previously budgeted advertisement.)

Case Study Forty-Two: Budget Battles

The Challenge: Managers of a bank want to increase the business's public profile.

The Strategy: Contact a local school district at the beginning of the school year and offer to sponsor a money management contest for high school students, challenging them to manage a family budget for the duration of the school year. Each participating student would be given the same amount of money and the same fictitious family. Fixed expenses (such as utility bills) would be identical for all participants, as would mortgages and maintenance costs. Periodically through the duration of the contest the students would have to deal with unexpected expenses, and periodically they would be given modest financial windfalls.

The students would have free rein on what to do with their money. They could save it, they could invest it in anything trackable, such as stocks, bonds or bank savings accounts. They could also keep the money in cash, or they could use it for gifts and entertainment. Every transaction would be logged.The grand prize at the end of the contest would go to the student who most successfully managed the family budget, keeping the family afloat and finishing the most amount of money.

The Rationale: As of 2026, thirty US states require students to take financial literacy courses to graduate. Students may be steeped in algebra, trigonometry, statistics, and calculus, but how many of them know how finances work in their own families? How many know where to get the money to put students through college while at the same time having enough to replace the roof? A financial literacy contest such as this could become a high-impact ongoing event that could attract parental interest, student involvement and television coverage. The bank could be seen as a tentpole of financial literacy, attracting goodwill, new accounts and future customers. The grand prizes could be college scholarships. The bank could make this an annual event and underwrite college scholarships

The Cost: Money for the grand prize and other prizes, money for administrative costs, and, if the bank so chose, funds to underwrite annual college scholarships. The possibilities are seemingly endless when it comes to PR campaigns for banks. Garret Reich writes an article published in 2022 in *Marketing Strategies* that afforded some examples:

- **Digital Bank Monzo and the London Bus:** "Talk about meeting people where they're at. UK-based Monzo added entire buses to its marketing repertoire and it got popular fast."
- **Barclays and 'Moneyverse Matchmaking':** "Barclays Bank UK took a different approach to advertising in a video format. Instead of sponsoring a television show, it produced its own mini-dating show, called 'Moneyverse Matchmaking.'"

And then there was Community First Credit Union's Mega Coloring Book in Florida. An article on Austin Williams' site, states, "Built for CF-CU's sponsorship of the Seawalk Music Festival, the activation successfully brought the Florida credit union's Just Be Yourself brand platform into the community in an engaging way that incited audience participation and generated social media and talk value beyond the event.

It featured a giant two-page spread of a coloring book (more than six feet tall and ten feet wide) with images evoking Florida's music and seaside nature and the location of the free festival. Attendees were invited to pick up one of several multicolored four-foot crayons and add their artistic talents to the collaborative mural."

Chapter Thirty

About Your Image

Authentic PR can only go so far in burnishing the image of a business. Just like a computer program, a business needs regular updates. Think of a bank decades ago, and you may think of George Bailey. The setting would be a row of teller windows with bars and behind them a cadre of professionally dressed tellers ready with a smile and a cash drawer. In those days, banks had the image of community institutions populated by bankers who managed Little League teams, joined service organizations, and showed up at all the "right" community events. There was a community cohesion that lent itself to brand loyalty.

The advent of drive-through-banking began the distancing of customers from the custodians of their money. The smile that the teller window was replaced by a tinny voice and the whoosh of a vacuum tube pulling in the cylinder that contained the paperwork. The ATM transformed banking into a more solitary pursuit that involved the customer and a machine. Inside the bank, there were still cubicles where bankers could greet you and offer you a cup of branch water while waiting to discuss your mortgage application, but the number of teller windows had started to shrink. As banking migrated online, the number of teller windows declined further, and banks adopted ultra-hip designs that made the teller area look like the future ticket window to the International Space Station. Global banking transformed the image of banking from pillar of the community to multinational behemoth. The cubicles were gone, replaced by a few offices in the bank where homeowner-hopefuls could fill out applications that asked for almost everything except their blood types. In the middle of what used to be the teller area there may be a round table with chairs where you and the banker can belly up to the wood and talk about your life savings.

Capital One, the company that wants to know what's in *your* wallet, has tried to keep up with the times by opening Capital One Cafés, places where you can come in for a cup of coffee, a rest…or a mortgage. People can wander in, sit down, type on a laptop, and maybe, if they're so inclined, apply for a credit card or a loan. Capital One began as a digital company, but it hit on the café idea as a way to lower the wall in a way that would appeal to contemporary tastes.

As the company puts it, "Capital One is reimagining banking—welcome to the *Capital One Café!* The idea: Create a welcoming space where banking meets living. Where everyone can relax, refuel and unwind, whether they're Capital One customers or not. Together—Cafés and our Café teams—play a unique role in our communities, one that runs deeper than customer finances." Each café is populated with café ambassadors, who are empowered to help in any way they can, whether or not the problem or question involves finances.

Capitol One states, "Whether someone wants to charge their phone, hang out and study, meet a friendly face, or grab a cup of warm comforting coffee, our cafés are open to everyone (you don't have to be a customer.)"

Just add banking and stir.

There's a yearning for banks to recapture that sense of community. Intelenet CEO Bhupender Singh is quoted on *Worldwide Business Research* as saying, "Although there is a rise in online banking, with fewer customers opting to go to branches, banks need to be strategic in the way they accommodate customers. Not all customers want to go solely online for the handling of such sensitive information. This is where banks can look to be really distinctive in the way they harness technology to direct financial advisers to customers' doorsteps."

Not every bank, and certainly not every branch, has the wherewithal open a chain of cafes, but the lesson is clear: customers want to interact with their banks, just not the way their parents did.

Chapter Thirty-One

A Child's Garden of Public Relations

A business never stands taller in the public's mind than when it helps a child. Some of the most venerable institutions devoted to helping children and saving their lives are also among the most visible. Think St. Jude's Children's Research Hospital and the Shriners' burn centers, for examples. Kids have a lot in common with startup businesses: they're vulnerable, they're hopeful, and they look for guidance. Children face a lot of challenges as they head to adulthood. Any business in whatever sector can become a worthy member of the community by making a difference in a child's life.

Michelle Ubben posted eight examples of campaigns focused on children in an article, "These 8 Kid-Centric Campaigns Will Make You Want to Work in PR." One such campaign was Explore Adoption, the goal of which was to find families for foster children who had waited the longest to be adopted, such as, in her words, "teenagers, sibling groups, kids with disabilities." The campaign strategy was to offer people the opportunity "to hear the real-life stories of adoptive parents." According to Ubben, "This gratifyingly successful campaign drove web traffic and calls to help Florida achieve back-to-back record years for public adoption."

Another campaign, "Waterproof," was directed at pool owners at aimed at reducing the number of child drownings. Even the smallest gesture can transform a child's day. If you watch football games that take place at the University of Iowa, you may be familiar with the Hawkeye Wave. According to a description posted on the Iowa Hawkeye Athletics site, "The Hawkeye Wave is the Best Tradition in college sports. When the Kinnick clock hits zero at the end of the first quarter, seventy-thousand + football fans turn their attention from the field to UI Stead Family Children's Hospital. In unison they wave to the pediatric patients and their families watching the game. The patients and family members view this genuine act of kindness as life-changing, inspiring, a wave of hope."

Case Study Forty-Three: World's Most Important Art Auction

The Challenge: Owners of an art supply store want to support a local children's hospital.

The Strategy: Arrange with the children's hospital to offer their patients the opportunity to paint a picture and have it sold at auction. The pictures could be hung in the art supply store for a couple of weeks to a month before they are sold. The auction would be held at the hospital, and it would be real. Each picture would be titled and named by the artist who drew it. The auction would be held at the hospital so that patients and their families could watch it. The auctioneer could either be a professional or an amateur, though it would add realism to have a professional donate his or her time to the cause. Proceeds would go to the hospital, and the artists would receive a trophy or a plaque commemorating their work. The auction itself could fit any budget, depending on who was willing to donate time and how elaborate the prizes were.

Conversely, the auction of the children's art could be held in conjunction with an actual auction of original art and could be held in a local gallery. The point is, to be as realistic as possible. Either way, the event could be streamed on Facebook, X, Instagram, the store's website or any one of a number of other sites. If possible, the purchasers would meet the artists and have the paintings signed. The paintings could also be at displayed at the art supply store or at the gallery and sold, after which the purchasers could meet the artists and have the paintings signed. The displays of the paintings, the auction and the signings would all lend themselves to television coverage. For that reason, the auction should be held on a Saturday or Sunday, the days when radio stations, television stations, news websites and newspapers generally look to event stories to fill their news holes.

The Rationale: This is an opportunity to tap into the creativity of children who might not otherwise have an opportunity to display their talents to the world. Every moment is precious to a child who is hospitalized. Anything that can fill their minds with hope is a good deed, as is anything that can help fund the facility where they are receiving potentially life-saving treatments.

The Cost: Art supplies, refreshments for the auction, awards for the artists, and incidentals. Ideally, the art supply house would be responsible only for art supplies. Partnerships with a trophy supplier and a catering service could lower the cost.

Case Study Forty-Four: Going, Going, Gone

The Challenge: Owners of a sports-oriented business hope to raise money for a charitable cause and raise brand awareness.

The Strategy: Team up with Little League Baseball or the local youth sports league to stage a baseball game pitting parents against kids. To even the strengths of the teams, parents would have to throw and bat with their non-dominant arms and hands. The righties would be lefties, and vice versa. The goal would be a slapstick comedy of errors on the part of the parents, while the kids pursued precision pitching and sleek, over-the-fence baseball. Proceeds from ticket sales would go to a nonprofit or charity chosen by the business. This would normally be a spring or summer promotion in colder climates. A winter version might involve bowling, basketball or badminton.

The Rationale: For millions of people around the world, the crack of the baseball bat is one of the first sounds of spring. Its distinctive "thwack" ricochets through city parks, leafy suburbs, and off-the-grid sandlots. Baseball is a game of moments. As a business, wouldn't you want to be associated with a moment when a ten year old sends the ball sailing into the sun and disappearing into the high grass beyond the fence? Wouldn't you want to be there when that kid's parent, a leftie batting right-handed, loops the ball into foul territory for the third time? For the crowd, it would be a good time in the first stirrings of summer. For your business, it would be win-win.

The Cost: The key to the success of this promotion is cooperation with Little League Baseball or a local sports league. They would generally have insurance to cover most contingencies in any of their games. Same for security. If the business decides to cater the event with the usual dining fare at a baseball game, it could bear that cost or cooperate with a local restaurant that would welcome the publicity associated with feeding the crowd.

There is no downside to raising money for kids. They are the future. If you're "good will hunting" as a business, you can't go wrong by funding the future.

Chapter Thirty-Two

Building a Campaign

In the digital age, apps can play a significant role in public relations, not only for the firms that are in the PR business, but also for the businesses that are waging *Authentic PR*. A number of PR-oriented apps focus on three areas: automation, campaign creation, and news aggregation. For public relations firms, these are critical tasks, but they can be just as helpful to a business, especially one that is new to the market and needs visibility. In the article, "14 Apps Recommended by PR Professionals," published by the Forbes Agency Council, Jacob Hanson of PR with Panache! states, 'A true marketing automation platform connects PR results to marketing campaigns, allowing PR professionals to leads created, nurtured, and qualified." This is one aspect of authentic public relations that businesses sometimes overlook. It's one thing to have a snazzy PR campaign, quite another to measure its impact. *Authentic PR* is data-driven PR. It's analytics PR. Anyone who doesn't pay close attention to the results is missing out.

Other automation apps can cut down the workload for routine office tasks, such as record keeping. *Case in Point*: Splashtop, described by Ahmad Kareh of Twistlab Marketing, as "a great way to access your computer from your phone to gain access to your resources and craft a swift response." Then there's Mailtrack. Darian Kovacs of Jelly Digital Marketing & PR, states, "Mailtrack is one of the best tools for PR professionals (and even those in sales) as it tells you if and when a reporter has opened your email. It also tells you if and when they've clicked on the link to your email." This sort of information can be indispensable for public relations firms and businesses. If you know that a reporter has checked your email, your response may be different than if your message or other content was unopened.

In the article, "The Best PR Tools and Apps for Public Relations Professionals," Wesley Matthew lists "Apple or Google News" as number one, and that, "both customise news content based on interests and preferences, and both are easy to use."

Of course, one breakthrough that can't be ignored is artificial intelligence. Android afficionados may prefer Gemini, which is integrated into the Google operating system. Among other things, it can generate a news release with a prompt. Prowly offers a package that is more specifically PR-oriented. According to Prowly, "ChatGPT and other bots are a great help in PR work. As per industry standards, the most popular applications of AI in PR include:

- *Idea Generation (77.8 percent)*
- *Content Creation (72.4 percent)*
- *Research: (53 percent)*
- *Reporting (10 percent)*
- *Monitoring (8 percent)*

Even though you may not be in the public relations industry, there's no harm in using professional software such as this to emulate what they do. After all, you *are*, in a sense, in the public relations business because you're doing PR on your own, without paying for a firm's input. My friend Jerry Edling asked ChatGPT to come up with a public relations campaign. It responded:

- **Sustainability Awareness Campaign:** *Goal*—Raise awareness about environmental sustainability practices. *Approach*—Partner with eco-friendly brands or local sustainability experts. Share stories of businesses reducing their carbon footprint, host community cleanup events, and use influencers to spread the word about eco-friendly habits. Incorporate interactive social media content, such as quizzes or challenges encouraging people to reduce waste.
- **Mental Health Advocacy Campaign:** *Goal*—Increase awareness of mental health issues and resources for support. *Approach*—Feature real-life testimonials from people who have faced mental health challenges. Partner with mental health organizations to promote support resources. Host free virtual workshops on managing stress, self-care practices and improving mental well-being. Create a hashtag for people. Create a hashtag for people to share their mental health journeys.
- **Local Business Revitalization Campaign:** *Goal*—Support and bring attention to small local businesses post-pandemic or during economic downturns. *Approach*—Spotlight different businesses each week on social media. Share success stories and behind-the-scenes looks at the businesses' daily operations. Organize pop-up events or collaborate

with food trucks, artists and local vendors to create a "local pride movement." Encourage consumers to shop locally and tag businesses on social media for exposure.

- **Community Empowerment Through Education:** *Goal*—Promote the importance of lifelong learning and educational resources. *Approach*—Launch a campaign that promotes access to free online courses or resources. Feature interviews with community leaders and education advocates. Host a series of workshops aimed at different age groups. To inspire continuous learning, from financial literacy to creative skills development. Creative a social media challenge where followers share their learning experiences.
- **Public Health & Safety Campaign:** *Goal*—Inform the public about preventive health measures, such as vaccinations or healthy habits. *Approach*—Collaborate with healthcare professionals to share accurate, evidence-based information. Use testimonials from medical staff or people who've benefited from public health initiatives to build trust. Develop a series of short educational videos for social media and community television that break down complicated health information in easy-to-understand ways.
- **Employment Engagement and Corporate Social Responsibility (CSR) Campaign:** *Goal*—Boost employee morale and demonstrate the company's commitment to giving back. *Approach*—Share stories of employees participating in volunteer activities or community outrach projects. Create a *day in the life* video series of employees working on charity projects. Launch a matching donation program for employees and invite the public to participate. Promote a sustainable company culture and initiatives aimed at corporate social responsibility.
- **Product Launch with User-Generated Content:** *Goal*—Generate excitement around a new product or service. *Approach*—Encourage customers to share their experiences through photos and videos on social media, using a branded hashtag. Offer exclusive early access or special discounts to loyal customers in exchange for reviews. Host a competition where users can submit ideas for future product improvements or creative ways to use the product. Use influencers to help launch the product and spread awareness.
- **Diversity, Equity and Inclusion Campaign:** *Goal*—Promote a more inclusive and equitable society. *Approach*—Develop content showing diverse voices in your organization or industry. Share data and research on how diverse teams lead to better outcomes. Host panels or roundtable discussions. With experts in diversity and inclusion topics. Launch an internal training program on DEI and share progress publicly.

- **Social Responsibility for Youth:** *Goal*—Encourage youth to engage in social causes and volunteerism. *Approach*—Create a mentorship program where young people can volunteer and develop leadership skills. Partner with schools and youth organizations to provide opportunities for community service and activism. Use social media challenges to encourage young people to contribute to social causes. Feature young advocates and their projects to inspire peers.
- **Event Promotion with an Interactive Twist:** *Goal*—Attract attention and boost attendance for an interactive event. *Approach*—Create a scavenger hunt or international contest leading up to the event, with clues posted on social media. Livestream key moments of the event or host Q&A with notable speakers. Offer special giveaways for attendees and create VIP experiences that encourage people to engage.

Case Study Forty-Five: Yes, And...

The Challenge: The government of a city with a history of racial and ethnic tension hopes to highlight the benefits of diversity and reduce the level of friction in the community.

The Strategy: Stage an improvisation contest. Invite members of the community to enter multicultural teams of improvisational actors in a competition that will test their abilities to act out scenarios that were submitted ahead of time by members of the public. A panel of judges would select the scenarios to be used in the contest. The scenarios would aim to highlight areas of miscommunication and tension in the city and challenge the improvisational teams to come up with scenes that lead to a solution.

The Rationale: Improvisational actors do not say no. Their core principle is *Yes, and…*, meaning that when an actor says something, the person or people to which he or she is talking will always agree with the premise and then add something. In the words of Jude Treder-Wolff, writing in the article, "Playing the Long Game: Applying Improv Tools To The Work of Anti-Racism," published on *Medium*, "There is a kind of magic that happens when improvisers co-create an imagined reality so seamlessly it seems hard to believe it is happening on the spot." Everyone's ideas are accepted. This creates a dynamic that has the potential to dilute the power of stereotypes and prompt the actors and the audience to learn new ways of communicating. Trederwolff states, "The work of anti-racism begins with recog-

nizing that structural racism exists." But that may not be a settled question among all the participants in a frank dialogue. The key is to balance hostility with honesty and to keep in mind that perception is reality. Treder-Wolff states, "The skills improvisers deploy to make creative magic and produce a dynamic story together without knowing what it will be ahead of time, are positive, useful tools for maintaining the focused attention and sustained awareness necessary for structural changes to take place over the long term." And businesses can play a key role in putting into effect these structural changes while elevating their profiles as peacemakers in the community.

The environment should be structured but spontaneous. Recruiting partners (such as the owners of he venue where the improvisations take place) can help defray the costs. This is an opportunity that is not only good business; it can effect real change in the community.

The Cost: The venue, light refreshments, security and publicity.

Case Study Forty-Six: The Ugliest Vehicle Contest

The Challenge: Owners of an automobile dealership hope to raise their profile and their standing in the community.

The Strategy: Hold an ugliest vehicle contest on a summer weekend afternoon that would pit junker against clunker for a nonprofit. According to Fernando Zeledon, who has created events like this for decades, the first step is to find communities where unusual car clubs cluster. According to Zeledon, those are the types of places that are likely to have a large-enough venue for the event (not to mention enough interest to bring it to critical mass). The next step would be to approach that community with the idea and enlist the support of city leaders, local businesses and service organizations. (Never forget the service organizations. Their primary focus is community improvement.)

Selecting a venue could be a challenge. This step is more easily accomplished in a smaller town, a smaller city or a suburb, where land is more plentiful. According to Zeledon, this sort of promotion is not generally suited for a large city, but it might be accomplished in a suburb of that city. Once support of political leaders, business leaders, and service organizations have been secured, it should be a relatively easy to get all the necessary permits. An ideal venue would be a fairground, which may be owned by the county or the city and administered by a nonprofit organization.

Publicizing the event should be a "full court press" involving social media, articles on newspaper and magazine sites. Some television stations have community bulletin boards that list upcoming events. Don't forget to tap this resource to try to draw a larger crowds. Call the station and speak with a producer or someone at the assignment desk. Find out how to get listed. (Note: You should have a "go-to" producer at each television station with whom you have already developed a relationship.)

The event would begin with a parade of the vehicles through the city to the venue where they'll be displayed. A high school marching band might play them in or be the lead unit in the parade. Revenue for the nonprofit could come from ticket sales, food sales, and entry fees. Another potential revenue stream is an auction of the ugly cars. Proceeds could go to the nonprofit, or the vehicle itself could be donated to a vetted vehicle donation program, with the owner getting the tax break and the dealer offering one checkup to make sure the vehicle is travel-ready.

The Rationale: This sort of campaign is aimed at bringing a sense of fun into the community, not to mention a touch of irony. Straightforward parades may be fun. Summer holiday parades can be a great opportunity to enjoy the sunshine and the blare of the brass as the high school marching band toodles its way down Main Street, but there's always the possibility that one of the entrants, hauling a float that celebrates the American Dream, just laid off half their workforce. A satirical parade takes away all the pretentions. It doesn't inflate. It *de*flates. It's a parade without pomposity. For the owners of a dealership, celebrating ugly vehicles is a way of poking fun at the potential future appearance of their new cars.

The Cost: The key to making this sort of community-wide or regional campaign affordable is partnership. The dealership would take care of initial costs, such as permitting; but restaurants would donate food, the owners of the venue would provide the facilities and the government would be responsible for security. Communities come together when people are in need. The fires in Los Angeles in January of 2025 are a prime example.

It might be helpful to review at this point what public relations is and what it is not. In the words of DePaul University, "Public relations focuses on maintaining and promoting the image of a company.

Advertising focuses on persuading an audience to purchase a product or service." If you're paying a television station, radio station, website, newspaper, you aren't engaging in *Authentic PR*. That's not to say you have to rule out advertising as part of your overall strategy. If you're having a two-week tire sale or lowering prices on cars ahead of next year's model, an advertising campaign would certainly be appropriate, but that isn't public relations (that's advertising). The only costs involved in *Authentic PR* are those paid to third parties to make the event possible. If costs are higher, you can reduce them by partnering. Not only does partnering defray the cost, it creates an excellent opportunity for networking.

Now, you begin your search for the perfect PR campaign with an awareness. (That's the term Paul Biebel used when he described the first step of the scientific method to students at Dickinson College.) There are many parallels between the scientific method and public relations. In both cases, you're trying to get to a deeper truth. Science proceeds by making connections that were previously unknown. Businesses survive by doing the same thing. Making those connections keeps you on top of or ahead of trends. If you know your business really well, you should know its core principles, its ethics, its limits, its aspirations, its flaws, its selling points, and the dreams of those who founded it and run it. Keep those in the back of your mind and take a walk. Enjoy the sunshine or the winterscape. Let the ideas percolate. If you get an idea, write it in your notes app, dictate it to an app, or write it down. You may think it's locked solidly in your mind, but it may not be. If it isn't recorded or documented, it could be gone.

That having been said, some of the best *Authentic PR* is the spontaneous kind: food to the fire line, winter coats delivered to the homeless shelter, emails to US troops on holidays, or any sort of spontaneous gesture in the midst of (or after) a natural disaster. It can be as quick as a flash mob and as a long as a parade down Main Street.

Adrian Falk, founder of Believe Advertising & PR and a Forbes Councils member, wrote an article, "5 Tips for a Successful PR Campaign."

The list:

1. Establish your objective and goals.
2. Know your target audience.
3. Identify the right platform.
4. Find creative Angles.
5. Keep track of progress.

To this list, I would only add what I would call the "Three Rs" of *Authentic PR*: Relationships, relationships and relationships. It is "who you know."

Chapter Thirty-Three

Fire, Police, and PR

Fire departments and police departments have their own needs for public relations. They're arguably the most visible public servants anywhere, and the type of work they do can necessitate split-second judgement calls that can have wide ramifications. In a connected age, first responders sometimes need a rapid response from public relations. People who run businesses can help in this effort by coming up with effective campaigns that highlight the work of fire departments and law enforcement while demonstrating to the public that the business plans to be a good corporate citizen.

Of course, firefighters and police have their own public relations initiatives. Michael Capoziello, in the article, "5 Ways to Create Positive Public Relations," says, "Today's fire service, especially the volunteer fire service, is under a lot of scrutiny from the public at large." And the key is accessibility:

1) Open Your Doors to the Community More Often: There was a time when fire departments held open houses where they allowed kids to sit in the driver's seat on fire trucks and performed some demonstrations of their firefighting capability. Holidays are an excellent time to do this, perhaps in conjunction with a community day event. Fire departments have never been more capable or professional, but too many have forgotten that open houses are an excellent way to generate good will.

2) Create Ways to Reach the Community via Media: According to Capoziello, his "department has been active with the various newspapers that have served our community since 1930. The various incarnations of the newspaper column have covered fire prevention tips as well as various happenings of the department during the month." He suggests having a website and a Facebook page. "Your website can be as elaborate as showing your alarms in real time with links to actual radio transmissions or as simple as listing basic information about your department."

3) After-the-Fire Care: Here the focus is on the families of fire victims. According to Capoziello, they need to be informed about what to expect after the fire or, at the very least, be given a packet of information explaining what will happen. This is essential to the family and good for the department's relations with the community.

4) Adopt-a-Hydrant Program: According to Capoziello, this type of program enlists "individuals and groups (Boy Scouts, civic associations) to care for a hydrant that may be located near their residence or organization."

5) Carry Pet Oxygen Masks: Capoziello says, "We have all seen photographs of firefighters in the process of administrating oxygen to rescued animals on the fireground." He suggests purchasing "specially designed O2 kits for dogs, cats, ferrets, guinea pigs and birds."

A business could get involved with any of these. A good public relations strategy is essential to firefighters and police, to protect and preserve their reputational advantages. A good authentic public relations strategy should call attention to the heroics that sometimes go unnoticed in crisis situations: the officer who defuses a domestic argument, the firefighter who rescues a pet out of a burning garage, the hostage negotiator whose social skills are as powerful as a pistol.

In the article, "Navigating the Future: Key Public Relations Strategies for Law Enforcement in 2024, Wayne Delk, writing in *The Media Matrix*, listed seven what he called "key public relations ideas that law enforcement agencies need to adopt":

1. *Embracing Digital and Social Media*
2. *Fostering Community Engagement*
3. *Transparency and Accountability*
4. *Training in Crisis Communication*
5. *Leveraging Positive Storytelling*
6. *Proactive Media Relations*
7. *Focus on Internal Communication*

Case Study Forty-Seven: Halls of Justice 1

The Challenge: Create an effective internal communications strategy for a city police department.

The Strategy: Create a digital newsletter that is emailed to all employees using the department's intranet or other internal communications systems. This newsletter would be strictly internal and would be interactive, allowing officers and other personnel to offer feedback, pushback, pitches, and suggestions. Some of the articles would be written by officers, including first-person accounts of how they overcame a specific challenge or solved a problem while on duty, and there would be regular columns and features. The newsletter could be published under the auspices of media relations or publications.

The Rationale: It's easy for a city fire department to become compartmentalized, especially in cities that have large assortments of patchwork neighborhoods and precincts with different cultures and varying law enforcement strategies. At a time when tight budgets and fights for funding are the norm, keeping departments unified should be a high priority, even though it may feel like a sprawling bureaucracy.

The Cost: In accordance with the department's size and budget and donations from private partners.

Case Study Forty-Eight: Halls of Justice 2

The Challenge: Owners of a restaurant want their eatery to become a fixture in the downtown part of the city, an area frequented by police and other government workers.

The Strategy: Create a hall of heroes inside the restaurant spotlighting the heroic actions of police. Hang portraits of the officers in a prominent place in the restaurant, with a special area reserved for pictures of officers who had died in the line of duty. One of the officers could be highlighted as the hero of the month.

Alert the media to the hall of heroes and pitch the story as local color. Also pitch it as a feature that could follow most crime stories in the rundown. Television producers value these kinds of stories as a way of giving their coverage more dimension. If the station has already run the story about the hall of heroes, the assignment editor could still send a reporter to that establishment to get reaction from law enforcement to a breaking news story.

The Rationale: If you've ever read the book *The Right Stuff* by Tom Wolfe, or if you've ever seen the film adaptation, you may recall the Happy Bottom Riding Club, which was an actual restaurant located in the Antelope Valley of California. The Happy Bottom Riding Club drew customers from Edwards Air Force Base, which was a site of flights by test pilots and played a role in aerospace. (Chuck Yeager broke the sound barrier over Rogers Dry Lake in the Mojave Desert.) Edwards Air Force Base was also the landing point for a number of space shuttle flights. The Happy Bottom Riding Club featured pictures of test pilots who had died while doing their jobs. It became a go-to spot for the aerospace crowd.

The lesson here is that restaurants and other businesses can become what you might call "fixtures in the neighborhood," and that can make them almost impervious to economic uncertainty, at least for a while. Changes in taste, the departure of certain hubs of the community can change that. But during the good years, it's important to project an authentic image of why the restaurant does so well, who goes there and why it is so integral to the community.

The Cost: Whatever it takes to print the pictures and put up a standout display. Iconic restaurants exemplify authentic public relations by just being. They have history, and they have been around long enough to know their customer bases and conduct their business just the way they are. All the hype and the pretense of their grand openings are long behind them. Whether they stayed true to their original promises or have morphed into something else, they have an authenticity that has been honed by longevity.

For example, The Original Pantry Café in Los Angeles was opened in 1924 and was at one time owned by a mayor of the city, and it featured hot beef sandwiches with every meal. In a downtown area that was virtually devoid of restaurants, The Original Pantry Café was like a warm hearth in the night, serving American food, and, on at least one occasion, holding a contest to win tickets to Dodger Stadium and sit in the mayor's box. The sign outside may have looked East Coast, but this was a California dream.

Another California tradition is In-N-Out Burger, which has fewer than ten items on the menu. It has Bible verse citations on the inside bottom rim of its cups, and the french fries are made fresh. Given the lengths of the lines at In-N-Out Burger, they must have enough potatoes to sink the Spanish Armada, and you might be waiting in line for some time to get your order.

The sign at Bob's Big Boy in Burbank, California takes you back to the *American Graffiti* era of car hops, sleek, fuel-busting cars, juke boxes, milk shakes, and blaring AM radios. Its décor seemingly hasn't changed since the 1950s. Even the light fixtures are pure post-war suburban. The original Bob's Big Boy is still on the menu, and the statue of him outside the restaurant seems ready to protect and serve.

A historical marker stands outside the Hamilton Restaurant in Carlisle, Pennsylvania, commemorating the home of the Hot-Chee Dog, as mentioned early in this book, and described in an article by Megan Talley on AB27's site as "a chili cheese dog that's been served at the Hamilton since its opening, but was officially named in the 1960s." At one time, it was open into the single-digit morning hours and catered to the night appetites of college students, while today it is open for breakfast and lunch.

Notice the characteristics shared by these establishments. They've all been around for decades, they each have at least one unique dish, and, most of all, they're each tied to the community in a particular way, if only by location. When it comes to restaurants, or any business, the key to effective *Authentic PR* is to find a niche in the community.

Case Study Forty-Nine: Happy Days

The Challenge: Owners of a 1950s-style restaurant hope to draw a crowd on Friday nights.

The Strategy: Hold a classic car night on Fridays.

The Rationale: Nostalgia is a shortcut to a customer's emotions. Older generations can relive the era, while younger generations can discover it. At a time when DoorDash and Uber have replaced car hops on roller skates, a look back once a week can be a great way to move forward.

The Cost: Labor costs (for more servers and chefs).

Anything that can bring a community together, whether through engagement with police and firefighters, encounters between people who live in different neighborhoods or eateries that light up the imagination is *Authentic PR*.

Chapter Thirty-Four

If You Are the Media

It could happen. You could decide to start a local newspaper and website, an alternative weekly or a video news channel centered on a community. More homegrown journalism is the norm as traditional models decline. Think of journalism as a puffball. Where once a dandelion stood, now a puffball will host the seeds that will start new growth potentially in all directions. Where once a standard model of journalism stood (the morning newspaper, AM radio, news weeklies), the digital age is sending the seeds of new forms of journalism in all directions. Entrepreneurs are starting to catch on and are investing in new forms of journalism. Media is migrating from network and cable to streaming and digital, and that makes the field more accessible. Websites, podcasts, blogs, and YouTube channels are all available to you to get your voice heard.

Take CNN, for instance. Compared to CBS, NBC, and ABC, CNN is a startup. It was founded in 1980, more than thirty years after broadcast television began to enter homes in the US Cable television has always been its mainstay, but viewership of cable television has been declining over the years, as has viewership of network television. CNN President Mark Thompson, as cited by Oliver Darcy on CNN's site, states. "[T]echnology and audiences are on the move again" and writes about how linear television is dying while digital products balloon in size. Shira Ovide, writing for *The Washington Post*, states, "As recently as about fifteen years ago, about 85 to 90 percent of households in the United States paid for TV channels from a cable company or a satellite TV provider like DirecTV. That's about as close as it gets to 'everyone' in America doing something.' She writes, "Now, barely half of American homes pay for TV service from a cable, satellite TV or internet-like cable company such as YouTube TV, according to cable industry analyst Craig Moffett of Moffett Nathanson research."

Local television news is in peril as well. Marshall Malone, in "The Digital Iceberg: Is Local TV News Dying?" recalls a "senior leader" at the station where he worked as saying, "Think of us like the Titanic, heading straight to the iceberg. After nearly five years in TV and over a decade in digital marketing, I couldn't help but cringe because I knew that the reality was much worse. We had already hit the iceberg and begun sinking."

He continues, "What made this situation even harder to swallow was the leadership's dismissive attitude toward independent digital creators. They referred to them as "any Joe in the basement, producing news on YouTube or live-streaming shows. But these 'Joes' were raking in more views, engagement and revenues thn entire TV stations. Rather than seeing them as a new wave of potential collaborators, TV leadership viewed them as competitors. Completely unable to keep up with speed, agility and scalability."

Newspapers face some of the same challenges. According to the 2025 Medill State of Local News Report, the industry has been trending toward the rising influence of generative AI, increased mobile-first consumption and the widening of news deserts. According to the report, the number of US counties without a source of local news rose to 213. One-hundred-thirty-six newspapers had closed in the previous year, and the US has lost thousands of newspapers since 2005. Thirty-nine states have fewer than 1,000 local journalists remaining. Smartphones have surpassed television as the primary source for local news.

The point is that the money is moving from legacy journalism to digital platforms, and because the digital realm is so accessible, it's comparatively easy to get in. If you cater to the habits of news consumers in the digital era, you may have a promising business on your hands. If you follow traditional models, you may put yourself on the deck of the Titanic.

So, are you ready to become a digital journalist?

You'll need equipment and knowhow. The type of news venture you plan to create will determine the types of equipment you will need. Take podcasting. In "Your Essential Podcasting Equipment List for 2024," published on *Podkick*, Mary Achurra identifies seven pieces of equipment needed to get your voice out in cyberspace:

1. A Laptop with more random access memory a multi-core processor and a digital audio workstation.

2. A Microphone: Achurra recommends not using the built-in microphone on a laptop or a phone. One is a USB microphone that plugs into a laptop. She said, "The second, more professional type of microphone uses an XLR connection that routes your microphone through a professional audio interface recorder, or mixer." She also recommends a microphone arm and a pop filter."

3. Headphones: "To avoid triggering feedback, you might want to use headphones instead of a microphone." Or, if you can control the feedback, use headphones as an accompaniment to the microphone. This is a type of equipment that is open to personal preference. Some professional radio broadcasters use headphones with bulbous ends and cushiony interfaces between ear and headphone. Others prefer smaller types. Some like the headphones that seemingly plugs into your ear, while others like the kind that look like twentieth-century telephone receivers."

4. Mixer: "A mixer is not really considered podcast essential equipment for a simple setup. However, you may want to use one if your show features numerous hosts or guests."

5. Portable Recorder: This piece of equipment allows you to do field recording and integrate interviews with natural sound, giving your podcast sort of an NPR feel. Alchurra mentions the Zoom H4N Pro and the Tula Mic.

6. Camera: A camera allows you to record video versions of your episodes for platforms like YouTube or social media, where discoverability can be significantly higher than audio-only formats. This doesn't necessarily require a high-end setup—many podcasters begin with a smartphone or a basic webcam—but lighting, framing, and background should be considered to maintain a professional appearance.

7. Host: According to Alchurra, the host has two responsibilities: "to provide a place on the web where you can upload your podcast" and "to provide you with an RSS feed generator. This allows you to upload your podcast to numerous directories through an RSS feed." (RSS stands for *Really Simple Syndication.*)

A podcast can make you money if you're willing to explore different potential revenue streams. In a blog published on *Printiful*, Karlina Rozkaine writes, "In 2024, the number of monthly podcast listeners in the US has climbed to an impressive 135M." Rozkaine identified "9 ways to monetize your podcast":

- *Sell podcast merch*
- *Accept listener donations*
- *Find sponsorship deals*
- *Offer ad spaces*
- *Promote affiliate links*
- *Sell premium content*
- *Create paid memberships*
- *Publish your show on YouTube*
- *Host an event*

Case Study Fifty: The Front Page

The Challenge: A number of people in an area want to start a digital newspaper devoted to their community.

The Strategy: It could be as simple as creating the website, buying audio, and video equipment for home base, purchasing a portable field unit for live coverage of community events, and, if possible, soliciting some advertisers. But it's probably best if you can assemble a core team, including local influencers who can spread the word about the project. Hold meetings, agree on roles, come up with a format, and, most importantly, come up with a list of principles and ethics. If the news website is to be truly journalistic, those principles will include fairness, objectivity, and accuracy. If it's a partisan site or is aimed at supporting one point of view, it will still strive for accuracy and fairness. There's no room for "fake" content in *Authentic PR*. If it includes both news and opinion, the two should be separate and compartmentalized. This is one case in which siloing is helpful.

One possible strategy is to create a community Patch if yours doesn't already have one. In "The alternative to your dying local paper is written by one person, a robot and you," published on *Vox*, Peter Kafka writes, "…local media outlets—the ones that are supposed to tell you what's happening at your kids' school, the zoning board, or the statehouse, are truly in trouble: They lost their most valuable revenue stream many years ago, and since then they have been shrinking, and shrinking or folding altogether." He states later that, "against that backdrop, take a look at Patch, the all-digital news company you probably stopped paying attention to years ago, when AOL used to own the company. For better or for worse, it may represent the future of local news."

Patch operates hyperlocal sites around the US that are focused on individual communities. Typically, one editor will cover a number of patches. Any member of the public may post a story that will be reviewed by the editor prior to publication. Stories include both headline news and the types of stories a larger news outlet wouldn't cover. The key to success here is speed. Someone stuck in a traffic tie-up on an interstate highway might turn to Patch to get the latest. The Patch model is extremely potent in emergency situations, such as wildfires. Patch can publish a list of evacuation sites, escape routes, and closed thoroughfares while leaving the long-form pieces to local television, local radio, newspapers and their websites.

Starting a Patch site to cover your community (if one doesn't already exist) is one possible strategy, but there aren't laws prohibiting an original venture that's more elaborate. Perhaps your website includes both editors and reporters to enable field coverage of breaking news and governmental meetings. You would naturally want to cover those meetings, just as C-SPAN does at the federal level. You could integrate coverage of the meeting with a sidebar of comments from viewers so that you and any officials who may be watching could see reaction in real time. Your website might even include paid classified advertising, the loss of which sent print editions into searches for new sources of revenue. There could be space for editorials and comments. Essentially, your news website would be somewhat like the town square, a gathering point for ideas and commerce.

To reach out effectively, include a social media presence on your community news operation. Since people have been migrating to online news, it's essential to "cover all the bases" in cyberspace. And whatever the platform, make it interactive.

The Rationale: As preferred sources of news change, you may notice that newer, more digital sources are modeled after older sources of information. For example, hyperlocal sources such as Patch are essentially digitized and distilled word of mouth. It's a coffee klatsch with fact checking. While it is true that a number of news sources are either unwilling or unable to spread the truth, some sources are run by dedicated professionals who are committed to fairness despite budget challenges and community pressures. You could be one of them.

Hyperlocal news is under immediate pressure to "get it right." If a hyperlocal news source says it has stopped snowing, a number of its local subscribers could look out the window to see if the source was correct.

The Cost: According to a blogpost, "How to Start a News Website in 12 Easy Steps. published in 2024 on *Gravitec*, technically, you can start a news website in four easy steps:

1. *Choose a domain name and a web host.*
2. *Install WordPress with a preferred theme.*
3. *Set up WordPress plugins to expand your website functionality.*
4. *Create website categories, their structure and start publishing.*

The Cost: The website should cost under $10 per month. But according to Verti Vtechnosys Services Private Limited, the cost of a news website can also be affected by some factors including:

1. *Design Complexity*
2. *Functionality and Features*
3. *CMS Selection*
4. *Responsive Design*
5. *Data security*
6. *Scalability*
7. *Hosting and infrastructure.*

They claim costs can range from $10,000—$15,000 for a basic website; $15,000—$20,000 for something more elaborate.

Case Study Fifty-One: Putting Together a Podcast

The Challenge: Owners of a hardware store hope to raise their profile in the community.

The Strategy: Start a podcast (with video) focusing on do-it-yourself projects at home.

The Rationale: Have you ever seen the television show *Home Improvement*? Actor and comedian Tim Allen played Tim Taylor, a television show host who had a program titled *Tool Time*, which focused on do-it-yourself projects. *Tool Time* was co-hosted by a character named Al Borland, played by Richard Karn, who was occasionally the butt of Tim's one-liners. Anyone who is handy with tools could do a home version of *Tool Time* with a friend. If the chemistry is right, the podcast could go viral.

Just ask Joe Rogan. According to *OnTheFly*'s site, "*The Joe Rogan Experience* is the number one podcast in the world with three billion listeners and millions of subscribers from different podcasting platforms." Rogan's website notes that the podcast launched on December 24, 2009, helping to create the space of long-form conversation video podcasting. With over 2,000 episodes, an average of two to three hours in length each, the show has become a destination for open dialogue with a wide range of guests and perspectives, including standup comedians, athletes, authors, artists, prolific thinkers and scientists."

Rogan has been a standup comedian for decades. Admittedly, he had a head start on recognizability, having hosted the show *Fear Factor* on NBC and *Joe Rogan Questions Everything* on the Syfy Channel, but to maintain an audience of billions of people consistently is no mean feat. Just as a genius in a garage could theoretically duplicate he success of Bill Gates or Elon Musk, your basement or office could be the launching point for podcast profitability.

The Cost: According to *Podcastle*, starting a podcast as a hobby could cost around $100-$350, while podcasting as a business could cost from $500-$1500. Joe Rogan's podcast focuses on the guest, whoever that might be and whatever expertise he or she might have. That's one model for a podcast. Another involves niche casting or narrowcasting, a show or a series of shows devoted to one topic, whether that be coin collecting, golf, foreign policy, automobile repair, hair care, chemistry, weight loss, or football.

Chapter Thirty-Five

PR and Marketing—What's the Difference?

Turns out, the goals of public relations and marketing have been veering toward a merger. This connected age is also disconnected because the number of ways to reach people and make them aware of a brand has increased. One way to reach people is what I call "pop-up PR," a strategy that reaches people where they are at any given time. This strategy combines elements of both PR and marketing and uses varying levels of each according to the circumstances.

According to Forthea, in "What is the Difference Between Marketing and PR?" on *Meltwater*, "The line between public relations (PR) and marketing can become easily blurred, even by professionals in the industry. To keep it simple, marketing is focused on driving sales and doing so by promoting products, services and or ideas on channels like social media. Public relations (PR) is more focused on the maintenance of a positive reputation of a company, brand or person through the media."

Though here's where the boundaries are getting blurred. In "Social Media and News Fact Sheet" by Pew Research Center, "Digital Sources have become an important part of Americans' news diets—with social media playing a crucial role. Particularly for young adults. Overall, just over half of US adults (54 percent) say they at least sometimes get their news from social media, up slightly compared with the last few years. It's no longer enough to "cast a broad net" and see who ventures inside. Marketing and public relations are both indispensable parts of an overall strategy, and you need what law enforcement call a unified command to get both to work together. A post on *Thunder Tech*, "How PR and Marketing Pros Can Work Together to Drive Results," states, "Traditional public relations and digital marketing professionals have started to bridge the gap between the two industries, forming the 'integrated communications label seen in the mission of many agencies around the world. PR practitioners, brand managers, and public relations professionals are leading the charge in reputation management, brand management, and paid advertising. This collaboration is forming a new type of communications professional with redefined goals and best practices." *Authentic PR*, as practiced by individuals and businesses, is no exception to this trend. You have to keep an eye on sales and an eye on reputation if you're going to practice *Authentic PR*. You literally can't have one without the other. If sales slide, your ability to function diminishes. If your reputation slides, your ability to sell anything will diminish.

Case Study Fifty-Two: Step by Step

The Challenge: Owners of a company that sell hiking gear want to increase their visibility in the community and call attention to the essentials of safe hiking.

The Strategy: Recruit a number of docents to host hikes of varying levels of difficulty throughout the year. Offer rebates on clothing and equipment to those who sign up for and complete the hikes.

The Rationale: According to an article, "Hiking & Outdoor Equipment Stores in the US—Market Research Report (2014–2029)," by Christian Perdomo, "Hiking and outdoor equipment stores have seen impressive growth in recent years, fueled by a surge of participation in outdoor activities. As people sought refuge and recreation in nature, expenditure on hiking, camping, and climbing gear increased significantly, boosting overall recreation spending." For those who wanted to do more than clamber over wet rocks and listen for the sound of a loon, there were other hikes in higher price ranges.

In "High-end Hikes offer great food, comfy bed at the end of the day," published on CNN.com in 2017, Tara Donaldson writes, "While the modern hiker may spend days trekking miles up mountains, over rivers and through the woods, many of today's trekkers opt to skip toting their own packs and setting up camp at day's end. The more fabulous hikes often end with a gourmet meal and a trained massage therapist kneading out knots on a lodge's private terrace." Hikes today can range from plaid jackets, birding and lace-up hiking shoes to "roughing it' with $3,000. Binoculars, prescription sunglasses and marshmallows with a mango glaze over the campfire.

Because so many people enjoy hiking, a store that sells gear and has knowledgeable salespeople is likely to do well. The key is to move it from merchant to meeting point and transform it into a place in which the community can congregate. Hiking can make you feel that you have abandoned the sedentary life and developed the knowhow to negotiate the fringe of civilization (even if that fringe is a mile away from an interstate highway).

Offering the rebate is a marketing tool, while offering the experience of hiking is public relations. The rebate attracts customers to the store; the experience of hiking attracts customers to the brand. Think of the rebate as hardware and the hiking experience as software. Separately, they are essential; together, they can take your business to new levels.

The Cost: Labor expenses for the docents (which may be a barter arrangement involving store merchandise), the cost of the rebates and insurance for the hikes (if needed). There may be a workaround if you don't sponsor the hike but just make it an informal meeting.

Chapter Thirty-Six

How to Recover When Something Goes Wrong

What could possibly go wrong with a public relations campaign? The truth is, *many things can go wrong*. A campaign that sounds unbeatable in the boardroom, at the kitchen table or wherever it's brainstormed could contain a sort of "minefield" of potential trip-ups. Just ask Ronn Tomassian, who identified some campaigns in the travel realm that veered off course:

United Airlines' 'United Breaks Guitars' Incident

"In 2008, United Airlines faced a PR nightmare when a musician, Dave Carroll, had his guitar dmaged by the airline and was disssatified with their customer service response. His video, 'United Breaks Guitars,' went viral, leading to widespread criticism of the airline's handling of customer complaints and their poor customer service."

Singapore Airlines 'The World's Best' Campaign

"In 2017, Singapore Airlines launched a campaign based on being 'the world's best airline.' The campaign was criticized for being overly self-promotional and not addressing real issues, such as customer service complaints and in-flight experience. Problems."

Tourism Australia's 'Come and say G'Day' Campaign

"In 2014, Tourism Australia's 'Come and Say G'Day' Campaign faced criticism for its portrayal of Australia as a stereotypical laid-back destination. The campaign, which featured phrases like 'G'Day and stereotypical Australian imagery, was seen as lacking depth and failing to accurately represent the experiences Australia has to offer."

The Takeaway: The "United Breaks Guitars" incident should be a hard lesson about customer service. Everything you have done to build your business, stoke its image with PR campaigns and goodwill, and demonstrate your compassion to those who are less fortunate can go away in an instant with a customer service mistake—or, even worse, a customer service mistake that goes viral. You should tell your employees that discourtesy to a single customer will be regarded as a serious incident.

In my book *Broken Windows, Broken Business*, I discussed how making sure your business is freshly painted and well designed, has clean restrooms, and has great customer experience can propel it to success, while a business where the "little things" are ignored may no longer be a business within a short period of time. The most important factor is the human factor.

It's important not to rest on your past accomplishments. Singapore Airlines' campaign was singled out for criticism because it was perceived to be self-serving and smug, while Tourism Australia was singled out for being stereotypical. Keep in mind as you are developing your public relations campaign that it's not about the business; it's about the customer. If you remember that, you may be richly rewarded with revenue.

Case Study Fifty-Three: Searching for the Key

The Challenge: Owners of an automobile dealership decide to give away a car to celebrate their 30th anniversary in a city.

The Strategy: The dealership partners with a local radio station, the management of which agrees to give away ten keys in an on-air contest involving trivia questions about cars. Each winner gets the right to show up at a mall on a given day and draw one of the ten keys out of a locked box. They are to draw in the order in which they won the key. Only one of the keys will unlock the car. Whoever unlocks the car that wins it.

What Goes Wrong: Contestants all show up for the drawing, and dozens of shoppers encircle the automobile. One by one, contestants try the keys. *Nothing*. Then it gets down to where there is one key left. The final keyholder is assuredly the winner. *Nothing*. Contestants and spectators erupt into a chant. This really happened to a radio station in Florida.

The Fix: From the standpoint of the contestants, this's something that would have to be negotiated, possibly by redoing the contest as a drawing and including an additional vehicle as a prize. From the standpoint of public relations, the general manager of the radio station and the owner of the dealership should immediately record a public apology and post it on their businesses' websites and on social media. The sooner, the better, because silence is likely to be met with headstrong posts from the public denouncing the contest as a fraud.

Case Study Fifty-Four: There's a Fly in My Soup

The Challenge: A patron at a local restaurant finds a fly in her soup and posts a photo on social media.

The Strategy: Owners of the restaurant should post an apology right away on social media, assuring the public that they are aware of the situation, that they're addressing it, and that they are deeply apologetic of the situation. If a reporter or assignment editor at a local television station requests an interview, the owners of the restaurant should consent and meet the situation directly. Trying to avoid engagement would be like encountering a bear in the woods. If you try to run away, it will catch you.

The Rationale: To paraphrase the lyrics of a song, *Authentic PR* means you sometimes have to say you're sorry. An apology that's fair, judicious, and well crafted should be part of your toolkit when you own, operate, or represent a business. In "The art of Crafting a perfect apology in public relations," published on Agility PR Solutions, Nahia Davies writes, "Navigating a crisis situation requires a delicate balance of timing, tone and tangible follow-through actions. A poorly executed apology can further exacerbate the situation, leaving a brand vulnerable to sustained backlash and scrutiny." In the article, Davies identified a number of aspects of the ideal apology.

Timing of delivery: In Davies' words, "Timing is absolutely pivotal. Any delay in addressing the issue head-on allows the crisis to intensify and public outrage to swell." But she also writes, "[S]peaking too soon without fully grasping the facts can also backfire—there's a balance to strike."

Language and tone: "The language used in an apology should be straightforward, avoiding jargon or overly complex explanations that might obscure the message."

Follow-through actions: "An apology must be followed up by a clear plan for rectifying the error and preventing similar incidents in the future. This might include corrective actions, policy changes, or other measures that demonstrate a commitment to improvement.

The Cost: Zero.

There's no question that these are difficult tasks to accomplish. After all, you've worked tirelessly to maintain a good image for your brand and all of sudden years of work seem to evaporate, but the digital age is an age of vulnerability. If you're running a business, you need to factor that vulnerability into the cost, both tangible and intangible, of doing business. The time to do that is before a mistake goes viral. Be sure you can respond quickly, accurately, and completely to the current situation. Identify the social media sites on which you will respond and know how to do so quickly. Then, when a situation develops, you're ready to react. After you have apologized and announced your action plans, you need a way to track reaction on social media sites. There are tools to help you accomplish that. Prowly cites Cision, Muck Rack, Meltwater, Agility PR Solutions, Nexis News Desk, Mention, Brandwatch, and Brand24." If you have monitoring in real time, you can adjust and massage your message to meet the moment.

Case Study Fifty-Five: Be True to Your Word

The Challenge: A restaurant that lists sustainability and ethical sourcing as two of its core values is found to have been procuring food from a commercial farm that is reputed to exploit its workers.

The Strategy: If the sourcing error was inadvertent, the owner(s) of the restaurant should apologize immediately, on their website and on social media, and they should make themselves available to television stations, radio stations, and newspapers for interviews. In all cases they should explain in detail what went wrong and how they plan to fix it. If the sourcing was deliberate, the immediate response should be the same, but the recovery will be more difficult, and the wording in the initial statement will be different as well. Every statement has to be tailored carefully to the demands of the current situation. If the owner(s) of the restaurant discover that the commercial farm was exploiting workers and the restaurant neglected to do anything about it, the apology should acknowledge fully that the restaurant has broken faith with its customers and that there's no excuse for what was done. If the alleged exploitation was unknown to the owner(s) of the restaurant, then the initial statement should begin with an apology for not being diligent in managing its sourcing and then continue with a promise to do better. In either case, the apology should not be conditional. The restaurant should accept full responsibility even if another party contributed to the mistake.

The Rationale: Restaurants that claim ethical sourcing and sustainability as core values are constantly vulnerable to lapses in compliance with their own standards. For example, what if a longtime source for ethically raised food is sold and the new owner implements some new policies that are exploitative without the knowledge of the restaurant? Cases of food poisoning can also prompt a PR challenge. Chipotle Mexican Grill faced such a challenge in 2018. According to NPR, 647 people who dined at a Chipotle Mexican Grill in Powell, Ohio came down with a gastrointestinal illness. According to NPR, Brian Niccol, then-CEO of Chipotle Mexican Grill, said in a statement published by *USA Today*": "Chipotle has a zero tolerance policy for any violations of our stringent food safety standards and we are committed to doing all we can to ensure it doesn't happen again." The statement said, "Once we identified this incident we acted quickly to close the Powell restaurant and implemented our food safety response protocols that include total replacement of all food inventory and complete cleaning and sanitization of the restaurant."

This is an example of a procedural statement, which lets customers and the public know what's happening in an ongoing investigation. Businesses dealing with a situation or investigation should publish this kind of statement daily to keep the public informed, but the first statement released after or at the onset of an event after an event should include two words: "We're sorry."

The Cost: Zero.

Chapter Thirty-Seven

How to Start a Trend

Ever wonder how trends get started and why they end? Favored fashion designs come and go. Automobiles change shape and style. The music of one generation becomes the laughing stock of the next. Change is a constant in the world, especially a connected world, but trends have been changing since before the digital age. Powdered wigs in the 18th century gave way to powdered hair. Fedoras, the mark of any successful businessman in the 1950s, faded in the 1960s. Rap and hip-hop supplanted rock music to a certain extent. Leisure suits, which made their wearers look like record producers or cabana boys, became de rigueur in the 1970s, and then faded in the 1980s. Then came the *Urban Cowboy* trend from the movie of the same name, which prompted grown men to mount mechanical horses, pay for a ride and hurt themselves.

According to an article published on the London School of Design & Marketing's site, "Culture plays an important role in the creation of trends. It can be influenced by everything from art and music to politics and social movements. For example, the rise of streetwear as a fashion trend can be attributed to the influence of hip hop and street culture."

The article also notes the move toward sustainable development, which has become the guiding principle for a number of businesses. It also lists technology as a factor, stating, "with the rapid advancement of technology, new products and ideas are constantly being developed, leading to new trends." The site notes the rise of social media and influencers" and lists "consumer behaviour" as a driving force, and it gives as examples "the rise of e-commerce" and "the rising popularity of subscription services."

Do you sense that there is something more at work in the development of trends?

You may, for example, be familiar with quantum entanglement, the phenomenon in physics in which a change in one particle is instantly matched with a change in another, entangled particle, no matter how far apart they are. One particle cannot be described independent of the other. This only works at the atomic level, but what if people were similarly connected? Sure, they're connected through social media, but what if they're connected in a subconscious way?

If you're intuitive enough, you can sense subtle shifts in behavior. For example, suppose you go dancing at a club one night and one particular song fills the floor with eager dancers. Then, two weeks later, you go to the same club and the song that had filled the dance floor the last time you were there now empties it. This may be a clue that things have changed.

The point is, don't overlook your intuition as a guide to anticipating trends. As to predictions for the years ahead, ChatGPT anticipates:

- **Remote Work and Hybrid Models**: The shift to remote work, accelerated by the COVID-19 pandemic, is likely to continue evolving. Companies may adopt hybrid models that mix in-person and remote work, altering urban landscapes and commuting patterns.
- **Technological Advancement and AI**: Rapid advancements in artificial intelligence and automation will transform industries. This may lead to increased efficiency but also raise concerns about job displacement and the ethical use of technology.
- **Sustainability and Green Initiatives**: Climate change awareness will push businesses and governments towards sustainable practices. Expect more investment in renewable energy, sustainable agriculture, and green technologies.
- **Mental Health and Well-being**: There will be a greater focus on mental health, particularly in the workplace. Companies may implement more supportive policies and programs to improve employee well-being.
- **Social Movements and Equity**: Social justice movements will continue to gain traction, influencing policies and corporate practices. Issues of equity, diversity, and inclusion will remain at the forefront of societal discourse.

Take mental health and well-being. If you're new to a community, your company could become the first to implement a counseling program for employees. Your local newspaper website or television station may be interested in a feature about your program as part of a series about workplace trends in the years ahead. Or, it might lend itself to a larger discussion (perhaps a television panel or a town about stress in the workplace and the loss of jobs to automation).

Case Study Fifty-Six: A Holiday for No Reason

The Challenge: Owners of a business hope to raise awareness of stress in the office and promote a program that gives their employees occasional days off for no reason.

The Strategy: Announce ahead of time that a business is giving every one of its employees the day off on a certain day to allow them to relax, kick back, and enjoy life. Try to persuade other businesses to join in, through appearances in the media, chat on social media and word of mouth. If you're successful, this type of promotion could morph into a day when the entire town goes on vacation (with the exception of public safety personnel and hospital staffs). Schools could even consider closing for the day so that families could spend time together. That could be a long shot, but if it works, think of the value it would add.

The Rationale: Upheavals in how work is organized have taken away some of the foundations that workers had taken for granted for decades and, in some cases, centuries. The Industrial Revolution took millions of people off the farm and transformed them into specialists on the assembly line. The Information Age took away some jobs and replaced them with automation, and the advent of the internet made the hybrid workplace and the work-at-home model possible. Today, the largest corporations are devoted to technology rather than manufacturing, and the startup has become the foundational model for business. Some workers have become entrepreneurs, while others see uncertainty in their futures. Add all the stressors together, and you have the makings of a challenge to the quality of life.

According to OSHA:

- *Nearly one in five US adults live with a mental illness.*
- *Workplace stress hs been reported to cause 120,000 deaths in the US each year.*
- *Approximately 65 percent of US workers surveyed have characterized work as being a very significant or somewhat significant source of stress each year from 2019–2021.*
- *83 percent of US workers suffer from work-related stress and 54 percent of workers report that work stress affects their home life.*
- *For every $1 spent on ordinary mental health concerns, employers see a $4 return in productivity gains.*

Focusing a promotion on stress in the workplace is win-win. Workers like it because it can directly affect them and potentially increase their health benefits if managers of the company decide to commit themselves to that. Members of the public like it because it raises awareness of an ongoing problem. Managers like it because it helps in worker retention and benefits the brand.

The Cost: Loss of one day of production or service.

Case Study Fifty-Seven: The Sustainability Rally

The Challenge: Owners of a coffee shop that are known for its espoused commitment to sustainability hope to raise awareness and their profile in the city.

The Strategy: Hold a sustainability rally over the weekend in a city park or other appropriate venue. Serve free coffee in recyclable cups. Donate recycling bins to the city with your logo on them.

The Rationale: Virtue signaling by businesses can be fraught with perils, especially when those who run the business don't really believe in what they are espousing. DEI, for example (Diversity, Equity, and Inclusion) has had its heydays and its nay-days, but a company for which DEI or sustainability is an ethic, sharing that ethic with the public can be a powerful tool.

One caveat: You have to make sure that the rally itself is sustainable. If you leave the park littered with coffee cups or if some of the cups are made of Styrofoam, you are going to have some explaining to do. One photograph or twenty-four frames of an empty coffee cup lying in the park can sink all the good will you have tried to impart.

The Cost: The coffee, permitting, any insurance and security.

Chapter Thirty-Eight

The Customer Service Factor

If you own a business and you don't regard customer service as your first priority, you need to rethink your priorities. In my opinion, owners of too many businesses think their products, their perks, and their prices will somehow transform the people who encounter them online, on the phone, or in person. They also think their customers will laugh off the rudeness of a surly representative or sit patiently as an automated voice asks them over and over and over again if they would like to chat with a digital assistant. A friend of mine counted twelve such exhortations on a call to a wireless company. It isn't difficult to imagine that the strategy is, through promises of greater efficiency, to draw people toward chatting so that the company can lay off workers and send the savings to shareholders.

Two principles guide my hinking about customer service in the digital age. With regard to artificial intelligence the principle is, AI is inadequate. If you've ever tried to make a flight reservation or add a plan to your phone service, you may have experienced the frustration of trying to get a question answered. A friend of mine called a telecommunications company to see if he could add international calls to his cell phone service. The company's automated system didn't understand the question. Repeated tries failed to get the call to a customer service representative with a human brain who could handle the request.

The problem is that the algorithm or AI system used by that company wasn't sophisticated enough to handle the complexity of the conversation. If the problem had been simpler, the algorithm (or whatever was guiding the conversation) might have been able to understand and handle the request efficiently, but not this time. That sort of interaction leaves behind an angry customer with access to social media.

What's missing with AI? *Empathy*. Remember that word. In all your dealings with customers, whether on the phone, on social media, on Zoom, or in person, empathy should be ingrained in not only the training of customer service representatives. I advise employers and customer service representatives that courtesy is free. You don't have to pay anyone or be paid to be pleasant. A customer service representative should act like the customer's advocate, not the company's adjutant. They're there to guide the customer through the bureaucracy. In that sense, a customer service representative is like a trail guide who knows all the shortcuts.

Research bears out these assertions. In August of 2024, I state in a news release, "A study conducted by Stanford University highlights that AI-powered customer service systems, although efficient, often lack the empathetic understanding and personalized touch that human representatives provide. This research demonstrates that customers interacting with AI systems are more likely to feel frustrated and undervalued, decreasing customer satisfaction and loyalty."

Furthermore, an MIT report found that while AI can handle basic inquiries, it struggles with complex problem-solving and emotional intelligence. These deficiencies can result in unresolved issues and negative customer experiences, ultimately harming a company's reputation and bottom line.

Put simply, your attitude will affect your altitude. If you want to grow your business, don't let PR blunders weigh you down. Don't let a tense conversation between an employee and a customer weigh you down, and don't give artificial intelligence a "seat at the able" until it can handle more sophisticated conversations. Relegate it to the "children's table" for now. AI may be a real asset in other aspects of a business. For example, AI can easily go through reams of data and detect patterns in consumer shopping, supply chains, and economic fluctuations, but it isn't yet ready for full customer service. Smart business managers will use this technology when it's useful and wait for it to catch up before using it in other applications.

Think of empathy as the engine that will grow your business, and make sure that only human beings have the keys to that engine. Remember that the next time you hire someone who will interact with customers. In "6 Key Reasons to Prioritize Empathy for Your Business in 2024," published on Qualtric's site, states, "Empathy makes a profound emotional connection with consumers. When businesses understand their customers' needs, desires and pain points, it fosters a sense of trust and reliability. This emotional bond nurtures long-term relationships, leading to height-

ened consumer loyalty. By showing genuine concern and addressing their concerns, businesses can solidify their customer base, fostering loyalty that withstands competitive pressures." The six reasons identified by the article are "Deeper Consumer Loyalty," "Higher Customer Satisfaction," "Stronger Competitive Advantage," "Improved Brand Image," "Greater Innovation," and "Better Customer Retention."

If you talk down to your customers in any way, they're likely to take down your business, and collectively, with the right combination of influencers and social media, they have the power to do that. They also have the power to make your business.

What's your preference?

Chapter Thirty-Nine

How to Write a News Release

This is one of the essential skills for venturing into *Authentic PR*. Think of the news release as the synapse between nerve cells, the medium that carries information from one neuron to another. If you're not used to pitching stories or otherwise dealing with the media, news releases may seem like something only people in "the business" could generate. In fact, while there are some fundamental parameters you can't violate if you want to look professional, writing a news release is not brain surgery.

Start with the contact information, including the name(s) of the contact person or people, the email address, and the phone number. Follow the contact information with a clever headline. This is the most important part of the news release. Add a sub-headline if needed. Begin the story with a dateline (city and state), then move to the lead paragraph, where you need to include the basics of the story.

The paragraphs that follow should include the background of the event or news development, some quotes and some basics on the organization(s) involved. Toward the end you should include appropriate hashtags along with the web address and other sources of more information. Here's how it might look:

For Immediate Release

Look. Up in the Sky. It's a Bird. It's a Helicopter.
It's Thanksgiving Dinner.

Cincinnati, OH—It may be no surprise to see holiday turkeys boxed and ready to go at the supermarket. But imagine stepping outside and seeing these winged birds fling out of a helicopter and fluttering to the ground on Wednesday, the day before the Thanksgiving holiday.

Local radio station WKRP has hired a helicopter, rounded up dozens of birds and is prepared to fill the parking lot of an area mall after their brief flights to freedom from the aircraft and their soft landings in the outdoor parking lot.

"Is there a better way to get into the holiday spirit than by watching turkeys take flight in the sky?" asks WKRP General Manager Arthur Carlson, who dreamed up the promotion. "We hope to bring joy to the faces of all the people of Cincinnati."

Carlson kept the promotion hidden from most of his staff, informing only WKRP Sales Manager Herb Tarlek, who says he looks forward to Wednesday "as one of the highlights of my life."

WKRP News Director Les Nessman, recipient of five Buckeye Newshawk Awards, will be on the ground for the play by play. As a news director, this is the kind of story I live for," Nessman said. "A story with a lot of meat."

WKRP is owned by Lillian Carlson, mother of General Manager Arthur Carlson, and features air personalities Dr. Johnny Fever and Venus Flytrap. The station is programmed by Andy Travis, who came to WKRP from a station in Santa Fe, New Mexico and has also programmed radio outlets in Albuquerque, New Mexico and Amarillo, Texas.

WKRP# Cincinnati#ThanksgivinG #Turkeys

No doubt you've discerned that this is a hypothetical news release issued before the turkey drop promotion that went wrong on the show *WKRP in Cincinnati.* Imagine the television script that might have been written after the turkeys fell to their deaths?

MALINDA: A radio station publicity stunt that involved pushing live turkeys out of a helicopter went wrong today when the birds, which cannot fly, plummeted to the ground nd perished in a shopping center parking lot. Good Evening, Cincinnati. I'm Malinda Mayer.

SAM: And I'm Sam Molofsky. It happened in the Pinedale Shoping Mall parking lot, which is now covered with feathers and surrounded by yellow police tape.

VO: The promotion was the brainchild of WKRP General Manager Art Carlson, who was quoted in a news release yesterday as saying, "Is there a better way to get into the holiday spirit than by watching turkeys take flight in the sky? He added, "We hope to bring joy to the faces of all the people of Cincinnati."

WKRP News Director Less Nessman described the scene on the air.

SOT
CG: Voice of Les Nessman
WKRP News Director

"Oh, my God! They're turkeys! Oh, no! Johnny, can you get this? Oh, they're crashing to the earth right in front of our eyes! One just went through the windshield of a parked car! This is terrible! Everyone's rushing around pushing each other. Oh, the humanity!"

MALINDA (On Camera): Carlson said after the incident, "As God is my witness I thought turkeys could fly."

By the way, it wouldn't hurt if you knew something about television and radio jargon. Knowing the lingo could help you hone your pitch.

A VO is a voiceover. It is read by an anchor or reporter, initially on camera, but then over video. A VO/SOT is a voiceover followed by a SOT (sound on tape; in other words, a sound bite). A SOT is a sound bite with no video preceding it or following it. When video precedes the sound bite and more video follows it, that's called a V/S/V at some stations, a VO/SOT/VO at others or a VO/SOT at others.

A package is a complete story, with video and sound bites, that's voiced by an anchor (in which case it is called an anchor package) or a reporter. The reporter may be live on camera to introduce the package and then follow it live on camera or the package may run alone.

A tag is information voiced by the anchor or reporter after the body of the story has run. For example, when the story is about a brush fire or a mudslide, the tag may include information about shelters. Or the tag may say, "For more information, please visit our website."

A look live appears to be a live shot, with the reporter introducing the package at the scene. In reality, the entire story, including the lead and the tag, were recorded earlier, possibly because the reporter was scheduled to be off duty by the time the report aired.

Radio shares the basics of journalism with television and newspapers, but it has some lingo of its own. A voice wrap is a story recorded by a reporter or anchor that includes at least one sound bite. A reader is a story with no sound bite(s) that is read live on the air by an anchor. A voicer is a story without any sound bites that is recorded by an anchor or reporter.

A chyron is the text and graphics you may see on the lower third of the television screen during news or talk show broadcasts. It may identify the anchor(s), their interviewees, or the person currently talking. For example, in the story about WKRP, the "Voice of Les Nessman" is identified by a chyron, also called a CG, which stands for character generator.

A banner is a type of chyron or cg that gives a sub-heading to a story. (For example, "Deadly Brush Fire" or "Department Store Robbery.") While a chyron identifying the speaker in a sound bite may be on-screen for about three-to-five seconds, a banner will probably remain up through the entire story.

Chapter Forty

Internal Communications

Rev. Paul Clairville, pastor of Westminster Presbyterian Church in Burbank, California, likens the breakdown of communications in a marriage to the construction of a brick wall. With each argument or lapse in communication, you add a brick. When the first row of bricks is laid, the two people are still accessible to each other. But add layer after layer of bricks, and eventually, there is an opaque wall separating the two people who vowed to stay with each other "until death do us part."

If you own a business, especially if it has grown to a certain level, you may be building a brick wall between you and your employees without even knowing it. As businesses expand, people may tend to settle in to groups and cliques, then build a number of walls that can fracture team spirit. A breakdown in communications can create an underlying tension that erodes morale and makes employees hesitant to go to the office. Benjamin Laker, a university professor and a senior contributor for *Forbes*, writes in an article, "Culture Is A Company's Single Most Powerful Advantage. Here's Why":

"There are very few factors that contribute more to business success than culture. Although it is sometimes difficult to draw boundaries around the notion of culture in organizations, it remains widely associated with business performance by practitioners, consultants, and insurers." He states, "Today's market is hyper-competitive, and employees expect a lot more from the companies they work for. Employee expectations are closely tied to their values. When employers deliver on these expectations, they see more loyal and productive employees, which in turn improves business outcomes and propels growth. Companies with strong cultures have "reaped a fourfold increase " in revenue growth."

The lesson here is that business leaders are no longer necessarily "Pied Pipers," leading their employees to a bright future; they are facilitators, incorporating their employees' backgrounds, values, and aspirations into a dynamic team with a singular mission. That's the way to retain existing employees, attract new employees and inspire customers.

Laker cites Sprout's IPO as an example. He writes, "Just three months before COVID-19 hit, Sprout Social leaped to become a publicly traded company, marking the first Chicago-based IPO in nearly five years. This gave Sprout the capital and momentum to build on its success while differentiating itself in the social media software space.

"The onset of the pandemic forced many organizations to rethink their strategies and operations as a whole. Sprout's newly public team adapted quickly and provided employees and customers with the tools and resources needed to flourish through the uncertainty." According to Laker, Sprout's culture "proved to be the company's single most powerful advantage."

Using *Authentic PR* to build an organizational culture begins with shared values. The digital age is a sharing era. People share their thoughts on social media, they share trips to the airport on ride-hailing services, they share information in exchange for access. All of that makes people more connected but also more vulnerable than ever before. But remember one of key tenets of *Authentic PR*: Vulnerable is good. *Why?* Because it leaves an organization reliant on its key values. That's how Sprout Social made it through the pandemic, and that's how your organization can make it through uncertain times.

The key to building a strong organizational culture is to build a strong team. Corporate retreats that focus on team building and trust are invaluable in transforming your employees from a gaggle of people doing thumb calisthenics on their smartphones to a team in which everyone relies on each other. Trust hikes are a good example of the exercises that can create a team. In a trust hike, employees, managers, and owners pair off. One person in the pair wears a blindfold, while the other walks with vision unimpeded, The "seeing" member of the pair is responsible for telling the blindfolded one about any obstacles ahead and keeping him or her on course. Later, the pair can switch places, or everyone can change partners. It may sound simple, but there's a real risk involved. If the "seeing" member of the team gets distracted, the blindfolded one could get seriously hurt.

Another team-building exercise that can be helpful at a corporate retreat involves gathering everyone in a conference room or recreational space and putting four signs on the floor in the four or more corners of the room. Each sign displays one core value of the company. One could say "Diversity," while another might say "Risk Taking." Participants at the conference are then asked to go to the sign with the topic that interests them the most. A facilitator then guides the conversation at each sign. If one sign outdraws all the others or if the conversation at one sign brings up a topic that is better addressed at another sign, the conversation can migrate. No one is tied to a particular group once he or she migrates to a particular sign.

This is one way for owners and managers to discover what matters most to their employees and vice versa. The idea for the exercise is to use the values as a launching point for discussion on what really matters to team members, and that can lead to a stronger set of values, stronger because the people who run the company and the ones who make it run can all participated in their adoption.

In her article, "Company core values: 25 inspiring examples," published on Achievers, Kellie Wong writes, "The top factor of employee satisfaction is the culture and values of an organization. Over 75 percent of employees consider it 'very important' to work for a company with defined core values." Her examples of core values include:

1. Integrity
2. Innovation
3. Accountability
4. Honesty
5, Respect

The ones you and your employees choose will be all the stronger if they are chosen collectively. Of course, they'll be meaningless if they aren't followed. Any company, for example, can claim innovation as a core value. But where are the innovations in its product line?

Case Study Fifty-Eight: Honing the Core

The Challenge: The people who run a public relations firm hope to reshape their values to revitalize their business.

The Strategy: Take the staff to a corporate retreat away from the city and the office. The retreat would take place over a weekend and might begin with an icebreaker, during which members of the team would say their name and talk about their hobbies and other aspects of their lives outside the office. That might be followed by, "Yes, and…," the improvisational exercise in which each member of the team would articulate a core value that he or she hopes to have included in the final list. Then, everyone might go outside for a trust hike that would last until lunch.

At lunch, members of the team would be required to sit at a table with at least one person from another department. After lunch would come the exercise with the signs in the corners of the room. Each sign would display one of the most frequently mentioned core values from the improvisational exercise earlier in the day. Team members would then go to the corner with the sign displaying the core value that is the most meaningful to them. The group at each sign could then talk about why they chose it. Members of the group would be free to gravitate to another sign. The goal is to find the one core value that everyone regards as most important and to embed that value in the corporate culture.

The Rationale: An article, "35 Retreat Activities to Motivate and Connect Employees," published on *Indeed*, identifies "[d]evelopment of values" as one of the "Benefits of retreat activities for employees." It continues, "Various retreat activities inspire the development of values that help establish your company culture. Some of the key values that retreat activities promote are collaboration and communication." Retreat activities mentioned include:

1. *Have a welcome party*
2. *Play board games*
3. *Set up a corporate trivia*
4. *Create a scavenger hunt*
5. *Sing karaoke*

For a public relations firm, corporate culture is especially crucial because of the firm's job to project an image for various brands and people. If everyone isn't "on the same page," that image can get fragmented, and the work force can easily silo and the messages to the pubic can get fragmented.

If a company practices *Authentic PR*, there are some core values that are mandatory. Ethical behavior would be one. Candor would be another. Telling the truth without regard to consequences is another.

There's no room for "glossing over" in *Authentic PR*. It's the ethical core values that enable the enterprising core values, like innovation, to flourish. Embedding ethics in your core values will grow your reputation and build a foundation of trust. Start with that, and watch what happens to your business.

The Cost: Venue rental, food, training materials, and other associated costs—lodging, if needed.

Chapter Forty-One

Doing Well by Doing Good

Public relations may be associated in the public's mind with profit-making operations and individuals who are protective of their reputations, but charities and other nonprofits are just as vulnerable as for-profit organizations and public figures, perhaps more so. People tend to be skeptical about charities, wondering whether their donations are being used to help people or to raise the salaries of managers. There's almost a built-in climate of suspicion that charities have to overcome if they are to succeed in raising enough money to survive.

Authentic PR can challenge that with facts and total transparency.

Ellenor (stylized as ellenor) provides hospice services for adults and children in the UK. An article on ellenor's website, "The Importance of Public Relations for a Charity: How ellenor Engages with its audience—and Why It's So Vital," states that, "PR, at its core, refers to the set of strategies and tools a charity uses to influence public perceptions about it. It's the way a nonprofit organization speaks to its audience, projects its brand and raises awareness around its services to the public. It's about mitigating risk, managing reputation and finding ever more effective ways of reaching—and making impact on the community." Public relations can be valuable to charities in three ways: by protecting their reputations, by promoting their events and by attracting volunteers. And charities can use the same techniques as for-profits to do their own public relations and reduce their overhead.

In "PR Strategy for Nonprofits," published by The TASC Group, states, "Nonprofit public relations focuses on communicating the organization's mission, values, programs, and executive thought leadership to the public. This involves storytelling, media relations, social media relations and more. A strong PR strategy for nonprofits helps to build credibility, foster trust and attract support from donors, volunteers and partners."

A first move by the nonprofit should be to establish relationships with people in the media. Part of the pitch should focus on the work the nonprofit does in the community; the other part should focus on the sort of expertise the nonprofit can provide the station. People who run a hospital may be interested in getting media coverage of a cardiac care unit. They can also provide lists of cardiologists and other cardiac care experts upon which the producer(s) can draw for interviews and sound bites about breaking stories.

For example, a study published in a medical journal might state that there's a promising treatment for diabetes. A producer could then contact the hospital and get a specialist for an interview. The turnaround time for the interview can be a matter of minutes, since it can be done on Zoom or another platform. That means a television station could get a bulletin about the treatment and have a specialist on the air within ten minutes.

For radio, the process is simpler. A specialist could go on the air via telephone with no video or graphics needed. Preferably, the specialist would go on Zoom or a similar platform, since the audio quality may make it sound as if he or she is in the room with the anchor.

Chapter Forty-Two

Takeaways

- *Don't post cat videos on LinkedIn*
- *Market to the "alpha pup"*
- *Don't broadcast; niche cast*
- *Don't try to pitch a television producer less than an hour before air time*
- *Observe the "5:30 Rule"*
- *Use the most appropriate social media to reach the public*
- *If you run a company and something goes wrong, you're the one who needs to be on the scene*
- *When you apologize, take responsibility and say, "I'm sorry"*
- *Pop-up PR is the medium of the moment*
- *Don't be cautious; be creative*
- *Familiarity does not breed contempt; it breeds comfort*
- *Don't try to pitch a producer less than an hour before air time*
- *Do well by doing good*
- *Conscience drives commerce*
- *You are a brand*

Epilogue

Revolutionary and genius are two words that have become almost shopworn through hyperbole and overuse, but there are times when they're apt descriptors. *Case in Point*: the assertion that we live in revolutionary times. We're as fortunate as the millions of people who lived in the Renaissance and those who experienced such cultural upheavals as the invention of the movable-type printing press, the democratization of information flows on a continent-wide scale, the development of modern currency, the expansion of trade, and the byproducts of prosperity: art and literature. Some believe that we're in a new Renaissance now. Ian Goldin and Chris Kutarna state in their book, *Age of Discovery: Navigating the Risks and Rewards of Our New Renaissance*, that "the present age is a contest between the good and bad consequences of global entanglement and human development; between forces of inclusion and exclusion; between flourishing genius and flourishing risks."

Social media has already made possible global communication on a scale unprecedented in human history, and they make gaining visibility for any enterprise easier (because of free access), and more difficult (because of clutter). Businesses have unique potential now to go from the garage to the globe quickly and stunningly.

My previous books showcased the ingenious ways in which the business owners of those times were calling attention to their enterprises. From food on the fire line to trash bags on the beach, these solutions were innovative and effective. And they all involved chutzpah and a willingness to be different. But they were fashioned for their times.

It's a measure of how exponentially the world has changed that "those times" were decades, or, in some cases, years old. Think of all that's happened. First stages of rockets now return to the launch pad seamlessly instead of dropping into the ocean. Conversations with colleagues around the world, some of whom may not speak your language, are translated instantly. The internet providing the ability to look up any information you want about all of human history, and AI to assist in composing music with you, make a doctor's appointment for you and beat you at chess. The opportunities for business are boundless, but the risks are boundless, too. In the past, a scathing letter from a dissatisfied customer to a company might get scant attention. Today, a scathing post by a dissatisfied customer could go viral and bring down the business.

You have one defense, one quality that is respected by people throughout a highly polarized and divided world. That defense is *authenticity.*

If you think of authenticity as your defensive weapon of choice, think of this book as your supply line. Our purpose is to keep you armed with innovative solutions that can keep your business visible and vital in a revolutionary world in which innovation has become almost commonplace. This book will also be a sort of repair manual. It will show you how to face your mistakes and rectify them to keep the customer satisfied. It is a book that will carry into the future, as this decade of revolutionary change offers new opportunities and presents new challenges.

Authentic PR: How Transparency Can Transform Your Business invites you to succeed by being yourself. To the metaverse and beyond.

Index

access
customer expectations, 42–43
information transparency, 22
leadership visibility, 21
media access strategies, 34–36
in Six As framework, 42
see also transparency; visibility
acknowledgement
customer recognition, 42
role in loyalty, 42–43
in Six As framework, 42
advertising
contrasted with PR, 208–209
limitations of, 208
see also marketing; public relations
AI PR
ethical implications, 152–154
content generation, 155–157
authenticity risks, 154
see also technology
AM radio
technical characteristics, 36
historical significance, 36
see also radio
anchors (media)
limited decision-making role, 31–32
see also producers
assignment editors
role in story selection, 34
as gatekeepers, 34
see also media relations
aspiration
customer alignment with values, 42–43
brand identity and, 23
in Six As framework, 42

attention economy
competition for visibility, 60
media fragmentation, 31
see also visibility
audiences
fragmentation of, 31
digital consumption habits, 31
targeting vs. authenticity, 27
see also customers
authenticity
as brand foundation, 15, 23–24
vs. manufactured image, 19–20
and credibility, 26–27
and vulnerability, 24
as competitive advantage, 40
see also transparency; trust
Authentic PR
definition, 11, 13
evolution from Guerrilla PR, 11–13
principles of, 26–27
multi-channel approach, 27
for small business, 40
as response to cynicism, 26
see also public relations
Ben & Jerry's
values-based branding, 24
social mission protection, 24
see also values
blogs
see social media
brand / branding
definition, 15
personal branding, 19–21
CEO as brand, 21
perception vs. reality, 15
authenticity in, 23–24
storytelling and, 10
alignment with values, 23–24
see also personal branding
branding—personal
see personal branding

broadcast media
overview, 30–37
radio, 36–37
television, 30–35
see also media
campaigns
planning, 116
execution, 187–190
measurement, 190
see also strategy
case studies
role in illustrating PR tactics, 25–230
thematic grouping, 25–230
see also examples
cell phones
content capture, 28
risk of negative exposure, 28
democratization of media, 28
see also technology
CEOs
visibility expectations, 21–22
influence on brand, 21
see also leadership
community
engagement strategies, 40–41
local business advantage, 40
as commerce driver, 43
see also small business
content creation
digital strategies, 81–92
storytelling formats, 81
see also messaging
credibility
decline of trust, 26
rebuilding strategies, 26–27
see also trust
crisis communication
recovery strategies, 211–214
transparency in crises, 211
see also reputation
customers
expectations (Six As), 42
influence via reviews, 22
engagement strategies, 42–43
see also audiences

digital media
transformation of PR, 11
social media integration, 16–17
impact on transparency, 21–22
see also social media
disruption
startup vs. large business, 40
see also innovation
earned media
see media relations
engagement
customer engagement, 42–43
media engagement, 31–35
see also relationships
ethics
"do no harm," 62–64
transparency in ethics, 62
see also authenticity
experience economy
definition, 54
role in branding, 54–58
Facebook
amplification role, 16
see also social media
force multiplier
definition, 16
social media as, 16
see also amplification
gatekeepers
assignment editors, 34
producers, 31–32
see also media relations
geometric progression
goodwill amplification, 16
see also social media
Hello Deli
proximity strategy, 33
see also location
image
brand image, 181
authenticity vs. image, 19–20
influencers
digital influence, 124–130
credibility factors, 124

marketing
vs. PR, 208–209
transactional vs. relational, 208
see also advertising
media relations
building relationships, 31–35
pitching strategies, 34–36
timing considerations, 35
importance of producers, 31–32
see also public relations
messaging
consistency, 27
multi-channel delivery, 27
see also communication
personal branding
evolution, 19–21
CEO visibility, 21
social media impact, 21–22
see also brand
podcasts
PR opportunities, 30
public relations (PR)
definition (implied), *throughout*
evolution, 19–21
strategy frameworks, 26–27
see also Authentic PR
radio
AM vs. FM, 36
talk shows, 30
expert positioning, 36–37
reputation
building, 146
restoring, 146–147
see also crisis communication
Six As
attendance, 42
authenticity, 42
access, 42
acknowledgement, 42
attitude, 42
aspiration, 42
see also customers

small business
advantages, 40
flexibility, 40
community integration, 40–41
social media
amplification, 16
volatility, 21–22
role in PR, 16–17
see also digital media
television
strategy for exposure, 30–35
morning shows, 38–39
see also media
transparency
definition, 13
digital implications, 21–22
see also authenticity
trust
decline in institutions, 26
rebuilding strategies, 26–27
values
alignment with brand, 23–24
see also authenticity
visibility
importance, 60
strategies, 60–62
vulnerability
leadership trait, 24
see also authenticity

Glossary

Authentic PR

A modern public relations philosophy centered on transparency, credibility, and alignment between a business's values and its outward messaging. Contrasts with earlier "Guerrilla PR" tactics focused on impact over authenticity.

Brand (Personal / Business)

The composite perception formed in the minds of the public, encompassing identity, behavior, reputation, and communication style—not just logos or marketing assets.

The Six As

A framework for customer expectations:

Attendance—being present and engaged
Authenticity—being genuine and transparent
Access—openness to customers
Acknowledgement—recognizing customers
Attitude—alignment of values
Aspiration—shared goals and identity

Force Multiplier (PR)

A tactic or platform—especially social media—that exponentially increases the reach and impact of a message without proportional cost.

Geometric Progression of Goodwill

The compounding effect of positive experiences shared through networks, particularly via social media.

Media Gatekeepers

Individuals who control access to media exposure, especially producers and assignment editors rather than on-air talent.

Newsworthiness

The quality that makes a story relevant to media outlets—typically tied to timeliness, human interest, novelty, or expertise.

Personal Branding
The deliberate shaping of an individual's public identity, increasingly inseparable from business branding in the digital age.

Transparency (Digital Era)
The near impossibility of privacy in a networked world, requiring proactive honesty from businesses and leaders.

Vulnerability (Leadership)
A strategic and humanizing trait that builds trust by openly acknowledging flaws, values, and intentions.

Visibility
The degree to which a brand is seen and recognized; in modern PR, driven by multi-channel presence.

Authentic *PR* Toolkit

Authentic PR is not about access. It is about relevance, credibility, and timing. The following tools are designed to help you translate ideas into action—quickly, clearly, and effectively.

MEDIA PITCH EMAIL TEMPLATE

Subject Line:
Timely Story Idea: [Short, Specific Hook]

Email Body:
Hello [Producer/Editor Name],

I've been following your work on [show/outlet], particularly your recent segment on [specific example]. I wanted to share a timely story idea that may be a good fit for your audience:

[1–2 sentence description of the story—clear, specific, relevant]

Why this works now:

- [Timeliness / news hook]
- [Audience relevance]
- [Visual or interview potential]
- I'm available for:
- On-air interview
- Demonstration or segment
- Additional sources if helpful

I can also provide supporting materials (video, photos, data) immediately. Thank you for your time—happy to follow your schedule.

Best,
[Name]
[Business Name]
[Phone]
[Email]

PRESS RELEASE TEMPLATE

This release should read like a story—not an announcement.

FOR IMMEDIATE RELEASE

Headline: Clear, compelling, benefit-driven

Subheadline: Optional clarification or added context

City, State—[Date]

Opening paragraph: Who, what, where, when, why. Keep it tight.
Second paragraph: Expand the story. Why it matters.

Quote:

"Insert human voice here. Make it real, not promotional."
Third paragraph: Supporting details, data, or context.

Final paragraph: Call to action or next step.

About [Company Name]
2–3 sentences describing the business, mission, and relevance.

Media Contact:
[Name]
[Phone]
[Email]

THE 30-SECOND PR IDEA GENERATOR

If you're stuck, ask:
What just happened that we can respond to?
What problem can we solve publicly?
What do we believe that others don't say out loud?
What can we give away (time, product, experience)?
What would make someone stop scrolling?
If the idea feels safe, it probably isn't interesting.
If you wouldn't stop to pay attention to it, no one else will either.

SOCIAL MEDIA AMPLIFICATION CHECKLIST

Before posting, confirm:
Is it authentic?
Is it visual (or can it be)?
Is there a human element?
Would someone share this?
Does it invite interaction?

After posting:
Respond to every meaningful comment
Share user-generated content
Extend the story across platforms
Capture and reuse momentum

LOCAL MEDIA OUTREACH CHECKLIST

Identify the right show (not just the station)
Find the producer's name
Call at the right time (not near airtime)
Lead with the story, not your business
Offer visuals or expertise
Follow up once—then move on

TOP 25 AUTHENTIC PR TACTICS

These are not rules. They are patterns.

1. Tell the truth—especially when it's uncomfortable.
2. Make your customer the hero of the story.
3. Turn mistakes into moments of transparency.
4. Create events that people want to talk about.
5. Be visible—personally, not just professionally.
6. Don't wait for permission to act.
7. Use your location to your advantage.
8. Build relationships with producers, not just outlets.
9. Offer expertise, not promotion.
10. Think visually—television is a medium of pictures.
11. Think conversationally—radio is a medium of ideas.
12. Be early with ideas, not late with reactions.
13. Make your values clear—and live them.
14. Show the process, not just the result.
15. Let your customers speak for you.
16. Be consistent across every channel.
17. Avoid jargon—clarity wins.
18. Respond quickly—news moves fast.
19. Keep your message simple and repeatable.
20. Look for moments of surprise.
21. Align your actions with your story.
22. Be persistent, but not annoying.
23. Make it easy for media to say yes.
24. Don't try to control the narrative—earn it.
25. Remember: credibility compounds over time.

MEDIA CONTACT STRATEGY GUIDE

WHO TO CONTACT

Not the anchor. Not the reporter.
Contact the producer.
Producers decide:
What stories run
What guests appear
What segments get airtime
Assignment editors decide:
Whether a story gets coverage
If you reach the right person, you're halfway there.

WHEN TO REACH OUT

Morning shows → call after they air
Afternoon/evening shows → call in the morning
Never call right before airtime
Avoid chaotic news cycles unless your story fits the moment
Timing is respect—and respect gets returned.

WHAT TO SAY (AND NOT SAY)

If your idea can be copied by ten other businesses, it's not a story.

Say:
"Here's a story your audience will care about."
"Here's why it's timely."
"Here's what it looks like on air."

Don't say:
"I'd like to promote my business."
"We're the best at…"
Anything vague or generic
Producers are not looking for advertisements.
They are looking for stories.

HOW TO FOLLOW UP

One follow-up is professional
Two is persistent
Three is noise
If there's no response, refine the idea and move on.

WHAT MAKES A STORY WORK

Strong segments usually include:
A clear human element
A visual or experiential component
A timely hook
A takeaway for the audience
If your story checks those boxes, it has a chance.

FINAL PRINCIPLE

Media exposure is not about access.
It's about relevance.
Media doesn't reward effort. It rewards relevance.
If you are not, no amount of persistence will matter.

You don't need a large budget to practice public relations.
You need clarity, credibility, and the willingness to act.
That's *Authentic PR*.